The Life of Faith is an introductory systematic theology that simultaneously cuts its own swathe and sustains traditional confessional evangelical theology. The fruit of a master teacher who has spent decades serving theological students, the book does not follow the traditional loci of systematic theology, but has been shaped by the form of biblical theology developed at Moore Theological College. It is only a fraction of the length of traditional magisterial volumes (e.g. Shedd, Hodge, Bavinck, Berkhof), while being more overtly edifying. The work has the freshness of an author who in the 21st century is still engaging in evangelism: it smells of the gospel, of 'gospelizing', rather more than of the library, even while readers will sense the author's allegiance to the Thirty-Nine Articles. This is an excellent book for those just starting out in serious study of theology, and for those who want a refresher.

D. A. Carson
Emeritus Professor of New Testament, Trinity Evangelical Divinity School, Deerfield, IL

Students of the Bible are indebted to Dr Peter Jensen's clear, concise and thoroughly readable introduction to Christian doctrine. After 25 years of teaching theological students, Dr Jensen is well across the nuances and challenges of explaining the Bible's core focus and the appropriate human response, namely, a life of faith. This volume will be an asset to all who desire a deeper understanding of God and his word.

Dr Glenn N. Davies
Former Anglican Archbishop of Sydney

Every generation needs its own restatement and application of the whole sweep of biblical doctrine, and in *The Life of Faith* we are in the hands of a master pastor–teacher. Based on a lifetime of personal discipleship and theological study, Peter Jensen has provided us with a wonderfully accessible, heartwarming exposition of the gospel of Christ—with all that flows from it in Christian experience—that is both comprehensive and panoramic. Particular strengths include its logical clarity in argument, its engagement with contemporary issues and distortions, both cultural and theological, its penetrating correctives of "our own perceptions shaped by sinful human ideas", but above all its unapologetic commitment to the truth and unity of the Scriptures, with Christ as their focus. The glory of God shines from these pages, causing one's spirit to lift in praise and thanksgiving. You will want to come back to it again and again!

David Jackman
Founding Director, Cornhill Training Course, London
Former President, The Proclamation Trust, London

In 27 crisp and concise chapters, Peter Jensen surveys Christian doctrine, relying on the gospel as the essential source of knowledge of God, biblical theology as the pattern of his study, and personal and social application as the essential concomitant of the apprehension of theological truth. Dr Jensen offers his reader a masterful tour of the sweep of biblical doctrine with clarity, pastoral as well as theological insight, and the sense of his own warm companionship as a fellow learner at the feet of a common Master, who rules his people by his Spirit-breathed word. I warmly commend this immensely useful volume to parents teaching their older children, those involved in discipling new or mature believers, small-group Bible study leaders, and pastors thinking of offering a doctrinal sermon series or providing training to all sorts of 'ministers of the word' in a local church setting.

Kanishka Raffel
Anglican Archbishop of Sydney

This is a magnificent book. There is gold on every page. For those who benefitted from the blessing of being taught by Peter Jensen at Moore College it will be a must-have—if only to remind of privileges once enjoyed. Those who missed such riches now can play catch up. Knowledge of God is the beautiful theme—through the Scriptures, in salvation, as Lord and by faith. This is no dry textbook. Every page drives towards practical knowledge of the living God. It will fill your mind, delight your soul and, above all, enrich your relationship with God.

William Taylor
Senior Minister, St Helen's Bishopsgate, London

Those of us familiar with Peter Jensen's teaching of Christian doctrine at Moore College for more than a quarter of a century will rejoice that the benefit we received can now be enjoyed by everyone who reads this book. Peter has always been known to us as a deep and rich thinker, one who penetrates to the heart of theological matters, bringing to them a clarity of expression and an unswerving faithfulness to the word of God. In this volume, Peter teaches us to think out from the gospel, to test everything against the Scriptures, and to pause regularly to give thanks to the God who created us and saved us in Jesus Christ. Here is theology that warms the heart, directs the mind, and feeds the soul.

Mark Thompson
Principal, Moore Theological College, Sydney

"Love God with all your mind." One of the features of Christ's quotation of the Old Testament command "love the Lord your God" is that he adds the words, "with all your mind" (e.g. Mark 12:30). Peter Jensen's introduction to theology will help you do that it. It is full of godly wisdom about God and the gospel, and is persuasive, pastoral, and practical.

> **Peter Adam**
> Vicar Emeritus, St Jude's Carlton, Melbourne
> Former Principal, Ridley College, Melbourne

It is with great delight that I see *The Life of Faith* become available for the strengthening of Christ's people. The work of one of Australia's foremost theological educators and theologians, these studies began life as lecture notes used to help form a generation of pastors and Christian leaders, and many of us who experienced those lectures can testify to their effectiveness. These studies, having been forged and developed over decades of actual use and now completely reworked and updated into book form, are a great resource for anyone wanting a solid foundation in the Christian faith. This book combines a concern to express biblical orthodoxy in a fresh and insightful way with a blending of a pastoral heart and warmth with wisdom and gospel clarity. *The Life of Faith* is well worth anyone's time to read and digest so as to grow in their knowledge and love of God and his saving ways.

> **Mark Baddeley**
> Senior Lecturer, Systematic Theology, Queensland Theological College, Brisbane

Peter Jensen's aim in this work is to summarize what the Bible teaches—in other words, to present the Bible's doctrine. Readers will deepen their knowledge of the Bible, learning a sound way of reading it and applying it. Jensen is a master teacher. There is an admirable recognition of Scripture as a covenantal book provided by God to his people, with careful attention given to the biblical plotline. Even so, the insights of great ones of the Christian past are not neglected. Clarity of expression and acute theological insight characterize the whole project. A very fine work. I could sum it up as John Calvin meets Broughton Knox.

Graham Cole
Emeritus Dean and Professor Emeritus of Biblical and Systematic Theology, Trinity Evangelical Divinity School, Deerfield, IL

This work is the result of years of theological reflection. Informed by various sociopolitical, cultural, theological and scholarly developments in the past two centuries, it presents a strong case for Reformed theology in the 21st century. Those of us who grew up with Reformed theology in the 20th century will find this book refreshing. It serves as a reminder not only of our core beliefs, but also of what an informed and thought-through Reformed theology should look like today in order to be relevant and yet faithful to its foundational premises.

Bishop Jensen shows, compellingly, why some of the 'newer' scholarly discoveries have failed to sway him from his Reformed roots. He demonstrates how he has considered these new discoveries and given them fair considerations. For example, his treatment of biblical criticism shows how he welcomes scholarly advancements without compromising his belief that the Bible is the word of God.

Bishop Jensen presents his theology to us systematically, biblically, accessibly, and concisely. Its organization helps readers to see the contours, the width and the depth of his thought, all of which come together to form a theological framework that will bring great benefit to new learners of theology. I would highly recommend this book to those who wish to find an entry-level introduction to systematic theology.

Khee-Vun Lin
Principal, Anglican Training Institute, Sabah, Malaysia

The
LIFE
— of —
FAITH

An introduction
to Christian doctrine

PETER F. JENSEN

The Life of Faith
© Peter Jensen 2022

All rights reserved. Except as may be permitted by the Copyright Act, no part of this publication may be reproduced in any form or by any means without prior permission from the publisher. Please direct all copyright enquiries and permission requests to the publisher.

Matthias Media
(St Matthias Press Ltd ACN 067 558 365)
Email: info@matthiasmedia.com.au
Internet: www.matthiasmedia.com.au
Please visit our website for current postal and telephone contact information.

Matthias Media (USA)
Email: sales@matthiasmedia.com
Internet: www.matthiasmedia.com
Please visit our website for current postal and telephone contact information.

Scripture quotations are from the Holy Bible, English Standard Version® (ESV®), copyright © 2001 by Crossway, a publishing ministry of Good News Publishers. Used by permission. All rights reserved.

ISBN 978 1 925424 79 9

Cover design and typesetting by Lankshear Design.

To my three beloved sons,
Michael, Stephen and David

CONTENTS

Introduction — 3

Part one: Knowing the God who creates — 7
1. Knowing God in the gospel — 9
2. Knowing God by God — 23
3. Knowing the God who speaks, part 1 — 37
4. Knowing the God who speaks, part 2 — 51
5. Knowing the God who speaks, part 3 — 65
6. Knowing the three-personed Creator — 79
7. Knowing God the Lord, part 1 — 93
8. Knowing God the Lord, part 2 — 103
9. Knowing God the Lord, part 3 — 115

Part two: Knowing the Creator who saves — 127
10. Humanity and the gospel message, part 1 — 129
11. Humanity and the gospel message, part 2 — 141
12. The covenantal nation — 153
13. The humble Lord — 165

14. The crucified Lord	179
15. The exalted Lord	195
16. The Lord who is Spirit	207

Part three: Knowing the Saviour who is Lord — 219

17. The Lord who summons	221
18. The Lord who summons: our response	235
19. The saving Lord who justifies	247
20. The saving Lord: his choice	259
21. The life of faith: its context	273
22. The life of faith: its pattern	287
23. The life of faith: its resources, part 1	301
24. The life of faith: its resources, part 2	317
25. The life of faith: its resources, part 3	333
26. The life of faith: its hope	347
27. Christ the Lord and the end of history	361

Appendices — 377

1. The Apostles' Creed	379
2. The Nicene Creed	381
3. The Thirty-Nine Articles of Religion	383
4. Scripture index	399

Acknowledgements — 419

INTRODUCTION

This book is an introduction to Christian doctrine. For many years now, I have initiated beginners at various theological colleges into this subject. The material itself arose from my long engagement with theological students as they began their studies at Moore College in Sydney, where our aim was to provide an introductory overview which would firmly ground the study of Christian doctrine in the Scriptures. It was, of course, fully supplemented by lectures which went beyond the content of this book. At the same time, other learning was being done in ancillary subjects such as Early Church History and Philosophy, as well as the biblical studies. We always sought to be a fellowship of teachers dedicated to sharing the knowledge of God with one another and with the students so that together we could make God known in the world.

The chief aim of this book, then, is to summarize what the Bible teaches (its 'doctrine') about the great topics it contains. Doctrine seeks to extend our knowledge of the Bible and help us to understand it fully and accurately. It is an essential method of reading and applying the Bible. I have tried to show what the Bible teaches and how the different subjects interrelate with each other. I also aim to introduce the voices of those who, down though Christian history, have read the same Bible and had insights which we need to embrace.

My aim is to write in such a way that you can read the book

through, chapter by chapter. It is not a textbook as such, although you can consult it on various issues. But I am hoping to make the subject coherent and engaging.

It will help to spend a moment familiarizing yourself with the book's contents pages before you begin, in order to grasp the overall shape of the material and be aware of its aims. Each chapter begins with a 'key concept' that summarizes the heart of the topic. To help you catch the book's flow of ideas, these key concepts are gathered together at the beginning of each of the three parts.

At the end of each chapter, I have included a range of material to stimulate further thought, and an indication of where further work on the topic may lead. The quotations at the conclusion of each chapter are not necessarily directly linked to the topic under discussion; in some cases, they are simply intended to introduce you to some of the riches of our Christian and cultural heritage. The questions for further thought offer a variety of material: many are designed to help you summarize and reflect on what the chapter has covered; others will require you to consider ideas about which little has been said, in the hope that this opens up avenues for future learning. Not all of them are intended to be easily answered!

There is, of course, so much more that needs to be said. To help you move forward, I have continually referred to three other authors at the end of each chapter, and tried to relate their writings to the themes as they unfold. The books that I have used are:

- Gerald Bray, *God is Love: A biblical and systematic theology* (Crossway, 2012)
- Michael Horton, *Pilgrim Theology: Core doctrines for Christian disciples* (Zondervan, 2012)
- Bruce Milne, *Know the Truth: A handbook of Christian belief* (IVP, third edition, 2013)

Milne is from the Baptist tradition, Horton from the Reformed, and Bray from the Anglican. All are expounding Reformed Protestant theology in their own way and at slightly different levels. They certainly do not necessarily agree with each other, or with me, about everything. Each of these books will take you on to the next stage of your study and answer many of the questions which I am not able to take up in this introductory volume.

I also make frequent reference to works by Dr JI Packer, especially his *Concise Theology: A guide to historic Christian beliefs* (Tyndale, 2001), which is a simple (but never simplistic) way in to thinking about these great themes.

Any usefulness this volume has will be found in three elements. First, it concentrates on the indispensable biblical basis of the subject. Second, it orders Christian doctrine by the shape and flow of what may be called 'biblical theology'. Third, it suggests ways in which readers can advance in further knowledge of the subject, and so paves the way for ongoing growth.

We could have started the study of doctrine from a historical or contemporary point. But I have begun with the Bible because I hold it to be God's word, his revelation of himself and of his purposes in the Lord Jesus Christ. I hope you share this conviction—or at least that you share it by the time you've finished using this book. It is good to acquire the habit of turning to the Bible first, because it remains the supreme source and touchstone of truth.

"The fear of the LORD is the beginning of knowledge; fools despise wisdom and instruction" (Prov 1:7). Humility before the Lord is the prerequisite to knowing God. My prayer for us all is that we will begin and end with the fear of the Lord that leads to wisdom.

PART ONE

KNOWING THE GOD WHO CREATES

- We live to know God, and the gospel of Jesus Christ is the means by which we come to know him.
- We know God only because he makes himself known to us.
- God's revelation of himself is not simply through creation; he has spoken, and his speech is in Scripture. Through Scripture, God rules over us.
- Scripture is inspired by God, and hence a perfect and sufficient unity.
- Scripture is inspired by God, and hence infallible and inerrant.
- The God we know reveals himself to be the Father, the Son, and the Holy Spirit.
- The God we know is utterly free from all limitations except those inherent in his own righteous character.
- The God we know has, from his own righteous character, created all things and committed himself to the welfare and salvation of his creation.
- The God we know is both glorious and gracious in his righteousness.

1

KNOWING GOD IN THE GOSPEL

Key concept: We live to know God, and the gospel of Jesus Christ is the means by which we come to know him.

1. Introduction: Knowing God

God is, and we may know him. That is the Christian claim.

This is a bold assertion, especially at the present time. Scepticism is the contemporary mood; atheism has become a popular crusade; agnosticism is a fashionable mindset. It is common to believe that if there is a God, he is virtually unknowable. But if we can in fact know God, especially the God who is described in the Bible, it would transform our lives, answering many of life's riddles and making it possible for us to know how we are expected to live as human beings.

Indeed, the Bible asserts that knowing God is the goal or purpose of human existence—not just knowing that he exists or what he is like, but entering into a personal relationship with him. As Jesus said, "this is eternal life, that they know you, the only true God, and Jesus Christ whom you have sent" (John 17:3). Here is the good news: personal and corporate fulfilment is possible, and our vision of the future is filled with a sure and wonderful hope.

But how can we know the invisible and transcendent God? How can we know that he is there or that he has any interest in us?

The answer is, through Jesus Christ.

The confidence of the New Testament that we may know God arises from Jesus Christ's claim that he was sent by God, and from the belief of his followers that he spoke the truth. This is apparent from any reading of the New Testament itself. The central Christian message was called "the word of God", or "the gospel". The early Christians taught that when men and women received the gospel and believed it, they would come to know the true and living God. This is what we have seen in John 17:3. It is also what we see in the teaching of the apostle Paul.

Paul believed that God had spoken a word, and that by the publication and reception of that word we can come to know God. In a seminal passage, 2 Corinthians 4:1-6, he called this word "the gospel of the glory of Christ" (v 4) and said that it had the power to provide "the light of the knowledge of the glory of God in the face of Jesus Christ" (v 6). The essential content of this gospel was simply stated: "Jesus Christ as Lord" (v 5). John speaks of gaining "eternal life" through the knowledge of God, while Paul describes such life in terms of "light" and "glory". The gospel saves by relating us to God.

The Bible teaches that the fundamental human problem is not ignorance as to whether there is a God, but a profound alienation from God which has left us in darkness. Thus, the unbelieving are blinded by Satan and perishing under the righteous judgement of God (2 Cor 4:3-4). Their basic difficulty is not intellectual, but moral, spiritual and relational. That is why the biblical message is not a reasoned argument setting out the proofs of God's existence. It is not opposed to reason—indeed, it appeals to reason—though it also assumes the distortion of human thought through pride and self-sufficiency. Instead, the biblical message is the disclosure of one person to another—of God to us. Only thus can we be reconciled to God and so have eternal life.

We will look again at these matters in due course. For now, however, we only need to notice that as a matter of history, the authorized Christian teachers followed the lead of Jesus Christ himself and centred their message on what they called the gospel of Jesus Christ, which, they claimed, introduced people to a salvation-giving knowledge of God.

What was the content of this gospel and why should it be the instrument of human salvation? Let us start with Jesus himself, and his use of the word "gospel".

2. The gospel of the kingdom

In what was probably the first written Gospel, Mark, the word "gospel" appears in the opening sentence.[1] His whole book is described as "the gospel of Jesus Christ, the Son of God" (Mark 1:1), and he records Jesus using the same word in his summary of Jesus' teaching in 1:15:

> Now after John was arrested, Jesus came into Galilee, proclaiming the gospel of God, and saying, "The time is fulfilled, and the kingdom of God is at hand; repent and believe in the gospel." (vv 14-15)

Matthew's Gospel agrees and adds that John the Baptist had already preached the same message of the kingdom (Matt 3:2). In addition, however, John identified Jesus as the one who was anointed to bring the Spirit of blessing and the fire of judgement (3:11-12). Of course, both John and Jesus were speaking to an audience who understood

---

1   Throughout this book, I will follow the convention of referring to the books of Matthew, Mark, Luke and John as 'Gospels' (capital G), while the message will be referred to as the 'gospel' (small g).

their message of a coming kingdom; they were speaking directly to the powerful hopes of their Jewish contemporaries. These hopes arose from the promises God made in the Old Testament and were sharpened by their current experience of being under the rule of alien kings and lords.

The opening of Mark's Gospel is so significant that it is worth examining his record of Jesus' teaching very carefully. As we do, we see the following six features: that Jesus preached; that he preached the gospel; that he announced a coming kingdom; that the kingdom was the kingdom of God; that it was imminent; and that repentance and faith were called for as a means of being prepared.

Let us take each of these six elements in turn.

First, Jesus *"preached"* or 'heralded' his gospel—that is, he announced it before he argued for it. This tells us something about the nature of Jesus' gospel. It is the announcement of a coming event, and hence must first be preached before discussion is entered into. The stories of Jesus reveal that he did discuss, argue and question. But his first duty was to preach (cf. Mark 1:38). He was a herald rather than a philosopher, guru or moralist.

Second, Jesus *preached a "gospel"*—that is, he gave 'glad tidings' before he gave abstract ideas or maxims about how to live. The word "gospel" itself contains the idea of 'news' or 'tidings' and is therefore appropriate for announcing a momentous event. The news gave rise to explanations, claims and maxims, but its essence is an event, and hence it is reported in a document called a Gospel.

Third, Jesus *announced the kingdom*—that is, the word "kingdom" implies a monarch's 'rule' or 'reign'. It was an event to be declared because he was announcing an imminent convulsion in the history of his nation, Israel, and then the world. Jesus is speaking here of God's plans for the whole world. God's reign, while almighty and unassailable from one point of view, was disputed and rejected from another. The story of Adam's refusal to obey God stood at the beginning of the Bible as a constant reminder that this was the current alienated state of humanity. Israel was deeply conscious of this. Her own oppressed circumstances, under the rule of a foreign empire, exemplified both the hostility of the nations to God's ways and also the judgement of God against her. To the ears of his hearers, tuned by John the Baptist and conscious of such prophets as Daniel, Jesus was announcing that God would soon reverse their historical circumstances and begin to rule the world through Israel as he had promised in the Scriptures. "The time is fulfilled", said Jesus, because the promises of God have reached their goal at this moment and in this person.

Fourth, Jesus *announced the kingdom of God*—that is, the coming event was the gift of God before it was the work of human beings. The word "kingdom" has sometimes suggested to Christians that Jesus' interest was in a new political and social order, and they have then taken the next step to assuming that the new order is to be created by the work of our hands. True, there can be no doubt that God's reign has had profound political and social consequences in this world; nor can there be any doubt that we have our part to play in contributing to these blessings by doing the good works which he has prepared for us to walk in. But the fact that God's kingdom is at stake here reminds us that the human side is a response, and it is, first of all, the response of repentance and faith. All human response is partial and inadequate. But we must also remember that he described his kingdom as being "not of this world" (John 18:36). We do not bring in his kingdom; we do not create it. It his work, not ours.

Fifth, Jesus *warned that the kingdom was near*—that is, it remained in the future rather than the present, but was close rather than remote. This nearness gave his exhortation its urgency. As the Gospel narrative of Jesus' work and words developed, however, it became clear that the 'nearness' of the kingdom had an unexpected aspect. The kingdom was to be regarded as both present and future (see, for example, Mark 4:26-32). As time goes on, it is revealed that we are dealing with two comings of Christ. By his first coming, he introduces the kingdom (Luke 17:21); at his second coming, the kingdom arrives in its finality. Between these two events, Christ rules over his church and the world (Eph 1:15-22; 1 Cor 15:20-28).

Thus, in his plans, the present historical age will one day be succeeded by a marvellous new age; there will be such a sharp break in the continuity of history that a whole new order will emerge. Scripture calls this "the age to come", or "eternal life", or "new heavens and a new earth". But the preaching of Jesus announced the invasion of the age to come into the present age. The two ages, present and future, co-exist until his return, when the old age will disappear and the new will be here in its completeness and glory.

Sixth, Jesus *demanded repentance and faith in the light of the kingdom*—that is, the kingdom or lordship of God must be received before it can be lived. There was a tendency in Israel to believe that mere membership of the covenant people assured the individual of a place in the kingdom. Jesus and John both warned powerfully that the appropriate response to their announcement was repentance and faith—a radical inward change of allegiance, applicable both to the leader and the outcast. This alone could qualify even the Israelites, the children of Abraham by biological descent, for acceptance in God's kingdom and so reconciliation with God. Even genetic relationship to Jesus himself was to be no substitute for this (Mark 3:31-35). Of course, entrance to the kingdom was to be followed by a life of obedience to God the king.

Jesus' initial challenge to Israel, his summons to repentance and faith in light of the coming kingdom, remains at the heart of the gospel, but the rest of the New Testament develops, enriches and explains it. The death, resurrection and ascension of Jesus demonstrated both the triumph of the kingdom and the person of the king, not least in his outpouring of the Holy Spirit. Likewise, in due course it is revealed that the message of the gospel was for all people, not just Israel (Acts 1:8). Furthermore, as Jesus' words about fulfilment demonstrate, the gospel is inextricably connected to the existing Scriptures of the Old Testament. To comprehend the fullness of the gospel, therefore, we must turn to the teaching of the whole of Scripture.

3. The kingdom of the gospel

God rules the world by his powerful word. In the original creation story, God effortlessly brought all things to be merely through his word. The Old Testament frequently celebrates the continued rule or kingdom of God over all creation (e.g. Psalm 93). In the garden of Eden he is also depicted as the sovereign Lord, reigning over his human creation by his word. The rebellious fall of Adam and Eve is a rejection of his word and hence his rule. The successive covenant relationships with Abraham, Israel and the Davidic kings is the re-assertion of his sovereignty by his word. A covenant is a word of promise binding parties together in relationship.

The Old Testament covenants such as the ones between the Lord and Abraham, Israel and David are, however, incomplete and inadequate. They bring a knowledge of God, although it is fitful and shadowy. But they also contain promises of better things to come, when God will once more assert his public rule and the knowledge of God will be deep and satisfying (Jer 31:31-34; Ezek 36:22-36; Dan 2:36-45). Sometimes these promises are connected with one who appears to be a supreme human ruler in the line of David—a 'Messiah' or 'Christ' (see, for example, Isaiah 11:1-11).

The New Testament asserts the eventual complete and public triumph of God the King and a new creation in which righteousness dwells (e.g. Rev 20:11-21:1; 2 Pet 3:13). But the path to these triumphs is not an easy one, for it involves the fire of judgement, as was foreshadowed and experienced many times in the Old Testament. When Jesus announces the kingdom, he is, among other things, announcing judgement. As a result of human rebellion, the way to life lies through death. Human history is the working out of both grace and judgement until God's appointed end. The kingdom *has* come, but the kingdom *will* come.

In a sense, the Old Testament prophets said as much as all this. But the New Testament message is qualitatively different—and the difference is Jesus. In him, the promises and purposes of God have come to fruition (2 Cor 1:18-20).

4. The king in the gospel

John the Baptist pointed to Jesus as "the Christ", that is, the one who fulfils all the promises of God. Jesus put himself at the centre of his own message in an astonishing way. His parables of the kingdom revealed that, up to that point, the kingdom had come in seed, although not in fullness (e.g. Mark 4). They foreshadowed both the judgement and salvation of God.

The New Testament describes the death of Jesus in terms of God's judgement. Where Israel and the world should have suffered judgement, he drinks the cup of God's wrath alone (Mark 14:36) and so gives his life "as a ransom for many" (10:45). As with other divine judgements in the past, new life blossoms forth; here, however, the one person judged is such that the whole of history hinges on his death, and a new age bursts into the old with his resurrection. The forces of the old age seek "signs and ... wisdom", but the Christian gospel must, from now on, be the message of a crucified Lord (1 Cor 1:18-31), mightier than any miracle and wiser than the wisest of human beings.

The truth about Jesus is, of course, more extraordinary than our hearts can imagine, for he is the Lord of Glory, crucified by the rulers of this age (1 Cor 2:8-9), the one who receives the Holy Spirit (Mark 1:10) and gives the Spirit to his followers (Acts 2:33). In Jesus Christ, God is re-asserting his rule and so saving us; Jesus is the last Adam, the true image of God, the true ruler of the world, and the Son of God himself, from all eternity with God and God (John 1:18; 1 Cor 15:45; Col 1:15). Only as both God and man can he be Saviour.

It is natural, therefore, that the final presentation of Christ in the New Testament is not even the crucified or risen Christ, but the Christ who is seated at the right hand of God— the Christ who is called both Lord and King (Rev 19:16). He is only thus because he died and rose again; but in this historical time between his ascension and his return, he reigns as 'God's man', until all his enemies are defeated and the kingdom of Christ becomes the kingdom of God (see 1 Cor 15:20-28).

This is the reason that the New Testament evangelists could preach both "the kingdom" and "the Christ" (Acts 20:25, 8:5). These are not separate entities. When Paul asserts that he preaches Jesus Christ as Lord and King, he is doing nothing else than proclaiming the kingdom (cf. Acts 17:7; 2 Cor 4:5). In so doing, he makes exactly the same demand as Jesus did, namely entry into the kingdom through repentance and faith (Acts 20:21), although the focus of that faith is now explicitly Jesus. For Jesus, the kingdom is as precious as a treasure hidden in a field (Matt 13:44); for Paul, every human privilege was as garbage compared with "the surpassing worth of knowing Christ Jesus my Lord" (Phil 3:8). Jesus is the Lord of God's kingdom.

5. The blessings of the gospel

In the passage just cited, Paul claims to know "Christ Jesus my Lord". This is not at all alien to knowing God, for to know Christ is to know God (see John 1:18, 17:3; 2 Cor 4:6; 1 Tim 2:5). In Christ, the Father discloses himself to us and invites relationship. It is by sending forth the Spirit of his Son that God enables us to call him Father (Gal 4:6). The whole of Scripture is a many-sided testimony to the possibilities of this knowledge, or relationship, until it reaches an extraordinary fruition in the age to come (1 Cor 13:12). For now, the blessings of the gospel are ours "in Christ".

Much to the surprise of the original disciples, the blessings are available to all—Jew and Gentile alike—on the same terms of repentance and faith. The failure of Israel to know its Lord has paradoxically led to worldwide blessing in line with God's stated intentions (Gal 3:8; Romans 11).

Repentance and faith are called for because they are the basic relational attitudes essential for the knowledge of God. The New Testament contrasts them with the good works by which sinful humanity is forever trying to please God while keeping him at a distance (e.g. Eph 2:8-9). Nonetheless, it is a blessing of the gospel that the life of faith is one of good works which glorify God and re-assert our true humanity by showing what we were meant to be (Eph 2:10, 4:22-24).

Constant amongst the blessings of the gospel mentioned in the New Testament is forgiveness. Since the warning of judgement to come is so central to the preaching of the kingdom, it is not at all surprising that cleansing from sin, or forgiveness, should be so prominent (e.g. Acts 5:31, 10:42-43). The wonderful truth is that the judgement of the end is brought forward into this age and we are acquitted in this present time through faith in Christ.

Our forgiveness entails reconciliation with God brought about by the Spirit of God. By the Spirit, new life comes; by the Spirit, God himself resides within us; by the Spirit, we call God our Father and Jesus our Lord; by the coming of the Spirit, we know that God has accepted lost Gentiles; in the power of the Spirit, we bear fruit that the law on its own could not produce; and by the Spirit, we know that one day our fulfilment will come (see John 3:1-8, 7:37-39, 14:16-20; Rom 8:15; 1 Cor 12:3; 2 Cor 1:21-22; Gal 5:22-23; Eph 1:13-14). The Spirit is indeed the power of the age to come at work in this present evil age. He is never in competition with God's word, for he is the author and interpreter of that precious gift.

6. Conclusion

We began with the bold biblical claim that God is, and we may know him through the gospel. And we have begun to see what the message of the gospel is. But are there not other ways of coming to know God? Do we not believe in God through reason, or through experience, for example? The biblical teaching certainly refers to such possibilities. And in the next chapter we will discuss their strengths and limitations. But the Bible itself leaves us virtually no alternative than to place greatest weight in assessing its truth claims on the person and work of Jesus Christ. It is how we regard him, as we hear the message about him preached, that will determine our view of God and the world. Indeed the business of gospel preaching is to provide a defence and confirmation of the gospel by relating it in the language of the hearers to their experience and knowledge. But since the gospel is personal knowledge which demands of proud humans that they submit to Jesus Christ as Lord, we are conscious that reason and experience will not provide the final explanation as to why a person believes or not. That is why the theme of the next chapter is knowing God by God.

Because the gospel is the starting point for the Christian knowledge of God, I have taken that as the beginning point for our study of doctrine. Furthermore, it introduces us immediately to the flow of God's salvation history and its ultimate goal. The life of faith is lived between the first and second comings of Christ, and unless we understand where we are, what we have, and what our hope is, we will be impoverished. In the chapters that follow, we will never be far from this beginning or from the great end that lies in store for us.

Key verse
"And this is eternal life, that they know you, the only true God, and Jesus Christ whom you have sent." (John 17:3)

Quotation
"Good, mery, glad and joyfull tydinge, that maketh a mannes heart glad, and maketh hym synge, daunce, and leepe for joye." (William Tyndale [1494-1536, Bible translator and martyr] on the meaning of the word 'gospel', Prologue to the New Testament)

Key terms
- Gospel
- Kingdom of God
- Covenant

For further thought
- What other starting points might people propose in their study of doctrine? From what we have seen in this chapter, why should we begin with the gospel?
- "God is"—or, as he says about himself, "I am". Does this mean more than simply "God exists"? How might it differentiate God from human beings and from the rest of creation?
- John Calvin's Geneva Catechism begins: "What is the chief end of human life? To know God by whom men were created." Another catechism begins: "What is the purpose of your life? To love God as he loves me." The Westminster Shorter Catechism begins: "What is the chief end of man? Man's chief end is to glorify God, and to enjoy him forever." Why the differences? Which do you prefer?
- Have you seen examples of Christians over-emphasising the connection between God's kingdom and "a new political and social order"? What damage has this done?

For further reading

- For chapters 1-9 of this book, see JI Packer, *Concise Theology*, part 1
- G Bray, *God is Love*, chapter 1
- M Horton, *Pilgrim Theology*, introduction ('Why Study Theology?')
- B Milne, *Know the Truth*, chapter 1

2

KNOWING GOD BY GOD

Key concept: We know God only because he makes himself known to us.

1. Introduction

As we have seen, the Christian gospel claims to have the power to lead to knowledge of God through Jesus Christ. But this also opens the wider questions of whether God may be known by means other than the gospel and what we may know of him and his will by such means. Can reason or experience lead the way to knowing that God exists and what he is like? Can we know God by such means?

This issue has become all the more urgent with the rise of 'the new atheism', with arguments appealing to logic, scientific evidence, and morality. Thus atheists deny the logical power of proofs for the existence of God; they point to science as having explained all natural phenomena without any need to invoke a divine being; and they castigate religious believers for their gross follies and crimes as a way of discrediting religion as such.

This certainly raises the issue of whether the claims of Christianity can receive any independent verification from outside—for example, through proofs for the existence of the Christian God. We therefore turn now to the question of the claims and reality of alternative ways of knowing God, and we do so by considering the categories known as 'natural theology' and 'general revelation'.

2. Natural theology

A famous series of lectures named 'The Gifford Lectures' began in Scotland in 1888. Lord Gifford, under whose will the series is still conducted, wished them to promote the study of 'natural theology'. His definition provides us with a famous, succinct statement of what this term means. He understood natural theology to be the knowledge of God, pursued as "a strictly natural science, the greatest of all possible sciences ... that of Infinite Being, without reference to or reliance upon any supposed special exceptional or so-called miraculous revelation. I wish it studied just as astronomy or chemistry is."[2]

'Natural theology', then, is theology without revelation. The word 'natural' here does not mean the study of nature (although ideas about God from nature may be included), but natural as opposed to 'divine' or 'supernatural'. What can we know of God from our own resources?

Natural theology has two broad areas of interest. In the first place, there is the question of whether a god or gods exist. The second question is how such god(s) as may exist can be described simply by using the power of the human mind and observation of the natural world. We will concentrate on the first of these questions.

The possible existence of God has been puzzled over by some of the greatest intellectuals from earliest times. In Western theology and

---

[2] M Davie, T Grass, SR Holmes, J McDowell and TA Noble (eds), *New Dictionary of Theology: Historical and Systematic*, 2nd edn, IVP, 2016, p 268.

philosophy, for example, various 'classical' proofs for the existence of God have been advanced, debated, refuted and re-formulated. Broadly speaking, they fall into four categories.

a. The cosmological

This argument begins from the idea that some higher being is required to account for the world (or 'cosmos') as we have it. One type of cosmological argument arises from the observation of causality in our world. Everything has a cause, but there must be a 'First Cause', for there can hardly be an infinity of causes. This would apply whether we are thinking of the First Cause at the beginning or rather the first sustaining cause of all that exists. This First Cause is named God.

b. The teleological

Originally this argument had to do with the purpose or end (the 'telos') of all things viewed dynamically. More recently, attention has concentrated on design: the contention is that the world shows clear evidence that planning has taken place, which leads, inevitably, to the thought of a Designer, who is called God.

c. The ontological

The ontological proof examines the being ('ontos') or nature of God and concludes that, by definition, he must exist. For the very idea of God is of a being than which nothing greater can be conceived. But a real God is obviously greater (or more perfect) than an imaginary God. Hence, we cannot but think of God except as existing.

d. The moral

According to some thinkers, it is not possible to explain the existence of our sense of moral values without invoking the idea of God, who is the divine law-giver. Without God, there can be no objective right and wrong; there can only be subjective preference. But our experience of life tells us that some things are *always* right or *always* wrong. Thus there must be a source of morality, namely God.

Of course, this brief introductory classification of the proofs does not do them justice. Even at this stage, however, we can benefit from some preliminary comments about them:

a. None of them can be regarded as having 'worked' in the sense of creating universal conviction. From time to time, one or another is rehabilitated in a way which makes it more persuasive, but argument goes on vigorously from all sides.
b. Some would argue that to think of them as 'proofs' is wrong; it is better to regard them as 'evidences' and give them some explanatory power. Thus we may speak of design and ask what the alternative is. The dilemma 'chaos or God?' can clarify the mind, although it does not force a decision for one against the other.
c. Many theologians are critical of the whole process, whether it 'works' or not. They would argue that the 'God' of the proofs is not necessarily the God revealed in Scripture, and that natural theology relies on corrupt human reason to arrive at truth, an impossible undertaking that only inflates the human ego.
d. On the other hand, the sheer religiousness of the human race, and the attractiveness to it of the teleological argument in particular, have suggested to others that belief in God (or gods) is an innate human capacity, an indispensable part of our way of viewing the world. As Francis Bacon wrote in his 1612 essay *Of Atheism,* "Atheism is rather in the lip than in the heart of man".[3]

---

3   F Bacon, *The Essays or Councils, Civil and Moral,* Oxford University Press, 1999, p 38.

Some would argue that the denial of God is akin to the case of a person denying that all other persons exists—a possible but ultimately unbelievable view. Likewise, there appears to be some neurological research which suggests that belief in a supreme being or beings is simply inherent to the way our brains work. But this hardly advances the argument for the reality of what we believe.

e. The chief argument against the existence of a perfectly good and all-powerful God, as classically conceived, is the fact of evil. Independent thought, without revelation, may conclude from the chaos of the world that the evidence points to polytheism, or a weak God, or a God in process of maturing, or to no God at all.

At this point, however, it is important to note the Bible's contribution to the debate.

3. The Bible and general revelation

Scripture nowhere tries to 'prove' God's existence. It assumes it, and labels the practical atheist a "fool" (Ps 14:1). From this point of view, the Bible seems to endorse the idea that the knowledge that there is a God is simply common to human beings and hardly needs to be argued for.

Paul is willing to appeal to human experience of God and the world as a starting point when speaking to Gentiles:

> In past generations he allowed all the nations to walk in their own ways. Yet he did not leave himself without witness, for he did good by giving you rains from heaven and fruitful seasons, satisfying your hearts with food and gladness. (Acts 14:16-17; cf. 17:22-31)

In thinking of the guilt of the human race for failing to respond to the available light, he writes:

> For what can be known about God is plain to them, because God has shown it to them. For his invisible attributes, namely, his eternal power and divine nature, have been clearly perceived, ever since the creation of the world, in the things that have been made. So they are without excuse. For although they knew God, they did not honour him as God or give thanks to him, but they became futile in their thinking, and their foolish hearts were darkened. (Rom 1:19-21)

He also refers to the inner experience of humanity in our contest with conscience and hence our sense that there is a right and wrong that is objective, not merely subjective (Rom 2:12-16).

Paul's position is, therefore, that there is a widespread knowledge of God but that it has arisen not from natural theology, but from an intentional revelation of God to all humankind mainly through the natural world (cf. Ps 19:1-6). This we may call a 'general revelation' ('general' in the sense of 'universal, available to all'). There is no hint here that human beings on our own could undertake the task of demonstrating the existence and nature of God. Rather, God intends that his person and power may be observed through the experience of living in this world. However, this general revelation of God has been suppressed by human sin, and now finds expression in corrupt religion, especially idolatry.

In all of this, Paul is identifying an important factor: the question of God's existence and nature is not a simple question for mere rationality to solve. It involves the whole person (including the mind); it impinges so significantly on our deepest experiences, on the sort of persons we are and want to be, that cool detachment is impossible. Indeed, while some hold that the problem of evil makes religion impossible, others find that Christianity very powerfully addresses this challenge.

The reader of the Bible is not at all surprised, therefore, that natural theology is totally inadequate to decide with any finality whether God exists or how we ought to describe him. In particular, if it relies on an inflated view of moral and intellectual capacity, it can only lead astray. But if it is the exposition of what we may call the general revelation of God, it can be a way into the knowledge of God provided in the gospel. It can provide what we may perhaps describe as a 'rumour' of God, a means of calling on our own observations of the world to prepare us for the gospel. The evangelist should repeat the rumour, but to rely upon it would be fatal, for both philosophical and theological reasons.

4. Religious experience

Many would feel impatient with the rather abstract philosophical debate on other grounds. For them, the knowledge of God has forced itself upon their consciousness and they could no more deny God than deny their own selves. To 'prove' God is a needless exercise.

This position has the strength of more adequately reflecting the reality of a transcendent God, if there is such a being. It is inherently more likely that he will need to make himself known to us in an overwhelming experience than that he may be 'discovered' in the laboratories of the mind, given the inadequacy of reason even when faced with the physical universe. Indeed, it also suits the nature of 'faith' as understood in Christianity. Faith and reason are not opposed to each other, but faith better describes the relational emphasis of the knowledge of God.

Some theologians have even attempted to describe God in terms of common religious experience. In *The Idea of the Holy*, a famous work first published in 1917, Rudolf Otto described the widespread experience of God in terms of a numinous dread which both fascinates and overwhelms. This he saw as being at the heart of all religion. More recently, the Alister Hardy Religious Experience Research Centre, based in the University of Wales, speaks of housing "an archive with over 6,000 accounts of first-hand experiences of people across the world who had a spiritual or religious experience".[4] Its findings suggest that such experiences are widespread in the community, even amongst those who would not regard themselves as religious.

By its very nature, however, religious experience tends to be private and personal (whereas belief stemming from the gospel is both public and trans-personal). Furthermore, its private nature tends to place it beyond critical assessment. It can hardly be commended to others—it is no gospel—no 'news'—as such. Nor can it be clear that the experience of the numinous is an experience of God and not (say) the devil or a lesser spirit, or even a trick of our own consciousness. Furthermore, it has no necessary connection with righteousness: the 'holy' is not necessarily 'moral'.

5. Revelation and the gospel

In thinking about religion, many have concluded that the best way to a knowledge of God is through revelation—that is, through God's disclosure of himself. As Hilary of Poitiers (c. 315-367) wrote: "For He whom we can know only through his own utterances is a fitting witness concerning himself".[5] It is no accident that the Gospel of John reveals that Jesus is to be called "the Word" of God (John 1:1, 14). This reflects both the transcendence of God and his personal and relational nature. Whatever we may make of natural the-

---

[4] Alister Hardy Religious Experience Research Centre, *Welcome to the Alister Hardy Religious Experience Research Centre (RERC)*, University of Wales Trinity Saint David website, 2022, accessed 18 January 2022 (uwtsd.ac.uk/library/alister-hardy-religious-experience-research-centre).

[5] Cited in G Hunsinger, *Evangelical, Catholic and Reformed: Essays on Barth and other themes*, Eerdmans, 2015, p 61.

ology and general revelation, the fundamental nature of the gospel of Jesus Christ means that it is a special revelation, centred on a person who is both God and man. This means that the key question for us all is the one posed by Jesus to his disciples: "Who do you say that I am?" (Mark 8:29). Rather than work out in advance how God has spoken, we must approach the actual gospel to see whether we can answer the question that it poses about who Jesus is.

6. The gospel of Jesus Christ

As we have seen in chapter 1, the gospel claims to be a word from God which brings us to a true and saving knowledge of God. The only way to discover whether the gospel is authentic is to examine it on its own terms. As with human enquiry, the object of investigation must be allowed to determine the angle of approach.

It is worth noting in a preliminary way that the gospel claim has a twofold aspect:

a. It preserves the 'Godness' of God. That is, by stressing God's initiative and grace, it emphasizes his character of transcendent almightiness and fatherly pity. We are invited into a relationship.
b. It reflects the sinfulness of man, in that although he is highly religious, and perhaps innately god-conscious, his corrupt mind is incapable of finding out the truth about God. Revelation is needed not just because we are human, but because we are sinful.

This twofold aspect corresponds exactly to the saving heart of the gospel. The way of *knowing God* and the way of *being saved by God* do not contradict one another within the Christian view. They both depend on God's grace and human incapacity. The gospel is internally coherent at this important point.

But the gospel further commends itself by being centred on

Jesus Christ, and it is by the truth about him that its claims stand or fall. In so commending him, the gospel invites assessment along three different lines.

a. First, in his relation to Israel

Jesus does not fit into the pattern of a lonely religious genius teaching people about God. He saw himself (and was seen by his followers) as the fulfilment of the plans of God as begun and recorded in the Old Testament. The prior question about Jesus has always been "Are you the one who is to come …?" (cf. Matt 11:3). The Jewish nation as a whole answered in the negative, but many gave a positive verdict. The Old Testament is not the invention of the early church; it stands apart from Christians as such. It is all the more impressive, therefore, to be able to ask whether Jesus fulfils the Old Testament's hopes and expectations.

b. Second, in his own 'words and works'

When set in the context provided by Israel, the life and teaching of Jesus are utterly remarkable on any account. His words have entered and even helped shape hundreds of languages. Stories such as the Good Samaritan and the Prodigal Son are familiar around the world. Jesus' teaching is extraordinary for the way in which he speaks truth in few words, but truth which enters the soul. Even those who have opposed or derided him have felt the fascination and power of his life. Furthermore, his was a life (and death) which conformed to his own words. He rebukes hypocrisy without fear; he mixes with the outcasts and transforms their lives; he prays for the forgiveness of those who are crucifying him. His teaching has had enough power to shape entire civilizations, and enough force that entire cultures can be measured by it. As the American sage Ralph Waldo Emerson once said, "The name of Jesus is not so much written as ploughed into the history of the world". One of the apparently odd things to notice is that Jesus revealed himself as not merely the prophet of the kingdom (as was John the Baptist), but the King of the kingdom (Luke 17:20-21). Such a self-identification led to his execution. But there were those who believed it and confessed that he is indeed God (John 20:28). This is the issue of revelation—is Jesus Christ the very Word of God?

c. Third, in his resurrection

It is a mistake to think that the resurrection of Christ can be 'proved' in some absolute sense. Nonetheless, it can be investigated, and the evidence for it examined and sifted. The Christian faith invites this examination and declares that Christianity would be nullified if Christ had not risen (e.g. 1 Cor 15:13-19). As long as no *a priori* decision is taken that no miracles ever occur, the evidence remains substantial and impressive. As Professor CFD Moule asks:

> If the coming into existence of the Nazarenes, a phenomenon undeniably attested by the New Testament, rips a great hole in history, a hole of the size and shape of Resurrection, what does the secular historian propose to stop it up with?[6]

7. Conclusion

Ultimately, assessment of Jesus today will be as it has ever been: mixed. When Jesus enquired, "Who do people say that the Son of Man is?" he was told "Some say John the Baptist, others say Elijah, and others Jeremiah or one of the prophets". Only Peter declared directly, "You are the Christ, the Son of the living God" (Matt 16:13-16). We do not need to doubt that Peter came to this mind by observing Jesus, by listening to him, by assessing him, by forming his own judgement. Yet when all that is conceded, we must also

---

6   CFD Moule, *Phenomenon of the New Testament*, SCM Press, 1967, p 3.

note the word of Jesus: "Blessed are you, Simon Bar-Jonah! For flesh and blood has not revealed this to you, but my Father who is in heaven" (16:17).

Even here, the initiative and grace of God is preserved, according to Jesus. We know God only because he has chosen to reveal himself to us and invite us into a relationship with him.

Key verse

For what can be known about God is plain to them, because God has shown it to them. For his invisible attributes, namely, his eternal power and divine nature, have been clearly perceived, ever since the creation of the world, in the things that have been made. So they are without excuse. (Rom 1:19-20)

Quotation

"When even the least drop of faith is instilled in our minds, we begin to contemplate God's face peaceful and calm and gracious toward us. We see him afar off, but so clearly as to know we are not all deceived." (John Calvin, *Institutes of the Christian Religion*)

Key terms

- Creation
- General revelation
- Special revelation
- Natural theology

For further thought

- Why is there something rather than nothing? What answer might atheism give?
- Which of the four points regarding the existence of God do you find most persuasive? Which do you find least persuasive?

Which do you think your non-Christian neighbours might find most or least persuasive?
- 'General revelation' is an important area of theological discussion. Is there a general light from God in the world, or is the world all darkness except for Scripture?
- What does the Bible say about other religions?
- One prominent question is whether the Bible is revelation, or simply a witness to revelation. Why does this distinction matter?

For further reading
- Westminster Confession, chapter 1, sections 1-4
- Bray, chapter 2
- Horton, chapter 1
- Milne, chapters 2 and 4

3

KNOWING THE GOD WHO SPEAKS, PART 1

Key concept: God's revelation of himself is not simply through creation; he has spoken, and his speech is in Scripture. Through Scripture, God rules over us.

1. Introduction

The renewed authority of God in our lives is integral to the Christian gospel. It was by disputing his authority that Adam and Eve committed the human race to enmity with God. It is through the gospel of Jesus Christ that we come once more to be in our proper place in submission to him. Our worship of him is the acknowledgement of his glory and his rule and of our creaturely status.

In the next three chapters, we examine *the word of God as the chief means by which God rules over us*. Just as in the beginning humanity repudiated his rule through his word, so now we see that he has re-instituted his rule over us by his word.

In the first chapter, we began with the gospel. Jesus' preaching was mainly focused on the gospel of the kingdom of God (e.g. Mark

1:14-15). After the ascension of Jesus, the gospel remains the gospel of the kingdom of God, but now the kingdom is focused through Jesus and on Jesus. It is the gospel of Christ, the gospel of *his* kingship—namely, that 'Jesus Christ is Lord'. To believe the gospel is to submit to the authority of God in Christ, to accept the yoke of his kingdom, and to be ruled by him at the cost of one's false desires and egocentricity but at the benefit of eternal life, of your true humanity. When we receive the gospel, the words of Jesus and his apostles form the basis of the promise and teaching of the New Testament (or new covenant), calling forth faith and obedience. But what of the Old Testament (or old covenant)? Does that still have any sway over us?

When we call Jesus by the title 'Christ', we are asserting that he fulfils the hopes and promises of the old covenant. One of the chief ways in which we assess the truth about Jesus is to see that he is essentially in continuity with God's action in the world, centred on Israel in the Old Testament. We must weigh him up in that context. Is he the one we are to look for? When we agree that he is in fact the Christ, the next question becomes: What is the relation between the authority of God in Israel and the new authority of Jesus Christ? If God ruled over Israel by his word, does this change now for us? Can we now forget Israel, or does Israel's old covenant experience of God's rule have an enduring place in the Christian church alongside the New Testament?

2. Kingdom and covenant

What do we learn to expect from the Old Testament? One of the most striking features of the first chapters of the Bible is the prominence of God's word. By his word the cosmos is created and by his word—and under the authority of his word—he establishes the first human pair in Eden. The calamity of the fall occurs when Satan sows doubt about God's word in Eve's mind.

The theme of the word of God ruling over the people of God continues as the story of the Bible unfolds. In saving his people, God re-establishes his rule with Noah, Abraham, Isaac and Jacob by entering into a covenant with them. A covenant is verbal; it is the formalization of God's rule in which he declares through promises his future intentions, and in the context of which his people respond by faith and obedience. They receive his covenantal word by faith (see Gen 15:6), and so begin the life of faith.

There are a number of covenantal 'moments' in the Old Testament. It is best to think of most of them as being the further outworking of God's foundational covenant with Abraham (Gen 12:1-3, 15:1-6, 17:1-14). The most extensive, and the one with most authority in Israel's national life, is the Sinai covenant (Exod 19:1-8, 20:1-17, 24:1-11). The Sinai covenant is, of course, a gracious provision of God arising from a great act of salvation. Like all covenants, it is entered by faith, but it is accompanied by an extensive provision for the path of obedience—the Law, or *Torah*. Thus, in offering the covenant, the Lord had Moses read the Book of the Covenant to the people. They responded: "All that the LORD has spoken we will do, and we will be obedient" (24:7). The covenant was then dramatically and tellingly sealed with the blood of burnt offerings sprinkled on the altar and on the people, and called "the blood of the covenant that the LORD has made with you in accordance with all these words" (24:8). The people are called God's "treasured possession ... a kingdom of priests and a holy nation" (19:5-6).

The people of Israel are thus constituted as a people saved by mercy and established under a covenantal constitution. The covenant does not age or grow weary; it cannot be repealed, challenged or altered by human decision; it remains God's ruling instrument. The prophets who come later are servants of the covenant, taking its provisions and applying them to the present life of the people in warning and in hope. The writings, in particular the Psalms, expound the piety of a covenantal people in different but not inconsistent ways.[7]

And yet, the disobedience of Israel, like that of Adam and Eve, cannot be overlooked. God does not fail in his promises, but the people fail so chronically that God finally promises a new covenantal provision: "I will put my law within them, and I will write it on their hearts. And I will be their God, and they shall be my people" (Jer 31:33). God still intends to use the covenant as a means of ruling his people; it is not 'new' in its substance, for, as Jeremiah says, law is still involved; but God promises a covenant new in its power to deal with human failure—a covenant which bring forgiveness and will operate from transformed hearts.

It is noteworthy, then, that the authority of the old covenant was the authority of God himself, and the words which he spoke at various times—especially through Moses—were regarded as determinative of the nation's very existence. They were to be carried in the ark of the covenant; they were to be carefully recorded; they were to be consulted; they were to be memorized; they were to be transmitted to the children of the community; they were to be practised and obeyed; they were to be the measuring rod of future revelation; they were to reform the nation when necessary; they were to be the heart of the nation's godliness. Where other nations carried with them the visible forms of their gods, Israel carried with it the word of God: "Then the LORD spoke to you out of the midst of the fire. You heard the sound of words, but saw no form; there was only a voice" (Deut 4:12).

The result was that Israel was a nation of the book, and that book was the Scriptures. Paul makes the point succinctly when he

---

[7] 'The writings' is a way of referring to certain Old Testament books (where the Old Testament is divided into three groups of books: 'the law', 'the prophets' and 'the writings'): 1-2 Chronicles, Ezra, Nehemiah, Esther, Job, Psalms, Proverbs, Ecclesiastes, Song of Solomon, Lamentations and Daniel.

describes Israel as those "entrusted with the oracles of God" (Rom 3:2; cf. 9:4-5; Eph 2:12).[8]

What should be noted is the diversity of ways in which the covenantal writings met the needs of the people. Fundamental to the corpus were promises, for all covenants are promises at heart. The prophets took the promises and interpreted the history of the nation through them. The prophetic histories, books such as 1-2 Samuel and 1-2 Kings, gave the nation identity and created hope for the future by showing how God kept his word despite the sin of the people.

The promises were also accompanied by law, which spelled out obedience, first in pithy demands such as the Ten Commandments, then in generalizing summaries such as 'the law of love' (Deut 6:4-5), then in case law and maxims which applied the law to particular circumstances. In turn, the law was reinforced by sermons and exhortations, such as those of the prophets. Likewise, poets and musicians provided Israel with authorized vehicles for godly praise and prayer; wise people and seers applied the law to wider situations of life such as despair and suffering and personal relationships.

It is right to say, therefore, that the Old Testament had the authority of God in Israel. Its authority is not merely didactic, for it contains a rich variety of writings which impress on the mind the ways of God and provides for his people in multiple ways. It is the covenantal provision of a great King for his nation.

Furthermore, this great King is a Lord who speaks. His encounter with his people is verbal; his words are recorded and continue to have power; he raises up and sends forth prophets who have the right to announce "Thus says the LORD". Contrary to many modern accounts about God, the God of the Old Testament is one who

---

[8] The Greek word translated 'oracles' (or 'words' in the NIV) is *logia*. This is the same Greek word used in the singular in John 1:1 ("In the beginning was the *logos* ...") and 1 Corinthians 1:18 ("For the *logos* of the cross is folly to those who are perishing ...").

has no difficulty in using words to communicate the truth about himself and his will for human beings:

> Then the LORD said to [Moses], "Who has made man's mouth? Who makes him mute, or deaf, or seeing, or blind? Is it not I, the LORD? Now therefore go, and I will be with your mouth and teach you what you shall speak." (Exod 4:11-12)

3. Jesus and the covenant

Jesus did not come to invent a new religion. He was born "under the law" (Gal 4:4)—that is, under the provisions of the old covenant. His announcement of the coming kingdom both arose from the promises of the old covenant and set up tensions with it. As he revealed to his disciples, his death on the cross would provide the blood by which the new covenant (that Jeremiah foreshadowed) would be inaugurated (Luke 22:20).

Despite these tensions, however, we must note first of all how strongly Jesus (and his apostles) received and endorsed the authority of the Old Testament, and regarded it as the very word of God with ongoing application, even under the changed circumstances of the coming of Jesus. In this connection, we note the following:

a. Jesus lived in obedience to the Scriptures. When challenged about alleged disobedience, he did not repudiate the covenant, but gave its true interpretation (e.g. Matt 12:1-14).
b. Jesus appealed to the Scriptures in controversy. In his dispute with the Sadducees, for example, he declared to them: "Is this not the reason you are wrong, because you know neither the Scriptures nor the power of God?" (Mark 12:24). He then asks them, "have you not read in the book of Moses, in the passage about the bush, how God spoke to him, saying, 'I am the God of Abraham, and the God of Isaac, and the God of Jacob'?" (12:26).

The original statement (from Exodus 3:6) was, according to Jesus, addressed not only to Moses but to his own contemporaries; it both *was* and *is* the word of God.

c. Jesus warned his contemporaries that they would be judged on their failure to keep the Scriptures (e.g. Luke 16:19-31).

d. Jesus identified God's word with Scripture, where he quoted Moses but attributed the words to God (e.g. Matt 19:4-5).

e. Jesus declared that the Scriptures ("the Law [and] the Prophets") would stand until the end (e.g. Matt 5:17-20).

f. Jesus did battle with Satan by quoting, believing and obeying Scripture, especially Deuteronomy 8:3: "Man shall not live by bread alone, but by every word that comes from the mouth of God" (Matt 4:4).

g. Jesus understood his whole mission in terms of the Scriptures and declared that the Scriptures had to be fulfilled, since they expressed the plan of God:

> Then he said to them, "These are my words that I spoke to you while I was still with you, that everything written about me in the Law of Moses and the Prophets and the Psalms *must* be fulfilled." Then he opened their minds to understand the Scriptures, and said to them, "Thus it is written, that the Christ should suffer and on the third day rise from the dead, and that repentance for the forgiveness of sins should be proclaimed in his name to all nations, beginning from Jerusalem." (Luke 24:44-47)

The summary just given represents only a fraction of the evidence that Jesus regarded the Scriptures as the very word of God with ongoing relevance to his hearers. Sometimes people suggest that Jesus was merely following cultural convention in his deference to Scripture. But Jesus was not one who accepted culture in this way;

he would have challenged this as readily as he challenged other conventions. In any case, the point really is that the culture of Israel was the product of God's covenant with Israel. Had Jesus challenged it, he would have been challenging the very word of God which gave his ministry its meaning.

The authority of Scripture as the word of God was also the teaching of the apostles. This is, if anything, easier to establish:

a. Paul called Scripture God's words (e.g. Rom 3:2) and identified what God said with what Scripture said (e.g. Rom 1:1-2, 9:17).
b. The apostles made clear that, as part of a true assessment of Jesus, the question of whether he fulfilled Scripture was of key significance. In their speeches to the Jews, they constantly appeal to Scripture as the inspired word of God and therefore necessarily to be fulfilled, believed and obeyed (e.g. Acts 4:25, 17:11; cf. 1 Cor 15:3-4).
c. The apostles taught that Scripture was inspired, or breathed out by God, using the instrumentality of his human servants (e.g. 2 Tim 3:16; 2 Pet 1:21).
d. The apostles verified the ongoing application and importance of Scripture in the Christian church (e.g. Rom 15:4; 1 Cor 10:11).
e. The apostles appealed to Scripture to verify their doctrine and their ethics (e.g. Eph 4:8, 5:14).

4. The effect of the new covenant

But what of the fact that such things as circumcision and animal sacrifices have now passed away for use by Christians? Does this passing away include the whole of the method by which God ruled his people in and through a written covenant? Is this what Paul means when he writes "but our sufficiency is from God, who has made us sufficient to be ministers of a new covenant, not of the letter [or 'not in a written code'] but of the Spirit. For the letter kills, but the Spirit gives life" (2 Cor 3:5-6)? Does this mean that God's method of dealing with us is no longer verbal and written?

To draw such a conclusion is to misunderstand Paul. The point of the new covenant is not that it ceases to be articulated in words, but that our response is not merely *external*. The power of the Holy Spirit writes the law *on our hearts* so that we delight in it (Rom 7:22), and by the power of the Spirit its requirements are fulfilled in us (8:4). Otherwise the Old Testament would become completely irrelevant to the gospel—which is hardly possible, given how deeply the gospel depends on the Old Testament for its validation, and given the way in which Jesus and his apostles refer to the Old Testament—and the whole nature of God's authority would be altered without notice. The dispute between Adam and God was over the word of God; the renewal of relationships sees the re-establishment of the word.

A further question, however, is whether Jesus and his apostles distinguished between Jews and Gentiles when it came to appealing to the Old Testament. Perhaps it may be appropriate to continue as Jewish Christians "under the law" while the Gentiles are freed from it, just as Jewish Christians may continue to circumcise their infant boys without this becoming a general rule for all Christians. But the way of salvation for all, both Jews and Gentiles, is by faith in Jesus, not by law-keeping.

In fact, there is ample evidence from the ministry of Jesus that his coming was to be accompanied by a change in the interpretation and application of the law. Together with his appeal to obedience to Scripture, Jesus:

- challenged contemporary interpretation (e.g. Matt 12:1-14)
- set some laws aside (e.g. Mark 7:19)
- added new injunctions (e.g. Matt 5:1-12; consider also Matthew 19:6-22) with equal status
- revealed new truths of an extraordinary nature (e.g. Matt 28:16-20).

Of these and similar passages in the Gospels, it must be noted, however, that they do not amount to a declaration that the old covenant is in error or must be ignored. The massive event of the coming of Jesus forces a new way of relating to the old covenant, both for Jews and Gentiles, but it does not overturn it. It is particularly the Sinai covenant which is re-assessed, but even here Jesus often binds the true significance of its injunctions upon his hearers, rather than overturning them (e.g. Matt 5:27-30). Even the food laws, which, in particular, are declared outmoded, remain in written form to testify still to the division between Jew and Gentile that is overcome in the gospel. Thus they have their place in our preaching of Christ (see Eph 2:15).

In short, while the ministry of Jesus is indispensable for a true understanding of the old covenant, it does not remove its ongoing validity as a witness to Christ and to the life of faith into which Christians enter. You do not properly understand Jesus—or God, or yourself—without the Old Testament. This view is vindicated by observing the post-Pentecost practice and teaching of the apostles, who were faced with the new fact of the church made up of Jew and Gentile. On the one hand, it is clear that they accepted the continuity of the old covenant revelation both in belief and command, and applied it to their converts, Jew and Gentile. On the other hand, they interpreted the old from the vantage point of the new, in particular from Christ: "To those outside the law I became as one outside the law (not being outside the law of God but under the law of Christ) that I might win those outside the law" (1 Cor 9:21).

It is hard to over-estimate the massive shift in perspective involved in receiving Christ. It was indeed a new age; they were a new creation, a "new self" (Col 3:10; cf. Eph 4:22). The coming of the Holy Spirit at Pentecost is at the heart of the revolution. This event testified dramatically to the invasion of the old age by the new. The Spirit brings the fulfilment of the promises of Jeremiah 31, with the Law internalized.

But the Spirit does not overturn the Law as such, or make redundant the written word. On the contrary, he inspires the word, and Jesus and the apostles assume at every point that both the words of the old covenant and their own teachings—spoken, and then written—will have ongoing and eternal validity (e.g. Matt 28:16-20; 1 Cor 14:37-38). The words of Jesus, accepted when we receive the gospel, form the basis of the New Testament. According to Paul, the church is built on the foundation of the apostles and prophets, with Christ Jesus being the cornerstone (Eph 2:20). The Scriptures bring faith in Christ and make the Christian complete for every good work (2 Tim 3:14-17). The Spirit is the sign and seal of Gentile membership of the church (e.g. Eph 1:13-14). But just as the new covenant is a development of the old, so the words of Scripture apply to the Gentiles as well as the Jews—always, however, through Christ.

5. Conclusion: the authority of Scripture

The authority of Scripture is a covenantal authority. God gives his word as part of his gracious provision for his people, and his word shares the dynamic nature of his kingdom.

John identifies Jesus Christ as God's Word—both with God, and God (John 1:1-3); Paul declares that all God's promises are summed up in him (2 Cor 1:20-21). In other words, Christ is the mediator of God's kingdom, the focal point of his covenant. It is on the authority of Jesus Christ that we believe that the Old Testament is the word of God and accept its binding power. The same authority of Jesus Christ is the foundation of the New Testament; it extends to the words of his apostles and prophets (e.g. John 16:12-15). As Jesus prays for the apostles on the night before his death, he tells the Father that he has given them his word and prays that God will "Sanctify them in the truth; your word is truth" (John 17:6-19). He then prays for all who will believe in him "through their word" (17:20; cf. 2 Pet 3:1-2).

In the first instance, this new covenant is with his church. In a secondary sense, it belongs to the individuals who make up the flock of God. At the heart of it is the gospel message: "Christ Jesus came into the world to save sinners" (1 Tim 1:15). A gracious, speaking God addresses us with this message of hope.

Key verse
Then [Moses] took the Book of the Covenant and read it in the hearing of the people. And they said, "All that the LORD has spoken we will do, and we will be obedient." (Exod 24:7)

Quotation
"God knows how to be active while at rest, and at rest in his activity." (Augustine, *City of God*)

Key terms
- Scripture
- Old covenant
- New covenant
- Law
- Prophets

For further thought
- Is there a danger of bibliolatry (the worship of the Bible) in identifying Scripture as God's word?
- Has Leviticus (for example) any ongoing relevance to the Christian?
- What is happening when people try to separate love for God from faithfulness to his word? Can this position be sustained? What relationship between a person and their words does this view suggest?

- What is the connection between ancient Israel and the church today?
- Luther used to put 'gospel' and 'law' in opposition to each other. Do they clash? Does the notion of 'covenant' help to reconcile them?
- How does the authority of God's written word relate to preaching?

For further reading
- Thirty-Nine Articles, article 7
- JI Packer, *"Fundamentalism" and the Word of God*
- Bray, chapter 4
- Milne, chapter 3

4

KNOWING THE GOD WHO SPEAKS, PART 2

Key concept: Scripture is inspired by God, and hence a perfect and sufficient unity.

1. Introduction: God's communication

In the preceding chapter, we have seen that the authority of God and his Son Jesus Christ is exercised by his written word, the Scriptures of the Old and New Testaments. He reveals himself to us and tells us what he requires of us, thus establishing his kingdom in our lives. In this chapter and the next, we will examine the doctrine of Scripture—namely, what Scripture teaches about itself. In essence we will see what is meant by the claim that Scripture is 'inspired'. If we are to interpret Scripture properly and apply its teaching to our lives, we need to understand its character as a book inspired by God.

When we examine the Bible to see how God communicates with humanity, we see instances of God speaking directly to a person, notably Moses (e.g. Exod 3:1-6). Indeed, we read that "the LORD used to speak to Moses face to face, as a man speaks to his friend" (Exod 33:11). Even in the former passage, however, reference is also made to an "angel [or 'messenger'] of the Lord" (3:2), and everywhere the emphasis falls on a certain indirectness of the communication in order to remind us of the majesty and otherness of God. This is a fitting reminder that "no-one has ever seen God" (John 1:18), not even Moses (Exod 33:23).

Communication even of this sort is notable and extraordinary, not usual, and the purpose is usually so that the prophet can pass on the message of God to others. The most common mode of communication from God to his people is, therefore, through a messenger, a prophet. The prophetic word was frequently oral. It would typically then enter the public record by being written, thus attaining a permanent place in God's address to Israel. It would be a mistake to think that prophecy has to display a certain form. In Scripture, the concept 'prophetic' is applied to a wide class of literature, including the writings we would normally call history, such as the books of Samuel and Kings. In such works we have the prophetic view of events.

In acknowledging the authority of the prophet to speak, we say that his utterance, spoken or written, is 'inspired'. Thus Scripture refers to the product of the prophetic ministry, the inscripturated word of God, as being "breathed out by God", a metaphor for inspiration (2 Tim 3:16; cf. 2 Pet 1:21). It is particularly associated with the ministry of the Holy Spirit. The term 'inspiration' is used in theology to imply that a human being and human language has become the vehicle for God's speech. An inspired book is both human and divine. Thus Acts 4:25 says that Psalm 2 is the product of the work of both the Holy Spirit and David. Hebrews 3:7 similarly attributes Psalm 95 directly to God, assuming the human authorship: "Therefore, as the Holy Spirit says ..."

Such New Testament language is grounded in the frequent use of the phrase "thus says the Lord", constantly used by the prophets of the Old Testament before they spoke. In the days of Jesus and the apostles, the inspiration of the Old Testament was acknowledged by the description "holy Scriptures" (or 'sacred writings'; e.g. Rom 1:2). That exalted phrase had begun to be extended to the New Testament writings even within the New Testament itself, as when the apostle Peter compared Paul's writings to "the *other* Scriptures" (2 Pet 3:16), and when Paul himself claimed to speak with the Lord's authority (e.g. 1 Cor 7:40; 2 Thess 3:14). While it was a matter of wonder that God should use such unworthy servants as prophets or apostles, they did not doubt that God spoke in their words.

The mode of the communication of God's word differed from occasion to occasion. The Bible is notably reticent about the methods used. It does not invite attempts to emulate God's spokesmen or to recreate the same experience they had in receiving the word. The word is given, not sought or invented, and God is not at the mercy of human whims. Whether dreams or voices or angels were used hardly matters; we know that sometimes the prophetic word was repeated by another prophet in a new situation; we know that one could even be unconscious of the significance of what he had to say and that he was prophesying (e.g. John 11:49-53). In short, the prophets may speak or write from the resources of their own minds, with God over-ruling their words.

Models of inspiration which, on the one hand, suggest automatic writing or, on the other hand, reduce it to the level of an 'inspiring' person or experience (as an actor may be 'inspired') fail to do justice to the concept. It is as certain that inspiration worked in and through the personalities of the human authors as it is that those personalities were not mere religious geniuses having their own say. What is being asserted is the reality of the divine/human authorship of Scripture so that we may trust it as the word of God in human speech. That best fits the covenantal nature of the Bible, made clear in the previous chapter.

The inspiration of Scripture determines its nature. We will now examine its uniqueness, its unity, its sufficiency and its extent. In the next chapter, we will continue to unfold the doctrine of the inspiration of Scripture by discussing its infallibility.

2. The uniqueness of Scripture

To accept the authority and inspiration of Scripture is to take up and accept certain positions, derived from the Bible, about other possible authorities and revelations. Notably, we need to position Scripture with regard to reason, experience and tradition. These fourfold sources of authority, when studied together, are sometimes called the 'authority quadrilateral'.

Only Scripture is inspired and so authoritative in an absolute sense—'the Bible alone' (or *Sola Scriptura*, to use the Latin phrase), as the Protestant Reformers taught. Dependence upon reason, experience or tradition may compromise that unique role or even subvert it. But the relation of Scripture to the other three sources of wisdom is by no means a thoroughly negative one, and we need to chart the connections carefully.

Human reason as such is not denigrated in Scripture. The presence of salvation begins the healing or renewal of the mind (Rom 12:1-2), and the gospel does not bypass the mind; the word of God appeals to it, and reason is invited to assess the word and submit to it. The mind in its maturity is a mind submitted to Jesus Christ:

> We destroy arguments and every lofty opinion raised against the knowledge of God, and take every thought captive to obey Christ ... (2 Cor 10:5)

> Brothers, do not be children in your thinking. Be infants in evil, but in your thinking be mature. (1 Cor 14:20)

Human reason is obviously one of the gifts which God bestowed on his creatures, and its daily use in pursuing our human callings is proper and fruitful. On the other hand, reason unfettered by revelation is prone to error as it comes closer to matters to do with God. We have already reviewed Scripture's generally negative attitude towards natural theology (see chapter 2). If, on the one hand, there is the general revelation through creation ("The heavens declare the glory of God"), on the other it is the word which brings light (Ps 19:1, 7: "The Law of the LORD is perfect, reviving the soul"). It is not the general revelation of God which is at fault, but the natural theology of sinful man and our unwillingness to see the splendour of God in the splendour of creation.

Our inability to find our way to God by unaided reason arises more from the sorry state of the human personality in its alienation from God than from a fault in the capacity to reason as such. Sometimes this personality is called the "heart"; sometimes the term "flesh" is used; sometimes the mind, the conscience or the will is on view. In all cases the perversity, corruption and bondage of the personality is made clear (e.g. Gen 6:5; Jer 17:9; Rom 1:21, 7:18). To expect that such a darkened mind can find God is to expect the impossible. Even the redeemed human mind is fallible and sinful, and that is why we need to submit to God's word in heart, soul, strength and mind.

Likewise with human religious experience. We note Paul's willingness to quote a pagan poet as testifying to the truth (Acts 17:28). Furthermore, it is true that there is a general revelation by God through nature, and there are even events which unbelievers see and in part understand (note the appeal to the nature and the impact of miracles in Acts 14 and 17). But it is also overwhelmingly clear that the Bible has a negative view of the religions of humanity, seeing in them mainly idolatry and error. It is only in the name of Jesus Christ that salvation may be found (Acts 4:12; 1 Cor 1:18-25). Even God's gift of spiritual experiences in the wake of the gospel are not elevated to the status of the revelation which he gives in his word; on the contrary, everything must be tested by the word (1 Cor 14:37).

When we rely simply on our intuition, it is no more likely to be correct than if we trust in reason or experience. There is a tendency in an individualistic world to justify our convictions and behaviour simply by saying "this seems good to me" or "this feels right to me" without having to offer any justification at all. We think that to offer such an explanation places us beyond challenge. But, of course, the corruption of the human heart is all the more likely to be at work if we are claiming intuition as our guide.

Human tradition which shapes the cultures in which we live is again both positive and negative. In particular the church tradition, insofar as it arises from an engagement with Scripture, often fruitfully enables us to understand and apply Scripture. *Sola Scriptura* does not imply that we should avoid the wisdom of the years. We need to learn from what our predecessors (and contemporaries) have thought about what the Bible means. Often, this is helpfully encapsulated in creeds and confessions.[9] Thus there has always been, historically and theologically, a close relationship between Scripture and tradition. Indeed, in one sense the Scriptures themselves have been 'passed down', which is the fundamental idea of tradition. But tradition can also overwhelm the voice of the Bible. This can occur in any denomination, but in Roman Catholic theology the Church is formally regarded as the guardian and interpreter of Scripture, and tradition is given a prominent role in delivering the truth. The Reformers rightly insisted that this compromised the authority of Scripture, and taught that the church, unlike Scripture, could err, and that its business was to submit to the Bible.[10] Indeed, they further stressed that the word created the church (rather than the church creating the word), in much the same way as the covenant had brought Israel into being. The church of God is ruled by the word of God in its midst (Col 3:16; Eph 2:20).

---

9   See, for example, the Thirty-Nine Articles of Religion, the Apostles' Creed, the Nicene Creed, the Westminster Confession of Faith, and the Heidelberg Catechism (among other examples).
10 See the Thirty-Nine Articles, articles 20 and 34.

3. The unity of Scripture

The initial impression that the Bible is simply one book is, of course, misleading. The invention of printing gives that impression to beginners. But its 66 books have many authors and three different languages, and are separated by up to 1,500 years in time. The literary styles show great diversity, as do the concerns and interests of the writings, from Song of Solomon to Revelation, Amos and Mark's Gospel. The Jewish Bible remains equivalent to the 39 books which Protestants recognize as the Old Testament. The judgement of Israel that Jesus is not the Christ involves a judgement that the 27 books of the New Testament do not form a group consistent with the Bible as they have it.

On the other hand, even at the historical level, there exists a unity in the 66 books of the Old and New Testaments. In the first place, many of the books are written from within a community of thought and practice shaped by the earlier and original works. Often they are commentaries and expositions of the earlier books and share a demonstrable comity of outlook. Most notably, the New Testament claims to be the fulfilment of the Old, and labours to show that it is. Secondly, the process involved in making this collection of books into the canon of Scripture worked self-consciously on a principle of looking for a fundamental unity. Thus the process specifically excluded works which were inconsistent with the outlook of the original works. This was a fundamental test as to whether a work was inspired by God and could therefore be joined with the ones already recognized as inspired.

In some modern theology there exists a divided approach. While the tradition of a unified, inspired Bible remains basic to much scholarly work on Scripture, many practitioners no longer adhere to a category of 'inspiration'. They would be better off, therefore, to use a far wider array of Jewish religious literature and not be bound to the ancient selection that was made, at least in part, on the grounds that this was the word of God.

Theologically the point at issue is the consistency of God who, in the words of Titus 1:2, is a God "who never lies". If God has inspired this literature, it must be as trustworthy as he himself is, and to be thus it must have a fundamental unity. This is presupposed in the categories used by Jesus himself, for example, when he calls on the witness of "the Law of Moses and the Prophets and the Psalms" (Luke 24:44), or when he reminds his adversaries that "Scripture cannot be broken" (John 10:35). At an even more significant level (also indicated in Luke 24:44), there is the great quarrel between Israel and Jesus—whether he and his word are the fulfilment of the Old Testament or not. For Christians to confess Jesus Christ and then to deny the unity of Old Testament and New Testament is to be involved in confessing a false Christ for false reasons.

Having said this, however, we must then comment on the sort of unity exhibited in Scripture. Already we have noted that it is possible for Jewish readers and others to reject the claim that Jesus fulfils the Old Testament. The unity which Christians wish to claim is a covenantal unity. That is, it arises from the rule of God over his people through covenantal promise and the multi-purposed literature which he provides for them—law, ritual, songs, history, prophecy, story, wisdom. A basic covenantal framework was provided for Israel as the nation church, and within it she was given the word which enabled her to worship God. Unity was not uniformity; in particular, unity does not imply that the Bible is merely a handbook of instruction.

The phrase 'progressive revelation' is used to describe a second important feature of the Bible. Since God's plans only gradually unfolded, he did not tell his people everything at once, but matched his revelation to his deeds. The new was always contained in and consistent with the old, but the old was often inadequate taken on its own. For example, God's name is only fully revealed in the coming of Jesus Christ.

The idea of progressive revelation raises the question of interpretation. The basic principle of interpretation is that, since the Bible is the word of God, it must not be interpreted in contradictory ways: "It is not lawful for the church to ... so expound one place of Scripture, that it be repugnant to another".[11] Scripture must interpret Scripture.

And yet this principle must not be used in a mechanical fashion. The partial nature of an earlier statement needs supplementing in fuller light; sometimes only an apparent contradiction can bring out the truth, and two propositions must be allowed to stand side by side, each bearing witness partially. To take an important example, there is a violent clash between Exodus 23:7 ("for I will not acquit the wicked") and Paul's insight that God "justifies the ungodly" (Rom 4:5), but it is a contradiction which throws light on the violence of the cross. Sometimes such statements must simply be allowed to stand as we admit that we do not yet know how they can be reconciled. Confident in the unity of Scripture—and in the perfect mind of the God who stands behind it—we can happily let ourselves feel the weight of such paradoxes without quickly dismissing them or rushing to find simplistic solutions.

In short, the principle of the unity of Scripture does not necessarily solve problems and should not lead to exegetical short cuts. But it functions to force the reader back to the text again and again, and to refuse to view any text in isolation from its ultimate context, which is the whole of Scripture. In this way, it is a vital commitment for those who wish to hear God speaking.

4. The sufficiency of Scripture

Scripture is thought of as 'sufficient' or 'complete' not in order to claim that it contains the answer to all life's problems, a commen-

---

11   Thirty-Nine Articles, article 20; cf. Westminster Confession, chapter 1, section 9.

tary on every ethical dilemma, or the groundwork of science, law and the humanities. The term points rather to Scripture's power to lead to salvation and to make "complete" for "every good work" (2 Tim 3:14-17). The contrast is not with reason or common sense, which must be relied on to give much information about the world, but with reason and tradition when they are treated as sources of revelation about God.

In Roman Catholic theology, "Both Scripture and Tradition must be accepted and honored with equal sentiments of devotion and reverence".[12] As we have already noted, the Protestant Reformers refused to countenance such a form of revelation beside Scripture, and adhered to Scripture alone. In today's world, the main danger for the doctrine of *Sola Scriptura* is not so much from the idea of tradition as a separate source of revelation, but from 'enthusiastic' religion (a technical term stemming from the Greek word *enthousiazein*, which means 'to be possessed or inspired by a god'), in which individuals claim to have access to prophetic revelations. Many see connections between this approach and some expression of the modern Pentecostal movement. Such 'enthusiasts' also troubled the Reformers and their successors in later centuries (e.g. George Fox, founder of the Quakers, who spoke of the "inner light" of the living Christ and, while esteeming Scripture, claimed to know things "in the light of the Lord Jesus Christ, and by his immediate spirit and power, as did the holy men of God by whom the Holy Scriptures were written").[13]

Both Roman Catholics and enthusiasts deeply reverence Scripture. At the same time, however, they add to it and, in so doing, distort its message. A further danger is that the written word will lose its

---

12 Catholic Church, *Catechism of the Catholic Church*, 2nd edn, paragraph 82, St Charles Borromeo Catholic Church website, 15 August 1997, accessed 12 January 2022 (scborromeo.org/ccc/p1s1c2a2.htm).
13 Christianity Today, *George Fox*, CT website, 2022, accessed 12 January 2022 (christianitytoday.com/history/people/denominationalfounders/george-fox.html).

attractions compared to the immediate and contemporary. This is especially so when new 'revelations' purport to give an understanding of the times in which we live and interpret them as dispensations in God's plan.

What is fundamentally at stake in speaking of 'Scripture alone' is our commitment to 'Christ alone', the doctrine of the sole sufficiency of Jesus Christ, the Word of God. The Scriptures themselves, as a covenantal book and as the expression of God's rule, culminate in Jesus Christ, "for all the promises of God they find their Yes in him" (2 Cor 1:20). Consider, likewise, the opening of Hebrews: "Long ago, at many times and in many ways, God spoke to our fathers by the prophets, but in these last days he has spoken to us by his Son …" (Heb 1:1-2).

The contrast between prophets and Son is paralleled by the contrast between "long ago" and "these last days". From the New Testament perspective we are in the last days, and the next great revelation will be the revealing of the Son of Man at his return. In the meantime, Christ is the one "in whom are hidden all the treasures of wisdom and knowledge" (Col 2:3). That is why Jude speaks of "the faith that was once for all delivered to the saints" (Jude 3). What we may know of Jesus Christ we may know from this source alone, and we must beware the great danger of adding to his portrait by imagination. It is wisdom to be satisfied with the goodness of God's Christ-centred revelation.

5. The extent of Scripture

The extent of Scripture has come to be known as its 'canon'; what does Scripture authentically contain? It is clear that in both Old Testament and New Testament, books were omitted which some felt should be included, and some were included that others felt should be excluded. To this day, the canon adopted by Roman Catholics and Protestants differs in that the Roman Catholic Church accepts various books in their Old Testament which were not part of the Hebrew Canon, but part of the wider collection of the 'Septuagint' (the Greek translation of the Hebrew Old Testament). As well, various lists of New Testament books are extant from the first centuries of the church.

It must not be thought, however, that the canon of Scripture has to be constructed from scratch. That has never been the case. There has always existed, even in the days of Abraham, that which is the indisputable word of God; the Christian in possession of "the Law of Moses and the Prophets and the Psalms", along with the Gospels and the testimony of the apostles, has the authority of the undisputed word of God.

The problem is not whether there is a canon, but what is its extent and how should a decision be made as to what it contains. To claim that the church decides the limits of the canon is to run the risk of making the church the mistress of Scripture. As well, it leaves open the knotty historical and theological questions of who represents the church in making such a decision and when the decision is alleged to have been made. Different councils and church fathers have different lists. If God has revealed the extent of the canon through the church or in some other way, his revelation has escaped the attention of many, and has not itself been given the status of Scripture.

What we are dealing with, therefore, is not an authoritative collection of texts, but a collection of authoritative texts recognized as such in the years during and after the apostles. Such matters as authorship, consistency with already acknowledged Scripture, and theological orthodoxy were used to include (or exclude) writings from the developing canon. That is, the early Christians did not think of themselves as deciding which books should be treated as God's word and which ones should not. They saw themselves as simply recognizing—formalizing—that which was already a fact. To this extent, the canon is a human judgement and therefore in theory fallible.

On the other hand, the same factor is at work here as in our recognition of Jesus as Lord. The Holy Spirit testifies to his own inspiring work and superintends the process so that his word is not lost, and he is the ultimate interpreter of holy Scripture. We should be confident that the Lord authenticates his own word and that, in his providence, the Scriptures as we have them are indeed "the oracles of God" (Rom 3:2).

―――――

Key verse
All Scripture is breathed out by God and profitable for teaching, for reproof, for correction, and for training in righteousness, that the man of God may be complete, equipped for every good work. (2 Tim 3:16-17)

Quotation
"It hath been an old complaint, even from the first time of the patriarchs and prophets, and confirmed by the writings and testimonies of every age, that the truth wandereth here and there as a stranger in the world, and doth readily find enemies and slanderers amongst those who know her not." (John Jewel, *An Apologie of the Church of England*)

Key terms
- Inspiration
- Sufficiency
- *Sola Scriptura*
- Authority quadrilateral
- Canon

For further thought
- If Scripture is inspired, what allowance do we make for the cultural factors involved in its creation?
- Consider reason, experience and tradition: how is each one important for our knowledge of God? What danger(s) might each one bring?
- Does it matter that inspiration has not left us with the exact text of the Bible?
- What is the relation between inspiration and translation?
- Are the arguments for biblical authority in this chapter and the last chapter examples of 'circular reasoning' and therefore invalid?
- What status should we give to knowledge in areas such as psychology, philosophy, economics and politics—areas on which Scripture touches, but which it does not treat exhaustively? Is there such a thing as 'Christian psychology', for example?
- Protestants sometimes refer to the 'self-authentication' of Scripture—that is, it does not need to be argued for or defended. Is this an appropriate view?

For further reading
- Thirty-Nine Articles, articles 6, 8, 18 and 20-21
- Westminster Confession, chapter 1, sections 5-6, 8 and 10
- Bray, chapter 5

5

KNOWING THE GOD WHO SPEAKS, PART 3

Key concept: Scripture is inspired by God, and hence infallible and inerrant.

1. Introduction

What was involved in producing the writings acknowledged as the inspired word of God? The method that God used involved both divine and human authorship. This is not to suggest an equal partnership or anything like it. God "who has made man's mouth" (Exod 4:11) is able to use the human capacity to speak to say what he wants said. Pre-eminently this is the case with Jesus himself. Given that we are dealing with "the oracles of God" (Rom 3:2), they necessarily reflect both his nature and his purpose: by *nature*, he is completely truthful and never lies; his *purpose* is to engage a people with truthful, understandable words of promise and command, words which they can trust.

And yet there is also a humanity to the Scriptures, since "men spoke from God as they were carried along by the Holy Spirit"

(2 Pet 1:21). Thus the Scriptures are written in human language and in particular times and places. Different literary styles are obvious. The twofold origin of Scripture needs to be acknowledged and observed if we are to understand the nature of the book by which God expresses his covenantal rule over his redeemed people.

The view of inspiration adopted in these chapters has, of course, been widely challenged. Many would prefer the Bible not to be identified so closely as God's word. They would regard what they see as the errors and blemishes of the Bible to be inconsistent with such a claim and, while still giving Scripture an honoured place as the chief source of Christian knowledge, would distance it somewhat from God's direct over-ruling power. The difficulty with such a view is that it does not do justice to the origin or function of Scripture in conveying the gospel. It departs from the grounds on which the gospel was accepted in the first place; and it does not reflect the attitude of Jesus himself to the Scriptures.

In the previous chapter, I noted some of the implications of inspiration in matters such as unity, sufficiency and the canon. This chapter resumes the discussion by consideration of the infallibility and clarity of Scripture and the role of biblical criticism.

2. Scripture as infallible and inerrant[14]

It is worth noting that the doctrine of inspiration and its consequence for infallibility is not a peculiarity of 20th-century fundamentalism or the invention of 19th-century so-called Presbyterian rationalists like Charles Hodge and BB Warfield. Theologian John Kelly writes on the attitude of the early church to Scripture:

> From Judaism Christianity inherited the conception of the divine inspiration of Holy Scripture. Whenever our Lord

---

14 For more on the infallibility of Scripture, see P Jensen, *The Revelation of God*, Contours of Christian Theology, IVP, 2002, pp 197-204.

and His apostles quoted the Old Testament, it is plain that they regarded it as the word of God ... It goes without saying that the fathers envisaged the whole of the Bible as inspired ... their general view was that Scripture was not only exempt from error but contained nothing that was superfluous.[15]

Thus Augustine, to take one example, gives many long sections of his famous book *City of God* to a historical exposition of the Bible, but he does not concede error, even though it conflicted in parts with other accounts. And it was not as though the Fathers were unaware of difficulties in Scripture; enemies of Christianity happily pointed them out. It was that their starting point was inspiration, and the difficulties must therefore be capable of explanation, at least in principle.

Some say that Protestant Reformers such as Luther and Calvin were happy to admit minor historical errors in Scripture, but that their 17th-century followers (the 'Protestant scholastics') tightened up the doctrine of Scripture until no blemish at all could be allowed. Whether this is an altogether fair account of either century may be doubted, but it is clear that the mainstream of Protestant thought in the 17th century accepted the view that Scripture was without error, and that in this they stood with the Fathers.

As observed already, there never has been a time when the Bible has been without its critics. But the 18th and 19th centuries introduced such a major revolution of thought about the Bible that it must be regarded as one of the great watersheds of history. It was an approach in line with new approaches to history itself, a way sceptical about the possibility of miracle and the supernatural ordering of events. New methods of seeing the Bible in its own context and also

---

15   JND Kelly, *Early Christian Doctrines*, 5th edn, HarperOne, 1978, pp 60-61; see also CE Hill, '"The truth above all demonstration": Scripture in the Patristic Period to Augustine', in DA Carson (ed), *The Enduring Authority of the Christian Scriptures*, Eerdmans, 2016, pp 43-88.

of offering critical reconstructions both of how the Bible came to be written and the history which it purported to recount were developed. The ancient critics were content to detail what they saw as inconsistencies, errors of fact, ethical blemishes and the like; the new critics, however, undertook a total review of the nature of Scripture with special attention to removing or explaining away the miraculous elements. Furthermore, these reconstructions emerged from within the Christian community, were taught and believed by Professors of Bible, and were largely accepted into systematic theology.

At the same time, major assaults on the veracity of Scripture were being developed from within the scientific community, which was, from around 1850 onwards, growing in prestige, influence and independence. In particular, the new understanding of human origins, associated especially with Charles Darwin, constituted a fundamental challenge to the way that Christians had almost always read Genesis 1-3. Where many Christians had once insisted that science conform to Genesis, they were now being forced to ask how Genesis conforms to science, or else abandon the Bible altogether. Of course, at this point the new critical and comparative studies began to prove illuminating.

Evangelicalism, which had been so prominent in Victorian England, was itself divided. It seemed unable to face the intellectual challenge. By the 1930s it seemed to be in intellectual disarray. It was not until after 1945 that its fortunes revived in the UK and the USA, where there grew a more scholarly evangelicalism. There remains at the heart of the evangelical movement worldwide, however, a split about its doctrine of Scripture, which is a legacy of its encounter with liberalism and biblical criticism. Using the words in a contemporary sense, the division is between those who wish to confess the *infallibility* of Scripture and those who believe that the *inerrancy* of Scripture must also be adhered to.

Discussion about the origins and significance of these words in themselves is not very helpful. The point is that, for some, whereas the inspiration of Scripture makes them conclude that the Bible is God's word and therefore thoroughly trustworthy and reliable in all that it sets out to achieve, they are forced by what they see as the phenomena of Scripture—that is, the way God has actually given it to us—to take the view that at some minor points where its teaching on faith and behaviour is not at stake, error may have been allowed by God. The chief question is what God intended to achieve, and his intentions are not put at risk by the problem of whether Jesus was entering or leaving Jericho (Luke 18:35; Mark 10:46) when he healed a blind man, or whether he told his disciples to take or not to take a staff on their journey (Mark 6:8; Matt 10:10). Despite such discrepancies, we must remember the purpose of Scripture. The Bible is not deceptive in what it is set forward to achieve.

Such a view does not necessarily entail the reconstruction of Scripture to which others are prone, and it has been held by some whose names are honoured among evangelicals. They would regard the major historical claims of the Bible as being within the ambit of what God intended to teach.

For others, however, this view is insufficient to guard all they hold to be essential. They favour employing the word 'inerrant' as well, to signify the quality of being "free from all falsehood, fraud, or deceit", hence asserting that holy Scripture contains "true and trustworthy utterance on all matters of which the biblical authors were moved to speak and write".[16] This would include matters scientific and historical in its scope. They would argue that the infallibilist position is too hard to maintain, being inconsistent with the purity of God's speech and vulnerable to the possibility that other doctrines may be lost. They would also say that historical details are intertwined with doctrine in God's revelation, and the idea that

---

16 'The Chicago statement on biblical inerrancy', *Themelios*, 1979, 4(3), accessed 13 January 2022 (thegospelcoalition.org/themelios/article/the-chicago-statement-on-biblical-inerrancy).

God intends to limit infallibility to faith and behaviour is impossible to sustain in fact.

In thinking about this issue, it is important to see that the two viewpoints are closer together than may at first be imagined. Indeed it is somewhat tragic that polarization has occurred, although it is right to be cautious about any teaching which casts doubts on Scripture being entirely the word of God.

The following points should be noted:

a. Both groups are speaking of the original 'autographs' as being inspired, not any copy or translation.[17] This means that no-one is arguing that infallible or inerrant copies of the Bible actually exist anywhere in the world today. Even scrupulously printed editions contain errors, and it is impossible to believe that we can return to the original purity of the texts involved. The idea of the original autographs remains important, however, so that in textual and exegetical work there is a concept of the original toward which we strive.

b. Both groups accept that we must interpret each part of Scripture according to its literary genre. Thus, for example, either side may consistently regard Genesis 1-3 as at least partially figurative.

c. Both groups agree that scriptural writers often use approximations, hyperbole, metaphor, and other ordinary features of language. Furthermore, both agree that many descriptive passages or phrases are 'phenomenalist' rather than 'scientific' — that is, they use the common observations and turns of expression of ordinary people, such as "the rising of the sun", without involving either human or divine author in error.

---

17 'Autographs' in this context is a technical term for the books or letters originally written by the hand of the authors.

d. Both groups agree that in the writing of the historical sections of Scripture selection has been used, and the whole story is not necessarily told. This, of course, is a feature of all historical writing; it should be noted, too, that ancient and modern methods in writing history were not exactly the same—the footnote had not been invented, for example. Truth and fraud remain as categories, but whether either is involved depends on a number of factors. Such things as topical arrangement of material do not involve error. So, for example, Matthew has grouped his material on healings (chapters 8-9) and then on parables (chapter 13).

e. Neither group claims to be able to explain the problems that remain. The infallibilists leave them without worry since they are not inconsistent with their position; inerrantists do not need to claim that they can actually reconcile all difficulties, but only that, in principle, they must be able to be explained. In order to illustrate their viewpoint, they can point to a number of alleged difficulties from the past that have now been resolved in the light of more knowledge, and they can offer possible or probable explanations for remaining difficulties. For example, to return to one example mentioned above, it seems there were two cities called Jericho: the ancient town, and one beside it built in Roman times. Jesus could therefore be entering Jericho (Luke 18:35) and leaving Jericho (Mark 10:46) simultaneously when he healed Bartimaeus. Such an explanation cannot, by its nature, show that the Bible is not in error at this point; but it does act as a reminder that plausible (or implausible though true) explanations may, in fact, be found, and that many of our problems arise from ignorance of the ancient world and the background circumstances of an incident.

When all this is conceded and the number of 'errors' and 'contradictions' which remain is examined, much of the offence is removed.

Furthermore, evangelicals will not concede that there are moral blemishes endorsed by Scripture, or that miracles cannot occur. Both groups are on their guard against the view that genuine history can only be achieved by reading the story 'behind' Scripture and adjusting the text to suit the reconstruction so obtained.

As far as I am concerned, however, I accept the inerrantist view. It seems to me that if we adopt the opinion not only that Scripture is inspired but that it constitutes the church in covenant relationship with God, we will hesitate before attributing error of any sort to it. Scripture is God's gift through human authors, and although it bears the marks of humanity, it is also, as the covenant document, not there to put to one side or pass judgement on. Our own ignorance and lack of discernment should constantly remind us of the limitations of reason. The effect of a difficulty for the inerrantist position is to stimulate continued exegetical and historical research and theological reflection in order to see whether there is some explanation. Infallibilists may well miss out on such helpful work because they see no need to engage in it. The view that the text is inerrant invites an appropriate response to a book which is unique. What really matters, however, is that we are called upon to trust the Scriptures, receive their message, and commit to living in obedience to them. To say that they are infallible and inerrant is to say that we may entrust ourselves to their message.

3. Biblical criticism

It is obvious from the brief outline given above that at the heart of the crisis over Scripture in the church is the rise of modern 'biblical criticism'. Earlier generations of evangelicals and Catholics saw the dangers of contemporary biblical criticism and reacted strongly. Some were very dismissive, refusing out-of-hand anything to do with historical and literary criticism. Others were convinced that the Bible could be exonerated before such attacks and, with varying degrees of success, used the methods of criticism to show that the radical critics were wrong.

Every thoughtful Christian is faced with these issues and should engage with them in a constructive and profitable way.

The word 'criticism' has a negative, carping and judgemental ring to it; but not necessarily so. In this context, it is better understood as "the art of estimating the qualities and character of literary or artistic work; the critical science which deals with the text, character, composition and origin of literary documents" (*Oxford English Dictionary*). As such, its purpose is to do justice to the work or piece of art or theatre under review and to assist other people to understand it. It may come to negative judgements (e.g. to do with origins or history, or in matters of taste), but its duty is to submit itself to the document in its own terms.

Biblical criticism is therefore capable of being thoroughly helpful. It can and does help us to see what the biblical books are about. There can be no doubt that progress has been made in appreciating the Bible during the past two centuries, and biblical criticism has enabled Christians to understand the nature of God's revelation in a way which has turned away the attack of non-Christians at a number of points. Proper biblical criticism is essential to good preaching, from finding the true text to understanding the genre.

The crucial point, however, is the axiom adopted by the critic. If the reader assumes from the very beginning that the Bible is a book like any other in its origin, that it is not the inspired word of God, the critical results will be vitiated. Criticism can only be fruitful when it appreciates the fundamental nature of what is being reviewed. We would regard as incongruous and mirth-provoking a review of *A Midsummer Night's Dream* which supposed that it was a Broadway musical, despite the respect we may have for both styles of work when properly viewed in the light of their fundamental nature. The prior adoption of a historical method in approaching Scripture—one which embraces scepticism about the miraculous, an inability to assign God a place, and a tendency to look for the psychological or social features by which the 'real' truth can be reconstructed out of literary remains—is simply wrong-headed. It seeks a theological justification in its appeal to Christianity as a historical religion which culminated in crucifixion; it neglects the equal truth that it is an eschatological religion in which its central figure was resurrected. The Bible is both historical and eschatological, human and divine; true criticism must respond to both.

The task of evangelicalism is to take a positive stance towards criticism without accepting the secularist pre-suppositions of many who now practise it. This can and must be done because of the value we place on Scripture, but it is not easily done. Some scholars are unduly sensitive to the claims of secularist critics, and spend more effort than is necessary in refuting positions based on unbelieving axioms. What's more, too rigid an 'inerrantist' position leads to ludicrous exegesis and theological nonsense; too loose an infallibilist position leads to a Christ other than the one whom God reveals in Scripture. We must be balanced biblical critics; that is, we must be intelligent readers of the text before us.

4. Scripture as clear

The scriptural testimony to itself is that it is expected to be heard, read and understood not merely by scholars, priests and experts, but by ordinary people. Thus Luke records that the Bereans "received the word with all eagerness, examining the Scriptures daily to see if these things were so" (Acts 17:11). This is exactly the presupposition of the New Testament epistles, in the course of which constant reference is made to the Scriptures as evidence for the truth of the Christian claims, and it assumed that the readers will be able to recognize these citations and verify the claims for themselves. Likewise, Peter urges his readers to "pay attention" to "the prophetic word ... as to a lamp shining in a dark place" (2 Pet 1:19).

Such a view of the clarity and accessibility of the Bible flows out of its character as the word of God, functioning to be the entirely trustworthy revelation of God to his people. Becoming a Christian involves believing in the scripturally attested gospel by the power of the Holy Spirit. The Scriptures contain many different styles of writing and vary in the clarity of their expression. But the central message of the Bible and hence the interpretative vantage point is the gospel of Jesus Christ; the parts, even the difficult parts, need to be read in the light of that whole.

The whole issue of how to read Scripture has received much attention from scholars. This discussion goes under the heading of 'hermeneutics', which could be defined as the art of reading or interpreting any document well. Part of such an art is the recognition of the sort of literature being read—a textbook, a poem, a novel, for example. The Bible is meant to be read as we would wish our own writings to be read and understood. The fundamental rule of interpretation, however, flowing out of the divine inspiration of the whole book with all its different parts and literary styles, is this: the Bible interprets the Bible. Thus, to take an obvious example, the Mosaic Law must be read through Christ as we receive guidance on the matter in the New Testament.

The apostle Peter writes of the way in which "our beloved brother Paul also wrote to you" and admits that in these Pauline writings "there are some things … that are hard to understand, which the ignorant and unstable twist to their own destruction, as they do the other Scriptures" (2 Pet 3:15-16). From this we see three things. First, the Scriptures are not all equally clear and easy to understand. In fact, they require careful reading, but God has not left us without help, since we benefit from the understanding of others. Second, Peter still expects his readers (or listeners) to engage with and benefit from Paul's writings; indeed, it is a challenge to us to engage with their meaning even more. Third, there is a spiritual element to reading the word of God: it is the ignorant and unstable who twist the Scriptures, and the antidote is to seek the knowledge of God which comes from an obedient and submissive heart. In the end, it is the Spirit of God who interprets the word of God to us and makes him known, just as the Spirit leads us into a knowledge of God through the gospel.

5. Conclusion

The sheer variety of Scripture may lead to bewilderment and despair. But the covenantal framework enables us to grasp its unfolding more easily; "all the promises of God find their Yes in [Jesus]" (2 Cor 1:20).

The covenant of God is ultimately the Word of God, Jesus, by whom he rules his church and all things. He is at the very centre of Scripture, and no sentence expresses that centre more clearly than 1 Timothy 1:15: "Christ Jesus came into the world to save sinners".

Whatever else we may find in the Bible—wisdom, morality, religious experience—if we do not find this, we do not have the Scriptures at all (cf. John 5:39-40). Here is the interpretative key to the Bible; and yet there is no Jesus Christ independent of the Bible. It is Christ who is the truth of Scripture and, paradoxically, only Scripture which can preach the true Christ.

In these opening chapters, then, we have been considering how we come to know God. In the next chapters, the focus shifts to the God we know through his revelation of himself.

Key verse

And count the patience of our Lord as salvation, just as our beloved brother Paul also wrote to you according to the wisdom given him, as he does in all his letters when he speaks in them of these matters. There are some things in them that are hard to understand, which the ignorant and unstable twist to their own destruction, as they do the other Scriptures. (2 Pet 3:15-16)

Quotation

"In the evening I went very unwillingly to a society in Aldersgate Street, where one was reading Luther's preface to the Epistle to the Romans. About a quarter before nine, while he was describing the change which God works in the heart through faith in Christ, I felt my heart strangely warmed. I felt I did trust in Christ, Christ alone, for salvation; and an assurance was given me that He had taken away my sins, even mine, and saved me from the law of sin and death." (John Wesley, *Journal of John Wesley*)

Key terms
- Infallibility
- Inerrancy
- Autographs
- Clarity (or perspicuity) of Scripture
- Hermeneutics
- Biblical criticism

For further thought
- Why is biblical criticism important for preaching?
- Is a knowledge of biblical criticism important for every Christian?
- What do we lose if we deny that Scripture is inerrant?
- Is there value in arguing for the inerrancy of the original 'autographs' when we don't possess those autographs?
- Charles Spurgeon is said to have remarked: "Defend the Bible? I'd as soon defend a lion! Unchain the Bible and it will defend itself!" Right or wrong?
- How should we deal with the difficulties we encounter when trying to understand parts of Scripture?

For further reading
- MD Thompson, *A Clear and Present Word: The clarity of Scripture*, chapters 2 and 4
- Bray, chapter 6
- Horton, chapter 2

6

KNOWING THE THREE-PERSONED CREATOR

Key concept: The God we know reveals himself to be the Father, the Son, and the Holy Spirit.

1. Introduction

We have been introduced to God by the gospel message of Jesus Christ.

But who is the God of the gospel?

When Jesus announced the nearness of the kingdom of God to his Jewish contemporaries (Mark 1:14-15), they knew which God he was speaking about: the one and only God who rules all time and space. Despite the "many 'gods' and many 'lords'" of the surrounding cultures (1 Cor 8:5), the revelation that there was one Creator who had redeemed a people for himself was at the heart of Israel's faith. This revelation released them from the multiplicity and capriciousness of the nature gods. Unlike their neighbours, they knew a great and saving Lord who alone ruled heaven and earth (e.g. Isa 45:21-22) and who had bound them to himself in covenant.

The oneness of God was liberating news.

This is the God of Jesus. Mark's Gospel emphasizes the continuity between the proclamation by Jesus and the promises of the Old Testament. John the Baptist's ministry fulfilled the prediction of Isaiah, for example, and when Jesus announced that "the time is fulfilled" (Mark 1:15), he was declaring that the moment created by the promises of God's prophets was at hand. The same passage builds on patterns of divine activity, speaking of the forty days of trial in the wilderness and, even more tellingly, presenting the familiar triadic picture of God being active through a human servant inspired by his Spirit (1:9-13). Here is a pattern exemplified by Old Testament personalities such as Moses, Gideon and David (Num 11:17; Judg 6:34; 1 Sam 16:13). This is the typical way in which the Lord does great things.

But the continuity is not exact. There also exist new and disturbing factors which alert us to the question of the identity of Jesus. For example, the quotation from Isaiah in Mark 1 proclaims the coming of "the Lord" and, although this may simply indicate the coming of the kingdom rather than the coming of Jesus, we must remember, too, the emphatic words of John the Baptist: "After me comes he who is mightier than I, the strap of whose sandals I am not worthy to stoop down and untie. I have baptized you with water, but he will baptize you with the Holy Spirit" (Mark 1:7-8).

John's status receives a glowing testimony from Jesus (Matt 11:11), and yet Jesus towers over John. The Lord took some of his Spirit from Moses and gave it to the elders (Num 11:17), but here we have one who himself baptizes with the Spirit. He is like Moses, but he transcends Moses. Already we are forced to ponder "Who then is Jesus?" even as we ask "Who is the God of the gospel?"

Take the description of the baptism of Jesus. Like Jesus, various Old Testament leaders were commissioned by God. Both Moses and Isaiah, however, were overwhelmed by the holiness of God and their own frail sinfulness. Jesus identifies with sinners in his baptism by John, but notably without a sense of sin. Furthermore, in the moment of commission we have the combination of Spirit, Son and Father: "And when he came up out of the water, immediately he saw the heavens being torn open and the Spirit descending on him like a dove. And a voice came from heaven, 'You are my beloved Son; with you I am well pleased'" (Mark 1:10-11).

It is true that 'the Spirit' is a familiar Old Testament expression for the presence and power of God. Likewise, the title 'Son' is not necessarily that of divinity. It describes both Israel (Hos 11:1) and her kings (2 Sam 7:14). But, in context, these verses leave us with the riddle of the single divine sovereignty announced by a servant of the Lord who has been raised to a unique height.

Who, then, is the God of the gospel? Some new thing is being revealed which centres on the question of the identity of Jesus. How does this God relate to Jesus Christ, and does the answer mean that there must be a divorce between the God revealed in the Old Testament and the one of the New? Since the gospel claims to introduce us to God, what can we say about him?

2. The gods of this world

God questions are, as always, set in a particular context. The nature gods which so appealed to Israel were tethered to the world. They personified the powers of nature such as storm, wind and sea, and were approached and manipulated through objects, or through the repetition of ritual. They were divided and divisive, but their appeal was great because they encouraged a functional religion which gave its worshippers a chance of harmony with the patterns of nature itself. Such religions as Israel encountered were typical of human attempts to live in harmony with the powers which control the world of nature and to use them to secure food, guard against illness and protect against magic.

There were a few who came by mere thought to a monotheism.

There was a strand of monotheism in the history of Egypt; so, too, amongst the Greek philosophers. But monotheism did not sustain the religious life of the ordinary person. What made Israel so extraordinary was not that its great thinkers had come to a generally accepted monotheism, but that, in the face of all the odds, not least its own waywardness, it had come to believe in the power, reality and uniqueness of the one Lord whom they knew and worshipped. This God relativized other divinities and eventually abolished them. Furthermore, the God who had revealed himself was free of the power of nature, was free of human influence, and was responsible for all things without being the victim of any. Unlike the gods of the nations, he was not divided; unlike the gods of the nations, he refused to be likened to images or worshipped through them; unlike the god of the philosophers, he was passionately involved in history and human affairs.

It is worth thinking about how the spiritual landscape of today's West compares with the landscape of the ancient world, or indeed, most of the world outside the West. The world into which the gospel goes today is very different, at least on the surface. Disbelief in the Christian God is our immediate context. This retreat from the Christian God is doubtless linked with a revolt against the churches which exercised social control for so long. The old tribal loyalties which gave us state churches and conventional state religion have shifted. The great world wars and lesser but bloody conflicts have played a part as well.

There is also, however, a systematic atheism, stemming largely from the 19th century, which has captured the minds of many and which has made Christian beliefs implausible by portraying them as wish fulfilment. At the same time scientific advance, particularly symbolized by the theory of evolution, has made religion appear to be pre-intellectual and infantile. Even morality no longer needs the underpinning of God, according to the newer views of humanity in the marketplace.

When people speak of God, it is as if they have heard a rumour of benign but remote divinity—so remote as to have no personal features at all. He, or rather 'it', does not impinge on their lives; it makes no demands and provides no support. And yet the retreat of Christianity has not been accompanied by a wholesale embrace of atheism. Far more common is a vague, often homespun, spirituality. For some, the vacuum is being filled by astrology, yoga or animistic beliefs; for others, materialism, sensuality, work, power, security-seeking or personal relations take God's place; others still find intellectual significance in ideologies such as Marxism.

From the Bible's point of view, the widespread revolt against God, whatever form it takes, is not inexplicable. It saw the religions of its own time as both untrue (indeed akin to wish fulfilment) and demonic (1 Cor 8:4, 10:20). It was conscious of human ingratitude to God (Rom 1:21). It sees humanity as caught up in a web of ungodliness inspired by Satan, whom it calls "the god of this world" (2 Cor 4:4). In the end, therefore, the battle is not with flesh and blood, but "against the rulers, against the authorities, against the cosmic powers over this present darkness, against the spiritual forces of evil in the heavenly places" (Eph 6:12). That is why, ultimately, the battle is the Lord's, for the spiritual powers of evil within and without the human race cannot be grappled with by the human race alone. They have political, social, economic and moral aspects and consequences, but at heart they are spiritual. The god of this world will only yield his hold to God himself in his kingdom: "He has delivered us from the domain of darkness and transferred us to the kingdom of his beloved Son ..." (Col 1:13).

3. The God of the kingdom

In a world of many gods, the revelation of the one true God was not by a simple declaration of his unique being. Rather, he covenanted himself to a single nation and revealed himself as a jealous

God, saying "You shall have no other gods before me" (Exod 20:3). This seems to be the point at issue in another pivotal statement, Deuteronomy 6:4: "Hear O Israel: the LORD our God, the LORD is one". This should probably be understood to be saying, 'the Lord our God alone is Lord' (cf. vv 10-15). The revelation of the uniqueness of God was given in the unfolding of history and relationships.

If there was any temptation to treat the Lord merely as a national deity—the one true God of Israel but only one amongst many national deities—this was more than corrected by both revelation and experience. Moses and the other prophets made abundantly clear that God was the sole Creator of heaven and earth (e.g. Genesis 1-2, 14:19; Amos 4:13). When Israel encountered the Lord at Mount Sinai, he assured them that they were his treasured possession while at the same time commissioning them to be "a kingdom of priests and a holy nation", suggestive of the role they were to play universally (Exod 19:6). Further, when Israel and Judah were devastated by their enemies, the prophets revealed that this was not a defeat for God, but the very work of God in judging his own people (e.g. Jer 7:12-15). New life could only come when the one true God of all the earth, who had chosen his own people, came once more to their rescue. The gods of the nations were empty; the sufferings of God's people arose from guilt in them, not impotence in their God.

The constant Old Testament witness to the oneness and power of God is thoroughly exemplified in the book of Daniel. In this book we see the clash, not only between God and the idols of prestigious Babylon, but also God and the political forces of the day. Daniel is far from Jerusalem, where the palace of God stood; it may have been thought that he was beyond the geographic influence of the Lord. As Daniel 1 reveals, however, Daniel's decision to honour God was honoured even in a foreign land. Daniel is superior to the magicians and enchanters, and proves that his God ("the God of heaven"; 2:19) has all wisdom, knowledge and revelation (2:20-23). Daniel, unlike the others, is inspired by God's Spirit (5:14).

When the kingdoms of men are portrayed as a mighty image of gold, iron and clay, a stone representing the kingdom of God ("a kingdom that shall never be destroyed"; Dan 2:44) brings the image down to the dust, wringing from Nebuchadnezzar this confession: "Truly, your God is God of gods and Lord of kings, and a revealer of mysteries ..." (2:47). God saves from the fiery furnace; God saves from the lion's den; God brings down Nebuchadnezzar in his haughtiness until he is forced once again to admit: "His kingdom is an everlasting kingdom" (4:3; cf. 6:26-27).

Given the emphasis in Daniel on the uniqueness and power of Israel's God, it is highly significant that Jesus so frequently uses a title drawn from the book to describe and explain himself. In Daniel 7, we read of the mysterious dream of the four beasts and the contest for dominion, with the award going to the 'fifth monarchy', "one like a son of man" (v 13), whose triumph is absolute and who in some way incorporates God's people (v 27), who will share his reign. Here we come to one of the most important New Testament developments of the Old Testament, for Jesus often calls himself "the Son of Man".

4. The King of the kingdom

There can be no doubt, then, that the Old Testament teaches that there is only one God, the Creator and Sustainer of all things. Nor is there the slightest doubt that the New Testament thoroughly endorses that revelation: "For there is one God" (1 Tim 2:5); "God is one" (Gal 3:20). The uniqueness of God is the ground of a profound cosmic and historical unity.

It is immediately apparent, however, that a change has occurred in line with the hints we have noticed in Mark. This change is illustrated by the use of the name "Father" for God in the New Testament. In the Old Testament, there exist some slight intimations that God may be known as "Father"; in the New Testament, it becomes almost normal for this name to be used. Two linked factors are responsible: first, in a way unique to himself, Jesus called God "Father" and could regard himself as a unique Son (e.g. John 10:17); second, such was the impact of his work that his disciples also began to speak of themselves as children of God, but, in distinction from Jesus, children by adoption (e.g. Rom 8:14-15; Gal 4:4-6). This distinction between Jesus and his followers is crucial.

We have used the phrase, "many 'gods' and many 'lords'" (from 1 Cor 8:5) to refer to the supermarket of gods available to worshippers in the ancient (and indeed much of the modern) world. The passage runs on as follows: "yet for us there is one God, the Father, from whom are all things and for whom we exist, and one Lord, Jesus Christ, through whom are all things and through whom we exist" (8:6). There can be no doubt of Jesus' distinctiveness from us, since he is the one Lord. What does the sonship of Jesus mean about his person?

For present purposes we will assume the true manhood of Jesus (see chapter 13). But to think of him as merely a man fails to do justice to the New Testament witness. What more does the New Testament force us to say of him? Is he, for example, an angel? The idea founders on the observation that angels refuse the worship which Jesus receives (cf. Hebrews 1). The titles "Son of God" and "Son of Man" show an exalted status, but do not themselves prove his divinity. But given that there is a unique element to his sonship, and in the light of all the evidence, there is no doubt that the New Testament writers regard him as divine. His dramatic and direct miracles point in that direction (e.g. Mark 4:35-41); so, too, his forgiveness of sins and his sovereign interpretation of the Law (Mark 2:9; Matthew 5); we also have the use of the Lord's name from Old Testament passages applied directly to him (e.g. Phil 2:9-11), and in several contexts he is identified as God (John 1:1, 8:58, 20:28; Rom 9:5; Titus 2:13).

While these sublime honours are being paid to Jesus, there

remains as well the New Testament's insistence on his distinction, in some sense, from the Father. The Son is not the Father by a different name. Nor does this difference merely involve his humanity; we are being told something here about relationship between Father and Son which goes back into eternity, into the way that things have always been: "In the beginning was the Word, and the Word was with God, and the Word was God" (John 1:1). There is an eternal relationship and an eternal ordering of relationships for which we must somehow account (John 10:30, 14:28; 1 Cor 11:3, 15:28). Indeed, the very revelation of God is involved, for the sonship of Jesus is the way in which we come to know what divine Fatherhood is like (John 14:7-10). However we may account for it, the New Testament confesses the unity of God and at the same time the full deity of both Father and Son.

5. The Spirit of the kingdom

What of the Spirit of God, also mentioned in Mark 1? The situation here is the reverse of the question of the Son. It is not the deity of the Spirit which is the question, but his person.

I have noted already that there is something of an Old Testament pattern in which God is active in salvation through a human servant inspired by his Spirit (e.g. Judg 15:14; 1 Sam 10:6). Isaiah portrays a messianic Son of David thoroughly endued with the Spirit of the Lord for his work (Isa 11:1-5). In such references, the Spirit of the Lord may be thought of simply as the Lord in his powerful presence, as we may think of his 'Wisdom' as his wonderful counsel and knowledge.

Therefore, we may also see the baptism of Jesus in this light (and so, too, his virginal conception). The New Testament confirms the Old Testament view that when you speak of the Spirit you speak of God himself (e.g. Acts 5:3-4), and the Spirit is God's powerful presence with Jesus. His deity is not the point at issue. In the case of

Jesus, we believe him to be in some sense distinct from the Father, but wish to know if he is God; with the Spirit the reverse applies. We understand him to be God, but is he a distinct person?

Once again, the New Testament speaks powerfully about the Spirit, throwing new light on him. The Spirit can be grieved (Eph 4:30) or quenched (1 Thess 5:19); the Spirit leads (Gal 5:18); the Spirit can be lied to (Acts 5:3-4); the Spirit "intercedes for us with groanings too deep for words" and has a mind open to the Father (Rom 8:26-27); the Spirit is sent to dwell with us, to teach and bring remembrance (John 14:17, 26); the Spirit bears witness (Rom 8:16); the Spirit is "another Helper" (John 14:16); the Spirit knows the thoughts of God (1 Cor 2:11).

It is not surprising, then, that in a number of New Testament contexts we find a triune formula, in which Father and Son are associated with the Spirit in a way that endorses both the deity of the Son and the distinctiveness of the Spirit: "The grace of the Lord Jesus Christ and the love of God and the fellowship of the Holy Spirit be with you all" (2 Cor 13:14). If the Son were not divine, his name would be blasphemously included in such a prayer; if the Spirit were not distinct in some way, he would not be conjoined with Jesus and God at such a point.

6. God the Saviour

It is most significant, therefore, that when Jesus gives his final instruction and speaks of the salvation of people everywhere, he should command that baptism be given in the "name" (singular) which is also three: "baptizing them in the name of the Father and of the Son and of the Holy Spirit" (Matt 28:19). Had he said 'names', it may have suggested three gods; had he said "Father, Son and Holy Spirit", it may have suggested one God with three functions. In the precise words he used, however, we find the equality, unity and distinctiveness of the persons summed up.

Further investigation of the New Testament reveals that it insists both on the oneness of God in essence and the unity of the persons in their distinction. Thus the Spirit is the Spirit of Jesus as well as the Spirit of God (cf. Rom 8:9; Gal 4:6). There is an order in the godhead, but not inequality or separateness. There is a difference in function (1 Cor 11:3), but inseparableness of nature, purpose, motive, love and will. To be indwelt by the Spirit is to be indwelt by Father and Son (John 14:17, 23). The work of atonement is the work of God—Father, Son and Holy Spirit—not merely the work of the Son (2 Cor 5:18; Heb 9:14).

7. Conclusion

What I have discussed so far is part of the scriptural raw material from which the doctrine of the Trinity emerged. You may have noticed already that I have begun to use language not literally found in Scripture to describe the 'three-ness' of God—for example, the word 'person'. Christians soon found that they needed a new vocabulary if they were to talk about the God of the Bible and were to avoid heresy. Over the years, words such as 'person', 'substance', 'economic', 'essence', 'co-inherence' and 'Trinity' came into use. Of course, there are dangers involved in the language deployed to speak the truth of Scripture. For example, the word 'person' in modern English has taken on a whole range of associations which are not part of the original. In particular, the idea of 'separate personality' now comes to the fore, and this could lead to tri-theism or the belief that we have three Gods; on the other hand, the suggestion of others that we use 'modes of being' in place of 'person' is equally difficult, as it suggests that the Trinity passes through stages of being, from Father to Son to Spirit.[18]

---

[18] I strongly recommend that you now follow this story further by reading chapter 4 of Michael Horton's *Pilgrim Theology* (Zondervan, 2017).

However, the language is vital, and it is important to know about it and also about the major heresies which it helped combat. Basically there were two: first, there was the heresy that Christ was not of the same essence as the Father, perhaps a man adopted by God and elevated, or a secondary God (e.g. Ebionism and Arianism). Second, there were the heresies which saw Christ as truly God, but as an aspect of God in which the one God appears as the different persons depending on the circumstances (e.g. Sabellianism). Hence the need to say, in the words of the Westminster Confession, "In the unity of the Godhead there be three Persons of one substance, power and eternity: God the Father, God the Son, and God the Holy Ghost. The Father is of none, neither begotten nor proceeding; the Son is eternally begotten of the Father; the Holy Ghost eternally proceeding from the Father and the Son."[19]

What the Bible reveals about our 'three-personed' God is, however, thoroughly wonderful. He alone is God, but he is not solitary. From all eternity, God is love within himself, so to speak, and something of the richness of what that means helps us to understand ourselves and our relationships. That we cannot comprehend the 'three-in-one'-ness should not surprise us. It is a constant reminder of how little we know and how much we should, like Isaiah, confess ourselves sinful and lost in the presence of so great a glory (cf. Isa 6:1-5). But we should never be ashamed or awkward about this, for the revelation of the majesty of our triune God is one of the glories of the gospel.

---

19 Westminster Confession, chapter 2, section 3. "Holy Ghost" is simply an alternate name for the Holy Spirit.

Key verse
"Go therefore and make disciples of all nations, baptizing them in the name of the Father and of the Son and of the Holy Spirit ..." (Matt 28:19)

Quotation
"Batter my heart, three person'd God; for, you
As yet but knocke, breathe, shine, and seek to mend." (John Donne, Dean of St Paul's, London, 1621-31)

Key terms
- Trinity
- Love
- Modalism
- Idolatry
- Son of God
- Son of Man
- Angels

For further thought
- Is the doctrine of the Trinity an embarrassment to Christianity?
- Would it be better not to use words like 'Trinity' which are not found in Scripture?
- Would erroneous views of the Trinity prevent a person being Christian?
- Is it possible that 'the Trinity' is simply God's way of revealing himself, and that in himself he is one rather than three?
- In what sense(s) is God 'jealous'? Why is this a positive attribute?
- It is worth starting to consider: What bearing does the doctrine of the Trinity have on our anthropology? On the Christian life? On how we understand the death of Jesus?

For further reading
- Thirty-Nine Articles, article 1
- Westminster Confession, chapter 2, section 3
- Bray, chapter 7
- Horton, chapter 4
- Milne, chapter 5

7

KNOWING GOD THE LORD, PART 1

Key concept: The God we know is utterly free from all limitations except those inherent in his own righteous character.

1. Introduction

Paul is rarely more sublime than when he prays for the Ephesians that they may "know the love of Christ that surpasses knowledge" (Eph 3:19); he recognizes the partial nature of our present knowledge as citizens of this age, but assures us that the time will come when we will know even as we have been known (1 Cor 13:12). True knowledge of God is, of course, basic to a relationship with him. Our knowledge, though rudimentary, is genuine.

Nonetheless, we must explore what it is that we have been graciously permitted to know of him, for what we know we confess as the basis of our faith, and we learn to trust him as he truly is.

Already, however, we have received a doctrine of God by starting with the gospel. The gospel is not only an instrument for arriving at a knowledge of God; it is a means of God's self-giving, and its very essence shows us that God is the one Lord in three persons, who speaks. The gospel points to the Scriptures, and these writings reveal that God is both independent of all things and committed to all; he is both glorious and gracious; he is both the one who rules and the one who serves. We believe that he is in himself what he is towards us: the Word has become flesh and dwelt among us, full of grace and truth (John 1:14).

Indeed, God's triune nature reveals these things. As the one Creator God, he is the independent source of all things. At the same time he is three, and demonstrates an interpenetration of love and dependence. Lest we should imagine that the list given above—independent and committed; glorious and gracious; ruler and servant (and remembering that it could be extended many times)—means that there is a duality, a tension in God, or even that our way of knowing him must be through a process of investigation, the fact of his triune nature shows that he is in essence at one in himself. Here is the joy of unity, harmony and love, not the tension of unresolved or competing motives and desires, let alone rival personalities.

2. God in his independence

By speaking of the 'independence' of God, I am seeking to do justice to the Bible's picture of him as free and unlimited, unable to be the victim of chance or malice, without rival or peer in the universe. This is also known by the technical word 'aseity'. Unlike every other being or thing, God exists 'from himself'.

Thus God is free in relation to the exercise of his power: he "works all things according to the counsel of his will" (Eph 1:11); "Is anything too hard for the LORD?" (Gen 18:14). Or as Job says to God, "I know that you can do all things, and that no purpose of yours can be thwarted" (Job 42:2). Whether we are dealing here with 'nature' (Ps 119:89-91), with spiritual forces (Eph 6:10ff), with human nature (Acts 16:14) or with history itself (Isa 40:15-17), all things work in accordance with his will. He cannot be frustrated or delayed. He is *omnipotent*, or 'all-powerful'.

The power of God is 'limited' in one way: he cannot do the logically absurd, such as making two times two equal five, or lifting an unliftable object. These are not limitations to his power but mere verbal quibbles, and can be ignored. It may be, however, that at other points where some imagine that God is limited, our ignorance is failing to detect a similar absurdity (see point 4 below).

How, then, can we describe his power?

First, God is unlimited in relation to time. He is the maker and master of time. This means that he remembers all things (Isa 41:22, 43:9), not with effort as we do but perfectly and instantly. As far as the present is concerned, he knows immediately all the occurrences in his creation as they occur (Prov 15:3; Luke 12:6). The future, too, is completely open before him (e.g. Ps 139:1-6; Isa 44:6-8), and his foreknowledge is complete.

Second, we would say that he therefore knows all things: he is *omniscient*. Nothing is hidden from him; no intellectual puzzle is too hard for him. The most secret aspect of the human personality is the thoughts of the heart, but these God knows and understands at once: "for you, you only, know the hearts of all the children of mankind" (1 Kgs 8:39; cf. Amos 4:13). Unlike us, he also understands himself perfectly (1 Cor 2:11). He is infinitely patient through the longest extent of time, and he is so painstakingly involved in creation that "with the Lord one day is as a thousand years, and a thousand years as one day" (2 Pet 3:8).

Third, his mastery of time means that history is in his hand. He not only foresees what is to happen, but plans it (Prov 16:9). When human history reaches its conclusion, he will judge all the earth with perfect knowledge of what has occurred (Rom 2:16; Matt 12:36-37; Ps 94:4-11). In fact, and even more importantly, God has no beginning and no end; he does not grow old or weary. Scripture speaks of the living God, meaning that nothing in all the world could ever assail him successfully—he is eternal and immortal, "the

Alpha and the Omega" (Rev 1:8; cf. 1 Tim 1:17, 6:16).

Fourth, inherent in his power over time is his power over space. In the Bible, God is regarded as being able to relate to his creatures and to exert his power equally and fully at any point of time and space (e.g. Matt 28:16-20; Psalm 139). This is so whether the location is within the human personality (Prov 21:1) or through the highest reaches of the heavens (Amos 5:8-9). He is untroubled when the whole earth prays to him at once, and is also able to reach out his protecting hand to the lost individual ("him who looks after me"; Gen 16:7f). Thus we trust the promise which Jesus makes at the end of Matthew's Gospel: "And behold, I am with you always, to the end of the age" (28:20). No time or space can defeat his word. God is *omnipresent*.

Having observed this scriptural teaching, it must be evident that God's relationship to time and space is very different from our own. Even the most casual thinker is puzzled by aspects of our experience of time, and we know that physicists speak of the interrelatedness of space, matter and time. If God perceives past, present and future with a perfect understanding, it is easy to think of him as 'timeless', or better, 'eternal'—that is, as existing without history or future but in identical relation with all that has been, is, and will be (indeed, in identical relation with all possible events past and future as well). This being so, most Christian thinkers seem to have adopted such a position, and wish to argue that the universe was created with time, there being no possibility of time as such until some part of creation came into being: "Thus there can be no doubt that the world was not created *in* time but *with* time".[20]

The problem is that all of this makes God's experience of relationships vastly remote from our own. For example, we experience change in relationships, but can a person be personal without change? Can the timeless God be personal? Even more significantly, the 'time-

---

20 Augustine, *City of God*, XI.6.

lessness' idea seems to have lost touch with scriptural categories in which God's eternity is not timelessness but unending life. Our immortality is to be a share in his (1 Cor 15:53; Eph 2:7), so it seems that our own future is not to be a 'timeless' eternity but 'eternal ages'. But does this mean that time has always been part of God's experience, too? (And if so, what of space?) Does that mean that time is not 'created', but has to do with the divine relations in the Trinity?

I favour the view that God is best described as eternal and immortal, transcending time, but perhaps it is foolish and unnecessary to adjudicate on these matters, especially when opinion is so divided about the human experience of time. Suffice to say that, whatever opinions we may have, we must hold that God is not at the mercy of time, but is its Lord and Master, so that whatever hold time has on us as frail human beings, it does not in the slightest hinder the purposes of God (cf. Psalm 90).

3. God's independence and creation

While the Bible represents God as being "from everlasting to everlasting" (e.g. Ps 90:2), it has no similar word to say about the universe. It makes clear that all things from greatest to least are the creation of God: "the heavens existed long ago, and the earth was formed out of water and through water by the word of God" (2 Pet 3:5; cf. Isa 40:28). In short, whatever ancient or modern cosmologies may teach about the eternity of matter or energy, the Bible regards God as creating *ex nihilo*, 'out of nothing'. He does not struggle to form the world out of pre-existing matter. He has no rival for his own eternity (cf. Heb 11:3).

The same truth applies to the spiritual forces, angelic or demonic, who are the servants of God but not his equals. They, too, are part of the created order, although the Bible is notably reticent to discuss their origin (Ps 148:2-5; Col 1:16). They are described as being involved with joyful praise at the creation of the world

(Job 38:7). The very name 'angel' (or 'messenger') speaks of their subordinate status (see Heb 1:5-14).

Nor do human beings create a threat to God's independence, although from the time of Adam and Eve ("you will be like God"; Gen 3:5) we have wished to do so. God, of course, has nothing to fear from such frail creatures, but the question of our influence on him may be asked from another perspective: what about the power of prayer? The people of Nineveh, for example, cried out to God in repentance, and "When God saw what they did, how they turned from their evil way, God relented of the disaster that he had said he would do to them, and he did not do it" (Jonah 3:10).

Something of an insight into prayer can be gained from Job 42:7-9, in which God both organizes and accepts Job's prayer. In the case of Jonah and Nineveh, it was the preaching of his word which led to repentance. There is, in other words, in God's way of ruling the world, the use of free agents to accomplish his purposes.

This raises, in fact, the larger issue of God's power—including his knowledge of all things—and human freedom. If God knows all, in what sense are we free? But if we are free agents in the sense that he cannot even predict our choices, how can he be God? The biblical revelation puts its emphasis on the power of God. What this means for human freedom must be considered elsewhere, but in any case we must remember that the biblical God is not just a series of philosophical concepts, but a relational, personal, self-revealing God.

4. God's independence and himself

As would be suggested by God's mastery of time and space, he is not limited as we are by a body. The frequent passages of Scripture that speak of God's hands, feet, face and other bodily parts are anthropomorphisms—that is, descriptions of the divine in terms of human analogies, helping us to understand him. In fact, God is best described as Spirit (John 4:24) and invisible (1 Tim 1:17).

But if God is not limited by a body, he is 'limited' by his own character. Consider some of the ways in which God manifests his character in the Bible:

a. He is the true God, who never lies. His is constant and faithful in relationships. He does not vary or change (John 4:24; Jas 1:17; Titus 1:2).
b. He is the good God, with no shadow or taint of evil. His goodness involves his purity, of course, but the purity of God is abounding, loving blessedness which seeks the good of the other (Hab 1:13; Matt 5:43-48; Mark 10:18).
c. He is the wise God, whose understanding is so linked with his goodness that he knows what is best and may be trusted to do it. That is why there is joy in obedience (Proverbs 8; Rom 11:33).
d. He is the just God, whose relationships are always marked by righteousness. He does not acquit the guilty, nor does he condemn the innocent (Exod 23:7). His justice is allied to his goodness in that he not only brings his right judgement to bear, but he also seeks to put right that which is wrong and to destroy evil. He is wrathful against sin while rewarding righteousness (Rom 1:18, 2:16, 3:19; Heb 10:30-31).
e. He is the loving God, whose mercy extends to the rebellious and sinful, and who upholds, sustains and saves his people. Ultimately the love of God is measured by the cross of Christ (1 John 4:10), leading to these decisive words: "Anyone who does not love does not know God, because God is love" (4:8).

If such a God is faithful and true, it is clear that there are limits to his possible actions. He cannot lie, for example, for to do so would be to lose that which makes him God. His constancy of character makes him worthy of our worship. It makes him the God of the covenant. This constancy must be borne in mind in relation to two important issues.

a. God and his law

In chapter 2, I observed that God's law is not independent of him. On the other hand, it would be wrong to conclude that he is, therefore, lawless, that he can simply declare murder to be right after all should he wish it. His law is an expression of his character, and his character does not vary. Were he to announce that telling lies was now permitted, for example, it would be tantamount to lying.

b. God and his freedom

It is somewhat strange to speak of God's character as though it were an object for examination separate from him. We are forced to it by the inadequacy of language. Nonetheless, we must say that 'character' implies settled habits or dispositions. Does this mean that God is not free? Is he free, for example, to sin? To answer positively to this question would be to betray a misunderstanding of freedom and its relation to character. God's freedom consists in his ability to be God—that is, to do the God-like thing in each circumstance. Contrary to the secular view of freedom, in which we can make any choice we like, true freedom assumes and requires limitations, or else it is destructive. You cannot play tennis without a net and lines and rules. But these things are not unfair limitations; they are what give us the freedom to play. To do without them would be to play some other game. Thus, were God to sin it would mean that he ceased to be godly; it would mean the loss of freedom rather than the exercise of freedom. In short, the 'limitations' imposed on God by his character are not real limitations, but are the conditions of true freedom.

God's freedom is basic to our own. Sin is slavery (John 8:34). When he sets us free from sin, we have the liberty of the children of God, liberty to be the persons we were designed to be. Integral to our freedom is our trust in the goodness and consistency of God. How wonderful it is, for example, to know that he never lies.

5. Conclusion

In speaking of God in his independence, therefore, it is clear that we can never forget God in his unbreakable promises to us. He binds himself to act in accordance with his word. In the next chapter, we explore how these commitments that the Lord has made are vital to an understanding of his work in creation and salvation.

Key verse
"The God who made the world and everything in it, being Lord of heaven and earth, does not live in temples made by man, nor is he served by human hands, as though he needed anything, since he himself gives to all mankind life and breath and everything." (Acts 17:24-25)

Quotation
"I shall set down the following two propositions concerning the freedom and the bondage of the spirit:
  A Christian is a perfectly free lord of all, subject to none.
  A Christian is a perfectly dutiful servant of all, subject to all."
(Martin Luther, *The Freedom of a Christian*)

Key terms
- Aseity
- Freedom
- Immutability
- Omniscience
- Omnipotence
- Omnipresence
- Immanence
- Transcendence
- Communicable/incommunicable

For further thought
- If we say, "God is like …", are there dangers that we are going to diminish him? Have we any other way of approach?
- Are we inappropriately limiting God when we say, "He cannot do the logically absurd"? In what sense(s) is God not 'free'?
- How does our world today define 'freedom'? How does this differ from the Bible's definition?
- Could you learn all you need to know about God from the New Testament alone?
- What is the relationship between the truth about God and faith?
- Does God ever change his mind? What parts of Scripture inform your answer?
- Many theologians have explored the difference between God's 'communicable' attributes (those which human beings may share) and his 'incommunicable' attributes (those that are his alone). Which aspects of God's character belong in each category?

For further reading
- Westminster Confession, chapter 2, sections 1-2
- Bray, chapter 8
- Horton, chapter 3
- Milne, chapter 6

8

KNOWING GOD THE LORD, PART 2

Key concept: The God we know has, from his own righteous character, created all things and committed himself to the welfare and salvation of his creation.

1. Introduction

The transcendent, independent God revealed in Scripture is also the God thoroughly committed in creation and redemption to his world. This dual aspect in our experience of God is indicated, among other things, by the revelation of his name.

Even today, a person's name will usually bear a meaning of some sort, a reminder of the time when the name and the character were understood to be closely allied. The name revealed the character, or suggested direction for an emerging character. Furthermore, even today the revelation of a name is a sort of self-giving which yields to the other person some power of rights over us. We are reluctant to give our name in some circumstances, for fear of what the name will open up to the person who has it. It may reveal who we are; it may identify our family; it may make it possible to trace us; it may mean that the other person will empower themselves by using our name.

These concepts were especially prominent in ancient culture, and even a cursory familiarity with Scripture will reveal the Bible's interest in the subject: "You shall not take the name of the Lord your God in vain" (Exod 20:7), for example; or, "you shall call his name Jesus, for he will save his people from their sins" (Matt 1:21; cf. Acts 4:12; Ezek 20:9).

Not surprisingly, then, the revelation to Moses of God's special name, Yhwh, is attended with great solemnity (Exodus 3-4):

> God said to Moses, "I am who I am". And he said, "Say this to the people of Israel: 'I am has sent me to you.'" (Exod 3:14)[21]

Much later, in a culture influenced by Greek philosophy, these mysterious words came to have a meaning which were thought to reveal God as the timeless one, eternally present, always contemporary; they were an insight into the God of the philosophers. But recent study has put the words back into their biblical and Hebrew context, and the announcement of Yhwh as the divine name is seen to refer to the *past* in which he made his promises, the *present* in which he is reminding them of his promises, and the *future* in which he will fulfil his promises.

This gave his people immediate access to him—a familiarity with God not vouchsafed to others—but it also reminded them that God's character would be revealed in the unfolding succession of his acts and words that were yet to come. History, not philosophy, is the key to understanding God. Without doubt this is far closer to the real significance of the revelation of the divine name.

Thus in the revelation of the name we see the twin aspects already observed of the free God who enters relationship, and of the

---

21 The four Hebrew consonants that form God's name in the Old Testament, Yhwh, are often lengthened to the name 'Yahweh' in modern usage, and also formed the basis of the older variant 'Jehovah'.

transcendent yet committed God. In giving us his name, he invites relationship, but such an invitation involves horrendous risks of the exploitation and abuse of his name (see, in addition to Exodus 20:7, Ezekiel 36:22f). On the other hand, the mystery of the name Yhwh indicates the depths and unrevealed purposes of God: 'I will be what I will be'.

His name, then, is an invitation to us to proceed to see what he has done and said as we try to grasp who God is toward us. In the broadest senses we know him as *Creator* and *Redeemer*; this chapter and the next chapter will follow these two great themes.

In so doing, however, we must remember the unity of creation and redemption, and that while we may distinguish them for the purpose of study, we must never divide them in reality. In particular, we must observe the unity they have in Jesus Christ, the Son of God. Christ is not only the world's redeemer, born to save us from sin; he is the one in whom, through whom and for whom all things were made (John 1:1-3; 1 Cor 8:6; Col 1:16). Creation is the sphere and even the object of redemption (Rom 8:21). That which we observe of the character of God in one sphere is also observable in the other, since it was always God's plan to have Christ as the head of all.

2. The act of creation

On his return to earth, one of the earliest Russian cosmonauts declared that God was absent from space. An American astronaut responded by reading Genesis 1 aloud as he hurtled round the moon. The reading of these ancient words was tremendously effective; they revealed a dignity which underlined their continuing power as the word of God in telling us the truth about creation.

a. The God of the creative act

In reading Genesis, it is important to recognize that it is aimed at the false cosmogonies of ancient culture. Other peoples believed, for example, that the world was born to the gods, or that it was created out of pre-existing matter.

The God of the Bible's first chapter is a God of purpose. The careful staging of the account, culminating in the creation of humankind and the day of rest, testifies to a God who is moving towards an end or goal. It is a contrast with those gods for whom the creation of the world is an accident, or a mere 'natural' event, or the result of struggle. With this God there will be an eschatology—a purposeful end of all things.

Equally, however, the account underlines the power of this purposeful God. He creates effortlessly, by a word. His creation is marked by variety and fecundity, by extraordinary invention. The Genesis story should be supplemented by the descriptions of creation in Job 38-41: "Where were you when I laid the foundation of the earth ... when the morning stars sang together and all the sons of God shouted for joy?" (Job 38:4, 7). The mind of God brings forth rain, snow, sea, stars, the Behemoth and the Leviathan. Before the glory of the Creator, Job can only repent in dust and ashes, confessing, "I know that you can do all things, and that no purpose of yours can be thwarted" (42:2).

Isaiah, too, dwells on the might of God and the impotence of man, stressing the universality of God's creative power. Nothing falls outside his hand, for he has created all things:

> Who has measured the waters in the hollow of his hand
>   and marked off the heavens with a span,
> enclosed the dust of the earth in a measure
>   and weighed the mountains in scales
>   and the hills in a balance? ...
>
> Behold, the nations are like a drop from a bucket,
>   and are accounted as the dust on the scales ...

> It is he who sits above the circle of the earth,
> and its inhabitants are like grasshoppers;
> who stretches out the heavens like a curtain,
> and spreads them like a tent to dwell in ...
>
> The Lord is the everlasting God,
> the Creator of the ends of the earth.
> (Isa 40:12, 15, 22, 28)

Indeed, God has not only created all things, but he created them from nothing (Rom 4:17).

When Scripture dwells on the creation and its Creator, it frequently celebrates not only his power, but his wisdom and goodness: "He does not faint or grow weary, his understanding is unsearchable. He gives power to the faint, and to him who has no might he increases strength" (Isa 40:28-29). When "the sons of God shouted for joy", they were praising the God who in his wisdom had made all things "very good" (Gen 1:31). This is in line with Romans 1:20, where creation reveals God's "invisible attributes", both his "eternal power" and his "divine nature". If our present experience is of a world in travail, this is not God's ultimate purpose, and nor should it dictate an approach to the material world which sees it as corrupt and evil (1 Tim 4:1-5).

b. The creation

What are the qualities of the created order? The creation bears witness to God's glory in its own subsidiary glory. The psalmists meditate on the earth which God has created, and wonder at what they see. But their thoughts immediately and properly rise to the wonder and glory of the source: "O Lord, our Lord, how majestic is your name in all the earth" (Ps 8:9). Psalm 104 is full of delight in the creation, but it is set in the context of praise: "May the glory of the Lord endure forever; may the Lord rejoice in his works ..." (v 31).

The creation is thoroughly dependent on God as its source and sustainer. It is never confused with God, as in pantheism, but it is held in being from moment to moment by the power of his arm (e.g. Ps 104:27-30; Heb 1:3). God did not need creation to complete himself; he created it from his sheer generosity (Acts 17:24-29).

The dependence of the creation on the one God who rules all things liberates us from belief in the independent power of spirits and demons, or of the potency to bless or curse objects in the world. Even meat offered to idols (and hence demons) can be received with a clear conscience, because it is quite incapable of tainting us (1 Cor 8:1-8, 10:19-31; Mark 7:14-23). It belongs to the Lord, who cleansed all things by his word: it is "good" (cf. 1 Tim 4:4-5). Furthermore, belief in the one God who is himself true, faithful and dependable assures us of a world which is fundamentally intelligible and rational. It encourages the scientific exploration of the world by freeing it of irrational and uncontrollable entities. In short, it cleanses it of magic.

At the same time, Scripture testifies to the goodness of the creation. It is a legitimate source of joy: God gives "wine to gladden the heart of man, oil to make his face shine and bread to strengthen man's heart" (Ps 104:15); "he did good by giving you rains from heaven and fruitful seasons, satisfying your hearts with food and gladness" (Acts 14:17). Indeed, the picture of the garden of Eden is one of fruitfulness and happiness in nature, and both the promised land and the new heavens and new earth are described thus (e.g. Isa 11:1-9). These things remain true even though human sin has impacted the world.

The dependence of the creation is, of course, only another way of declaring God's rightful ownership over all that he has made: "It is I who by my great power and my outstretched arm have made the earth, with the men and animals that are on the earth, and I give it to whomever it seems right to me" (Jer 27:5). The writers of Scripture are fully conscious of the moral dimension of this; the

Lord is the Judge of the whole earth, and no sinner will stand in his creation (e.g. Ps 104:35; Isa 6:3-5). In short, consideration of the Creator leads not only to the doctrine of creation but also to the response of the sinful human creature to the perfect, holy God.

c. The human creature

Like all else in creation, human beings exist by, through and for Jesus Christ (Col 1:16). According to Paul, their response to God as Creator ought to be honour and thanksgiving (Rom 1:21). The Lord does not need human worship (Acts 17:24-25), but, as our hearts tell us, when we acknowledge any goodness in this life, he ought to receive our praise and thanksgiving as his due. This includes seeking after him (17:27).

But the usual human response from the children of fallen Adam is idolatry—the taking of a part of creation, treating it as divine and using it to supplant the Creator. In this way the creation is perverted from its proper use. But the problem lies in the human heart rather than in creation itself. We humans have a profound ability to "suppress the truth" in our unrighteousness (Rom 1:18).

The worship of God liberates us from enslavement and restores us to the rightful place we had in Adam, where all things served him (see Rom 8:28; 1 Cor 3:22). While we await the final fulfilment of this restoration of Adam (Heb 2:5-9), the world serves us by painful as well as pleasant means. For our part, the stewardship of nature arises from obedience to the Lord of all things and by doing those good works he has called on us to walk in (Eph 2:10). This will certainly include the proper care of creation, treating all things in line with their purpose and nature in faith and love.

3. The nature of providence

By 'providence' we refer to the creative sovereignty of God as he continually sustains the world for our benefit and his glory. In the biblical way of thought, God "works all things according to the counsel of his will" (Eph 1:11). His wise purposes and his boundless power combine to ensure that his will is done in all things. It follows that in every moment and every circumstance we may be confident of the Lord's presence and ruling.

The scope of his providence is total. All nature, small or large, moves to do his will (e.g. Ps 119:89-91), but so do the forces of history (e.g. Isa 10:5-11) and even the incidents that we may regard as accidental (1 Kgs 22:20, 34, 37) or trivial (Luke 12:6-7). Even the smallest creatures and the least parts of our physical existence are in his hands (Matt 10:29-30).

It ought not to be concluded, however, that this removes the reality or responsibility of creaturely responses. God works in and with his creation, not against it, and uses such things as prayer and human effort to accomplish his purposes (e.g. 1 Cor 3:5-9). The winds and the storms are his servants while having their own genuine life and integrity. Even evil itself, while not being approved in the slightest by God, is used by him to accomplish his purposes (Acts 2:23). His good and loving plan encompassed and overruled the evil will of men (cf. Gen 45:8, 50:20).

It is especially important not to regard the work of God in the world as being frustrated by our evil choices, as though he is the helpless victim of wrong. Were we without revelation, the universe would present a most ambiguous appearance to the sinful heart. For every evidence of God's glory, we could also see most clear evidence of his wrath and judgement. We could have no confidence in his intention to bless us. It is only in the light of the gospel that we may be trusting of our heavenly Father and live the life of faith (Rom 8:28-39).

The greatest difficulty with any Christian doctrine of God the Creator is the problem of the source and prevalence of evil. The Bible gives no countenance whatever to the suggestion that God is either unable to prevent evil or is himself corrupt; we must never compromise God's power or his goodness. But neither does

Scripture offer us an account of the ultimate origin of evil. It is notable, however, that the Bible's whole theme is about the defeat of evil, and it certainly delineates the problem that we feel: "You who are of purer eyes than to see evil and cannot look at wrong, why do you idly look at traitors and remain silent when the wicked swallows up the man more righteous than he?" (Hab 1:13).

The answer of Habakkuk is typical of the whole of Scripture: God is both pure and powerful; he is working out his purposes—of that you may be sure; in the meantime, "the righteous shall live by his faith" (2:4). Yet this faith is not mindless acquiescence ('believing what you know is not true'), but a confidence based on the cross of Christ where evil had its say and was defeated in accordance with the foreordination of God.

In short, the Bible does not answer our questions about suffering specifically, but shows that we may wait on God for the answer. It never ducks the issue; and in the cross we see the Lord's righteousness at work, giving us confidence.

4. Creation and scientific work

It is commonly believed that the 19th century saw a great clash between science and religion, especially in the study of the origins and evolution of the species. This clash is often misunderstood, and propagandists portray it as the victory of scientific light over religious credulity, ignoring the way in which many Christians were (and are) part of the scientific enterprise. Indeed, it should be noted that the rise of modern science was given impetus by the re-emphasis on biblical truth in the 16th century. The idea that there is one sovereign Lord who rules all things consistently was (and is) profitable for scientific thought. Far from science and the Bible being enemies, they are partners, although from time to time work is needed to show how they interact with each other. Thus we must also guard against the tendency to 'discover' God only in the strange or bizarre events of life, as though he is a 'God of the gaps'. He is not to be reduced to being an explanation of what we do not understand, either in science or in daily life. God is in charge of the usual, the ordinary and the regular as much as the strange and unusual.

This also leads to a consideration of the doctrine of creation and the idea of 'miracles'. Since the work of David Hume in the 18th century, there has been a wholesale rejection of miracles in the Western intellectual tradition. A miracle is thought to interfere with God's orderly running of the world, to be a breach of the law of nature. It is thought, too, that no historical evidence would be sufficient to convince us of the truth of so extraordinary an event.

Part of the problem lies in the definition of 'miracle': do we mean any answer to prayer, for example? Or any event we cannot explain? Is it a miracle when by special timing an event occurs even though we can see why it does? For example, was it a miracle when God used "a strong east wind" to drive back the Red Sea so the Israelites could escape Egypt's clutches (Exod 14:21)?

These and similar questions will be pursued elsewhere, but suffice to say that the doctrine of God's sovereignty outlined above relieves some of the pressure felt by a more deistic view. The so-called 'laws of nature' are simply the observed regularities of God's dealing with the world to this point, regularities which he has the freedom to vary as he will. They include his capacity to create animals and objects which will act habitually in certain ways. A number of questions in this area turn on an unnecessary attempt to define miracles too closely; God is sovereign, however we experience that sovereignty. It may be better to reserve the word 'providences' for the Christian experience of God's fatherly care and to use 'miracles' of the great revelatory events described in Scripture. But this is a secondary classification.

5. Conclusion

In this chapter we have introduced difficult and demanding material—after all, God is God. It may all seem rather remote. But this is the God who has revealed his name and invites us to trust in him. This means that nothing can have more practical influence on the way we live than our understanding of God; nothing is more practical than good theology. The link between the reading of the Bible and the rise of modern science is not an accidental one. But, even more importantly, in everyday life our knowledge about and confidence in God dictates our character and our behaviour and impacts the world in which we live. The God of the Bible is trustworthy and strong. We learn to trust his constant providence in every aspect of our lives. As we do, we begin to fulfil God's design for humanity.

Key verse
"I know that you can do all things, and that no purpose of yours can be thwarted." (Job 42:2)

Quotation
"You must picture me alone in that room in Magdalen [College], night after night, feeling, whenever my mind lifted for even a second from my work, the steady, unrelenting approach of Him whom I so earnestly desired not to meet. That which I greatly feared had at last come upon me. In the Trinity Term of 1929 I gave in, and admitted that God was God, and knelt and prayed: perhaps, that night, the most dejected and reluctant convert in all England." (CS Lewis, *Surprised by Joy*)

Key terms
- Yahweh
- Miracles
- Creator
- Redeemer
- Providence
- Supernatural
- Pantheism
- Ex nihilo

For further thought
- "History, not philosophy, is the key to understanding God." What does this statement mean? How does it shape our approach to doctrine?
- What distinction, if any, should we draw between 'miracles' and 'providence'?
- If God is the Creator, has he left his imprint on the creation to such an extent that we can find out what he is like by studying it?
- How should we respond to the notion that science and Christian faith are antithetical?
- Has Christianity contributed to the present environmental situation? How involved in or passionate about environmental concerns should we be? Are there aspects of the secular movement that must be resisted?
- What are the expressions of modern idolatry? Can we use parts of the material world to worship God? If not, are we saying that matter is corrupt?
- "Nothing is more practical than good theology." Do you agree?

For further reading
- Westminster Confession, chapters 4-5
- Bray, chapter 12
- Milne, chapters 7 and 8

9

KNOWING GOD THE LORD, PART 3

Key concept: The God we know is both glorious and gracious in his righteousness.

1. Introduction

In chapters 7 and 8, we have seen that the God of the Bible is both free and committed. In this chapter, we take up a second pair of descriptive words and say that he is both glorious and gracious.

Consider one of the central episodes of the Bible, the giving of the law at Sinai (Exodus 19-20). The gathering of the people at the foot of the mountain was followed by the blast of a trumpet, the trembling of the people, and the mountain being wrapped in smoke "because the LORD had descended on it in fire" (19:18). The people were not to "break through to the LORD to look", lest they perish (19:21); their response was fear, lest God speak directly to them, so they asked Moses to be their mediator (20:18f). When Moses and the seventy elders ascended, "they saw the God of Israel. There was under his feet as it were a pavement of sapphire stone, like the very heaven for clearness" (24:10). Moses was then summoned up on to the mountain on his own, "and the cloud covered the mountain. The glory of the Lord dwelt on Mount Sinai, and ... the appearance of the glory of the Lord was like a devouring fire on the top of the mountain in the sight of the people of Israel" (24:15-17).

The meeting place between God and his people, the tent of meeting, was sanctified by his glory (Exod 29:43) as the Lord dwelt amongst his people. But while the Lord was giving detailed instructions to Moses about his dwelling place, the people rebelled and made and worshipped a molten calf. The wrath of God burned against the people and they were punished. The intercession of Moses prevented their complete overthrow, and ensured that God's presence would still be with them in their journey. Moses, seeking to be reassured, asked for the Lord's glory to be revealed to him, and the Lord granted his request: "Behold, there is a place by me where you shall stand on the rock; and while my glory passes by I will put you in a cleft of the rock, and I will cover you with my hand until I have passed by. Then I will take away my hand, and you shall see my back; but my face shall not be seen" (33:21-23).

In these events we see both the glory and the grace of the Lord. His glory is awesome, and yet in his love he approaches and relates to a sinful people. Yet even in his loving approach, there is the constant reminder of his 'otherness': "my face shall not be seen". Glory and grace are in constant, perfect interplay.

Not surprisingly, in view of the place of the name of Yhwh early in Exodus, the events culminate in a future revelation of the Lord's name. The promise contained in the 'I will be what I will be' now begins to be fulfilled, as the words and deeds of God have revealed what he is like. He passes before Moses and proclaims "the name of the Lord" (34:5):

> "The Lord, the Lord, a God merciful and gracious, slow to anger, and abounding in steadfast love and faithfulness,

keeping steadfast love for thousands, forgiving iniquity and transgression and sin, but who will by no means clear the guilty, visiting the iniquity of the fathers on the children and the children's children, to the third and the fourth generation." (Exod 34:6-7)

It is on this ground that Moses is bold enough to ask for pardon for the people.

The glory and grace of God are themes sustained throughout the Bible. Although it is an over-simplification to schematize all we may want to say under these headings, there is sufficient truth in it for the attempt to be useful. By so doing, we capture something of the dynamic of the biblical story. In one of the great moments in his Gospel, John sees the glory and grace of God in the incarnation of his Son:

And the Word became flesh and dwelt among us, and we have seen his glory, glory as of the only Son from the Father, full of grace and truth … For the law was given through Moses; grace and truth came through Jesus Christ. (John 1:14, 17)

2. The glory of God

The glory that separates

In praying for a sight of God's glory, Moses is reminding us that the glory of the Lord is precisely what we human beings do not have. The Lord's glory dazzles; it is his 'weight', his reputation, his greatness and his goodness. His glory communicates the essence of his being by overwhelming the observer. It warns us that he is set apart from us (Isa 42:8), a truth that is undeniably confirmed by the revelation of his triune nature.

Another expression for the same truth is that the Lord is 'holy'. In the first instance, this is a word that denotes a general 'otherness':

the Lord is not man. But it quickly comes to imply especially the *moral* otherness of God, for when humans come into the presence of God it is not even his awesome magnificence beside their insignificance that they first feel, but their moral unworthiness. Thus, classically, when Isaiah sees the Lord upon his throne, and hears the call of the Seraph, "Holy, holy, holy is the Lord of hosts; the whole earth is full of his glory" (Isa 6:3), his reaction is not merely to express his smallness, but to confess his sinfulness. The purity of the Lord is overwhelming to the prophet (cf. Hab 1:13; Ps 11:4-7); our sin is described as falling short of his glory (Rom 3:23).

The glory that consumes

The name of the Lord reminds us that he "will by no means clear the guilty" (Exod 34:7). The guilty and idolatrous people, having made the golden calf in the absence of Moses, had discovered that his anger was not merely directed at the pagan Egyptians but at his own people: "Now therefore let me alone, that my wrath may burn hot against them and I may consume them" (32:10). The Lord enacts a just retribution on those who sin against him. Given the human tendency to excuse ourselves for our sins, it is not surprising that the Bible, from Genesis to Revelation, reveals that God in his wrath takes just vengeance on humanity—that his justice is at the heart of the universe.

It is certainly true that he does not wish to punish (2 Pet 3:9); it is true that he is quick to show compassion (1 John 1:9); it is true that many sins contain their own punishment (Rom 1:28-31); and it is true that the Lord sometimes disciplines in order to correct (Heb 12:5-6; 1 Cor 5:6-7). But nothing can remove the solemnity of such passages as Hebrews 10:30-31: "For we know him who said, 'Vengeance is mine, I will repay'. And again, 'The Lord will judge his people'. It is a fearful thing to fall into the hands of the Living God." Nor is there any escape in the thought that the New Testament is less severe than the Old, or that Jesus is less severe than

Moses or Paul. It was Jesus who said, "if your eye causes you to sin, tear it out. It is better for you to enter the kingdom of God with one eye than with two eyes to be thrown into hell" (Mark 9:47).

We must insist, furthermore, that the Bible sees no embarrassment in this. Our instinct is to say that God's glory is somehow compromised by his wrath. But the Bible would see his glory as established in his wrath. The only passage in the New Testament in which the word "hallelujah" is used is Revelation 19, where it's used specifically to praise God for his judgement against Babylon, the great enemy of the people of God (Rev 19:1-6). It is precisely because of God's purity that Habakkuk cannot understand his slowness to punish (Hab 1:13). If God loves the good and the just, he must also bring vengeance to bear, for sin accumulates a debt which God cannot ignore (Rom 2:4-11). His justice is indeed good news; we have all longed to see wickedness and evil brought to judgement.

The problem is our own guilt.

The glory that saves

The glory of God is not only his awe-inspiring presence and power or his holiness and wrath; it is also expressed in his righteousness. In one sense the righteousness of God is simply his holiness, the mainspring of his wrath, his passion for justice which will redress wrong, reward the innocent and punish the guilty according to his perfect rules. But God's righteousness is more than that. God's righteousness is also his fixed determination to set things to rights, to make the world what he purposed it to be, and so fulfil his promises.

Thus, the righteousness of God actively seeks the salvation of his people. It is only by his righteous power that the fallen world will be set to rights and justice and mercy will reign. It is the supreme glory of God that he is a Saviour, and he never receives more glory or acts more gloriously or more righteously than when he is saving (e.g. Psalm 71). But God's glory is such that his salvation of some is in the midst of the downfall of others (consider the psalms from, say, 52 to 65).

It must not be imagined that God's righteous glory is inconsistent with his love. In the psalms just referred to, his steadfast love and goodness are celebrated constantly (e.g. 52:8; 54:5-6; 55:22; 57:3, 10; 59:10, 16; 61:7; 62:8; 63:3; 65:1-4). Indeed, his love is that which insists on justice—justice for the oppressed, weak and vulnerable, and a justice which takes seriously the dignity of every human being and his or her right to be judged with fairness. But this love also, astonishingly, provides for the salvation of sinners, in the cross-making kiss between righteousness and peace (85:10).

The glory that triumphs

Scripture teaches the uniqueness of God and hence the uniqueness of his glory. And yet, just as his people are called upon to reflect his holiness (and thus 'share' his uniqueness, such as in Leviticus 19:2), there are also links between humanity and the glory of God.

In the first place, of course, it is our duty to glorify him. This we do by the sacrifice of praise and thanksgiving and by the trusting obedience of redeemed persons (Rom 1:20, 15:7-13). It is both our duty and joy, and when Christ returns it will be in order "to be glorified in his saints" (2 Thess 1:10).

Secondly, we are now able to see the glory of God in a special place: "[God] has shone in our hearts to give the light of the knowledge of the glory of God in the face of Jesus Christ" (2 Cor 4:6). For Jesus Christ is "the Lord of glory" (1 Cor 2:8), the one who "is the radiance of the glory of God and the exact imprint of his nature" (Heb 1:3). Moses had a unique experience of seeing God's glory, but it cannot be compared with our experience of that glory. Moses' face was veiled after speaking with the Lord, so glorious was his appearance for some time; but we now behold the Lord unveiled, even though the new revelation surpasses the old and makes it fade away (2 Cor 3:7-11).

Thirdly, so marvellous is this sight of God's glory that we, like Moses, begin to reflect it or partake of it: "And we all, with unveiled face, beholding the glory of the Lord, are being transformed into the same image from one degree of glory to another" (2 Cor 3:18; cf. 1 Cor 2:7). Paul even speaks of our ultimate destiny as "an eternal weight of glory beyond all comparison" (2 Cor 4:17).

There is a bold parody that runs: "Glory to Man in the highest, for Man is the maker of things!" That we should be so glorified as to share an eternal weight of glory may be regarded as a religious version of the same sentiment. In this thinking, God is humanity writ large; the ultimate secret of the Bible is that humanity triumphs after all.

To any attentive reader of the Bible, such a proposal is absurd. If in the end humanity is glorified, it is only by the most extraordinary exercise of God's free power.

This breathtaking audacity in God is his grace.

3. The grace of God
Grace in essence

Unless the love of God towards us is understood to be grace, it is not understood at all. For at the very heart of the Christian faith is the recognition that we deserve nothing from God, that we are righteously punished for our sins. There is nothing in us to attract his favour and everything to attract his wrath. We are the alienated sons of the father in Jesus' parable (Luke 15:11-32).

Grace is first and foremost God's attitude of love to the lost and unlovely: "but God shows his love for us in that while we were still sinners, Christ died for us" (Rom 5:8). Paul calls this the "grace in which we stand" (5:2)—that is, the favour of God which we now enjoy. It is the same as being now able to call him Father, when before we did not know him and we could expect nothing but condemnation and wrath from him.

The Old Testament saints were conscious of the undeserved love of God sustaining them. But even the exodus was far less a source for their understanding of grace than what we now have in "the grace of our Lord Jesus Christ", who "though he was rich, yet for your sake he became poor, so that by his poverty you might become rich" (2 Cor 8:9).

Grace in choice

The history of salvation is marked by grace at every turn, since the day when the Lord God kindly clothed Adam and Eve to hide their nakedness (Gen 3:21). Whether we think of Noah, Abraham, Moses, David, Hosea or Israel itself, we see that what the Lord revealed as his name is true: he is "a God merciful and gracious, slow to anger, and abounding in steadfast love and faithfulness" (Exod 34:6).

We must note, however, that the Bible celebrates the grace of God in his prior choices. The election of Israel was sheer love (Deut 7:6-8). But this is merely an example of his electing love for all his people (including the Gentiles, which is especially amazing to the Bible writers):

> ... he chose us in [Christ] before the foundation of the world, that we should be holy and blameless before him. In love he predestined us for adoption to himself as sons through Jesus Christ, according to the purpose of his will, to the praise of his glorious grace, with which he has blessed us in the Beloved. (Eph 1:4-6)

By speaking thus of God's prior choice, the Bible underlines the sheer graciousness of it all, since it depends upon the love of God and not upon human merit or worth. It is in contrast to those versions of salvation in which human effort or goodness play a determinative role.

Grace in action

Of all the actions of God which may be attributed to his grace, none is more significant than the saving death of Jesus on the cross. In him, says Paul, "we have redemption through his blood, the forgiveness of our trespasses, according to the riches of his grace, which he lavished upon us" (Eph 1:7-8). According to John, the cross is the supreme manifestation of God's love (1 John 4:10). The love poured into our hearts by the Holy Spirit is our knowledge that God loves us, and the proof of this is the cross (Rom 5:5-6).

The gospel is based on what God has done for us in Christ, and this is the great work of his grace. Since, however, we are spiritually dead and unable to save ourselves, God completes his work of salvation by bringing us to new life. Salvation, then, is accomplished through the work of Christ and applied to us by his Spirit (Eph 2:1-10; John 3:1-8). In some circles, the idea of the application of salvation can lead to God's grace being treated as a 'power', rather than as God's love. The application of salvation is certainly the work of grace, but we must continue to remember that grace is fundamentally the expression of God's love.

Grace in triumph

Once the secret of grace has been understood, it becomes determinative for every aspect of the Christian life. It banishes fear, since it assures the conscience; it destroys pride, since its whole tendency is to attack human pretension and boastfulness. It is one of the most unpopular of all Christian doctrines since it is based on such a low estimate of human capacity. On the other hand, it is one of the most loved of all Christian truths because it binds up the brokenhearted and brings comfort to those who mourn (cf. Isa 61:1-2).

Paul sees our life as bounded by grace, not only in its beginning before the creation of the world, in its expression at the cross, and in its application in salvation, but also in the experience of heaven:

"that in the coming ages he might show the immeasurable riches of his grace in kindness toward us in Christ Jesus" (Eph 2:7). Our whole life before God is grace abounding, and it will continue to be so in the new creation.

To understand grace is also to understand that God does not in his grace give us a licence to sin. A genuine believer in Jesus Christ must be appalled at such a thought because he or she recognizes that it is sin which crucified the Lord (see Rom 6:1f). As the apostle says in Titus 2, "the grace of God has appeared, bringing salvation for all people, training us to renounce ungodliness and worldly passions, and to live self-controlled, upright, and godly lives in the present age" (vv 11-12). Grace is our teacher, not an excuse for disobedience; grace saves us from sin, but it does not leave us in sin.

4. Conclusion

Since the first chapter of this book, we have been focusing our attention on God himself. From the gospel of Jesus Christ, we have seen who and what God is, and who and what God is towards us. Our beliefs about God set us apart from other beliefs and values—and set us at tension with them. In what follows—the doctrine of humanity, of salvation, of the church and of the last things—we will never move far from the doctrine of God, for this is the foundation on which all else is built. On the other hand, we do not believe that we can study God in isolation from his works as described in Scripture. What we have to say in what follows will add to and refine the material already given. In biblical doctrine, all things are connected.

In all this, we must never forget that the knowledge of God is unique. It is uniquely practical, involving as it does the whole of our life here and in the age to come. It is also unique in that it calls forth our faith and obedience. Our study must proceed with reverence and prayer, or else it utterly misjudges its object.

Key verse

For by grace you have been saved through faith. And this is not your own doing; it is the gift of God, not a result of works, so that no-one may boast. (Eph 2:8-9)

Quotation

"'Twas grace that taught my heart to fear,
and grace my fears relieved;
how precious did that grace appear
the hour I first believed!

Through many dangers, toils and snares
I have already come:
'tis grace has brought me safe thus far,
and grace will lead me home." (John Newton, 'Amazing Grace')

Key terms
- Grace
- Glory
- Righteousness

For further thought
- Should we talk about God in such a way that his grace and his justice are in tension, or even in conflict?
- It is sometimes claimed that God is 'egotistical' to command us to praise and glorify him. Is this true?
- If we are saved by grace at every point, what place is left for human responsibility?
- "Naked I came from my mother's womb, and naked shall I return. The Lord gave, and the Lord has taken away; blessed be the name of the Lord" (Job 1:21). Is it right to say that we deserve nothing from God? Is this overly negative?

- The gender of God is much discussed today. Is our use of masculine language arbitrary and incidental, or is it part of the unchangeable revelation?

For further reading
- JI Packer, *Knowing God*, chapters 12-17
- Milne, chapter 9

PART TWO

KNOWING THE CREATOR WHO SAVES

- In God's sight, human beings are both precious and corrupt.
- God provides for humanity to be social and to have a future, but we are condemned even in our religiosity.
- In saving the human world, God first created a nation to live under his rule and provide the pattern for salvation.
- Into the chosen and covenanted nation is born the Saviour of the world.
- The humble Lord, rejected by his own people, lays down his life for the world.
- The humble Lord is exalted to the right hand of God, from where he rules over all things.
- The exalted Lord sends his Spirit as the one who will bring us to salvation through union with him.

10

HUMANITY AND THE GOSPEL MESSAGE, PART 1

Key concept: In God's sight, human beings are both precious and corrupt.

1. Introduction

The great French thinker Blaise Pascal described humanity as "the glory and shame of the Universe". In so doing, he captured something of the paradox that both the Scriptures and human experience set before us. It is commonplace to observe that the extraordinary technical achievements of humankind are matched by their sordid exploitation and abuse. To take an obvious example, the extraordinary achievement of the internet is the vehicle for unlimited pornography.

As we seek to describe and understand the biblical view of humanity, we ought also to be conscious of the fascination that the subject has for the secular world. Whole academic disciplines such as anthropology, sociology, psychology and politics are given over to this study—as are, in effect, history, law, medicine, linguistics and much philosophy. Whereas 'Divinity', or the study of God, was once a dominant study in the university, its place has often been taken by the study of 'religion'. We may have moved far from a heliocentric universe in physics, but we have shifted towards an anthropocentric universe in other studies.

Part of this fascination arises, of course, from the perennially interesting questions involved in the study of humanity. Where did we come from? How can we explain human behaviour? What goals are appropriate for the race and for the individual? Why do men and women create gods? What is our relationship to nature? What does the future hold? What should we say about the relationship of men and women, and of family life? The list of questions is endless, and the answers are legion.

In Western culture, the old power exercised by Christian thought has been challenged and largely overthrown. It has not, in my judgement, been replaced by a coherent ideology, but by a number of competing points of view about humanity. Whatever view is adopted, however, must take into account the sense of anxiety engendered both by the realization of the insignificance of humanity and the growing conviction that we have despoiled the planet, perhaps irreversibly.

The insignificance of our species (and of us as individuals) has been brought home by the dissemination of scientific information. The planet on which we live seems virtually infinite in the number and range of its vegetable and animal life. We have not yet catalogued let alone studied the living species. We are told that the earth's age is immense when compared to a human life-span or even to human history. But the earth itself, notwithstanding its complexity and hugeness, is tiny compared with the vastness of the universe and the numbers of its stars and galaxies. The human mind long ago ceased being able to provide any meaningful perspective on what we now believe about space and time.

Our own individual life seems impossibly random. It is usually one sperm out of millions which fertilizes the ovum. Each of the mother's egg cells, too, is unique, and by the time an individual is conceived he or she represents one of a huge number of potential individuals. When this one, unique person is born, he or she becomes simply one of the eight billion or so persons on a crowded planet, conscious that the death of individuals hardly counts amongst so many, and even the most famous of people is barely remembered beyond a few decades. Sheer luck seems to haunt our lives from beginning to end. We are forced to ask, "Who are we?" and even more poignantly, "Who am I?"

2. A starting point

In the study of humanity, it is tempting to abstract the object from its surrounds, as if a man or a woman could be observed best under "laboratory conditions". Even in the animal realm, this course of action yields partial results at best. Theologians have sometimes fallen prey to this error when trying to isolate what is meant by "the image of God", or endeavouring to construct a psychological picture of a human being from the elements in the Bible.

Our fundamental understanding of humanity must arise from relationship, and especially the human being's relationship with God. This is so because human beings are dependent on God—taking our source from God, being sustained by God, and having our only hope in God. It is only as we understand the purpose of God for human beings that we can establish the basis for a true anthropology and have any true perception of a man or woman's relationship with the world and with other human beings.

It has become customary in Christian anthropology to start with Genesis 1-3 and glean all that can be said from the teaching about human beings in those chapters. There is certainly nothing wrong with this starting point, for it sets humanity in the context of our origin and the purposes of God, and lays the foundations for a consideration of such vital matters as humanity and creation, humanity and God, humanity and work, humanity and marriage, and humanity and sin. But its very power is something of a trap; too much Christian anthropology becomes limited to the exploration of these chapters and, in particular, to the discussion of "the image of God", whereas the Bible as a whole has much to say about what it means to be human.

I propose to start, therefore, with the gospel, and see whether this will help keep a satisfactory balance and enable us to gain a fuller biblical perspective. In so doing, we should be aware at once that Genesis 1-3 will never be far away! If we begin with the gospel, however, we are beginning not with humanity in its innocence, but with humanity in our current experience—with humanity in need of salvation. Such a starting point may have some immediate value.

3. The individual addressed by the gospel
A precious individual
The fact that there is a gospel at all is overwhelming testimony that, to God, the human race is precious: "For God so loved the world, that he gave his only Son ..." (John 3:16). The incarnation, the Word become flesh, is proof of this, for it demonstrates the grace of God (2 Cor 8:9) to humankind. Jesus was born man, neither animal nor angel, and he remains both true God and true man forever.

But the greatest demonstration of all is the cross, for this supreme gift of God is the evidence of the extent to which he will go to find the lost sheep (Luke 15:1-10; Rom 5:7-8). Paul powerfully individualizes the cross at one point:

> I have been crucified with Christ. It is no longer I who live, but Christ who lives in me. And the life I now live in the flesh I live by faith in the Son of God, who loved me and gave himself for me. (Gal 2:20)

The future of humanity testifies to the same preciousness. We are not destined for annihilation; we are destined for eternity, and an eternity fulfilled in God, where we will know as we have been known (1 Cor 13:12). Even the fact of hell does not compromise this, for hell expresses the importance of the human creature to God, his determination to take us seriously and treat us righteously. Far from our persons—our thoughts, our words and our deeds—being insignificant, every human is taken with great seriousness and judged accordingly.

This divine estimate of human beings finds Old Testament expression in the way in which God insists that we treat each other:

> "For your lifeblood I will require a reckoning: from every beast I will require it and from man. From his fellow man I will require a reckoning for the life of man.
>
> "Whoever sheds the blood of man,
>   by man shall his blood be shed,
> for God made man in his own image." (Gen 9:5-6)

In passage after passage, we are exhorted to walk with justice and mercy towards all who are human. Whatever else "the image of God" language in Genesis 1:27 implies, it sets human beings off as unique, and uniquely precious to God.

The preciousness of humanity to God must be applied vigorously to the problems generated by our consciousness of insignificance. Nothing is more pompous, pretentious or absurd than the vision of humanity exalting itself as Lord of the universe—a "forked radish", to use one of Shakespeare's phrases. To this proud spirit, the revelation of our insignificance is salutary. But to those who are crushed by their nothingness and who are prepared to hear that their significance arises from the love of another who has created them, the gospel message is truly and wonderfully applied. It also constitutes a grave warning to those who hold human life cheaply, who put wealth or possessions or art or music or politics or ideas before persons. It is a rebuke to the humanistic spirit that has led to the slaughter of babies in their mother's womb, or the wicked preference for male children over female, or for the neglect of the aged, the isolated, the unemployed or the disabled.

A rebellious individual

There would not need to be a gospel if this beloved creature of God had not become his enemy (Rom 5:10). The very shape of the gospel—speaking as it does of the rule of God (or the lordship of Christ), the need for repentance, or the submission of the person to God—testifies to the fundamental problem of the race. We are out of touch with our Creator, indeed alienated from him, and while that situation exists nothing can go completely right, whether it is in our relationships with each other, with the world, or even in ourselves. Even our best endeavours are compromised by our sinful weakness.

We may see the *evidence* of the truth of what the Bible says in things such as our treatment of one another, the exploitation of the groaning, suffering natural world, our disdain for God's will even though we know right and wrong (Rom 1:18-3:20), and even human religion, which avoids the proper response to God in favour of the worship of beings less than God. We may see the *ground* for God's call for repentance in the fact that he made us, that we belong to him, and that he has every right to our worship (1:25, 2:6-7, 9:19-24). We may see the *origin* of human rebellion not in each individual will, but in an historical encounter between Adam and Eve and the evil one, in which our first parents deliberately put God's word to one side in favour of Satan's specious lies.

The biblical account of the origin of humanity is so selective that it is difficult to offer a commentary on how it ties in with scientific descriptions. We do not even know what time span it is taken to represent. It is open to several interpretations as there are matters the Bible does not address. But what the New Testament does not allow us to say is that the account is a parabolic or mythological rendering of the creation and fall of every person. Even if it is in some sense symbolic (which is by no means certain) or a parable, it is a parable of true history, of real events, just as Nathan's parable of the lamb was based on history (2 Sam 12:1-15).

We must also acknowledge that we look back on the events which have shaped us from our present position outside the garden of Eden. Only a glimpse has been allowed us, enough to be able to understand the truth. It is not intended to give us a comprehensive re-creation of our history as a race, but to establish the key truth that we need to know: that Adam and Eve, with whom we are all connected, rebelled against the word of God and so infected the race with rebellion and its consequences. This is called 'original sin', original in its beginnings with our first parents and original because it describes our nature as a result. What the world would have been like for an innocent people we do not know; suffice to say that it has proved an arena of trial and suffering for a rebellious people, and has suffered itself in our fall.

Some would say that our connection with Adam is primarily 'federal' or 'covenantal' (though perhaps the word 'judicial' is better). This means that he was our appointed representative, and that as our representative he involved us all in sin and guilt. Such a view helps explain why it is part of God's righteousness to treat us as being "in Adam" before we even become independent (Rom 5:12; 1 Cor 15:22). On the other hand, it hardly explains why we habitually and invariably sin.

Others would prefer the view that there is some inheritance of sin, a factor in the spiritual make-up of the whole race which is (humanly) ineradicable and which is transmitted to every generation. Such a view seems a better reflection of Paul's language in Romans 5, where it is participation in Adam, and in the "one man's trespass" (vv 15-18), which leads to death, rather than imitation or representation. On the other hand, such a view poses problems about guilt.

It is best to see Adam as both our representative and our spiritual progenitor. We accept his representative role in relation to such matters as the image of God, the meaning of work, and the basis of marriage; we should accept the same role in connection with sin and guilt. As our progenitor, however, his connection with us is constitutive of our being, as is demonstrated by the universality of sin and guilt. We are not born morally neutral, but already disposed to rebellion; we sin because we are born sinners (Ps 51:5).

An enslaved individual

Humanity was created to live in God's kingdom, and was never intended to be autonomous. Rebellion against God was suggested by the serpent, who is rightly understood to be the evil one (Gen 3:15; Rom 16:20), and human life since then has been susceptible to his influence and control. He is called "the ruler of this world" (John 12:31), and "the god of this world" (2 Cor 4:4); in the latter verse, he is said to have "blinded the minds of the unbelievers, to keep them from seeing the light of the gospel of the glory of Christ". In Colossians, the redemption secured by Christ is described in terms of being delivered "from the domain of darkness and transferred ... to the kingdom of his beloved Son" (Col 1:13). In Ephesians, Paul describes the unbeliever as "following the prince of the power of the air, the spirit that is now at work in the sons of disobedience" (Eph 2:2). The same passage also ascribes power over the unregenerate to "the world"—a reminder that Satan's hold is neither complete nor unchallenged. We cannot blame him for our misfortune, as though we are not responsible.

But human beings are also enslaved to sin: "everyone who practices sin is a slave to sin" (John 8:34). The most telling picture of this enslavement is in Romans 7: "I have the desire to do what is right, but not the ability to carry it out" (v 18). But the Bible tells the same tale throughout: "every intention of the thoughts of [humanity's] heart was only evil continually" (Gen 6:5); "The heart is deceitful above all things, and desperately sick; who can understand it?" (Jer 17:9). However clear and right the call to repentance, it cannot in itself break the power of sin, which exists at every level of the human personality. The mind, the heart and the will are all infected. To take a biblical example, the wonderful privilege and grace bestowed on Israel contrasts with her inveterate wickedness.

Such observations bear directly on the question of the will. As JI Packer helpfully explains, humans are free agents in the sense "that they make their own decisions as to what they will do, choosing as they please in the light of their sense of right and wrong and the inclinations they feel".[22] The difficulty is that our inclinations are twisted by sin and so the will is not free to turn to those good things which we do not desire now that sin has twisted us. We are free agents, but we are enslaved to our own desires and approve of them. We lack wisdom, and we do not long to be righteous.

Even the law of God, which is holy and righteous and good, is part of that which traps the sinner. Paul points out, for example, how sin uses the law to suggest other sin (Rom 7:7-12). Furthermore, those who adopt a false attitude to the law, relying on it for salvation, find themselves cursed by their inability to satisfy its legal demands (see Gal 3:10, 4:1-10; Col 2:14). That which promises life turns out to bring death.

A corrupt individual

Human enslavement to sin constitutes an irreversible corruption. By this I mean that the problem is from within the heart, the

---

22 JI Packer, *Concise Theology: A guide to historic Christian beliefs*, Tyndale, 1993, p 85.

centre of the person. It is not merely that faced with a succession of choices between good and evil we sometimes choose one and sometimes the other with little reason, the inner person being neutral. On the contrary, the Bible views us as comprehensively distorted and biased towards the evil.

There are two emphases to note here. In the first place, our sin is inwardly situated:

> "Do you not see that whatever goes into a person from outside cannot defile him, since it enters not his heart but his stomach, and is expelled? ... What comes out of a person is what defiles him. For from within, out of the heart of man, come evil thoughts, sexual immorality, theft, murder, adultery, coveting, wickedness, deceit, sensuality, envy, slander, pride, foolishness. All these evil things come from within, and they defile a person." (Mark 7:18-23)

Secondly, our sin arises spontaneously: "I would not have known what it is to covet if the law had not said, 'You shall not covet.' But sin, seizing an opportunity through the commandment, produced in me all kinds of covetousness" (Rom 7:7-8). Covetousness, forbidden in the tenth commandment, is false desire, a desire which arises from the already sinful heart. Sin is not merely an action or failure to act, but an evil desire of the heart. It may never manifest itself for the world to see even while thoroughly polluting the person at the level where God perceives (see also Gen 6:5).

Human corruption is summed up in Paul's writings by his use of the word "flesh" (*sarx*), by which he means not our physical component but the bias toward sin found in every human being, and manifesting itself in "sexual immorality, impurity, sensuality, idolatry, sorcery, enmity, strife, jealousy, fits of anger, rivalries, dissensions, divisions, envy, drunkenness, orgies, and things like these" (Gal 5:19-21).

4. Conclusion

It is crucial to observe how significant is our view of the human being as sinner. To state the obvious, our understanding of what God did through Christ's death on the cross depends upon our understanding of how desperate is human spiritual sickness. If we take the view, for example, that we are only sinners through following the example of others and that we can choose to be good, the cross may become a great example, but it will not be an atoning sacrifice. Likewise, if we think that people are basically good, we will be far more optimistic about the power of humanity to create a utopia in our own strength. Much therefore depends on how we understand the human situation. The grace and glory of God's work reflects the impotence of humanity to save itself.

Key verse
And he said, "What comes out of a person is what defiles him. For from within, out of the heart of man, come evil thoughts, sexual immorality, theft, murder, adultery, coveting, wickedness, deceit, sensuality, envy, slander, pride, foolishness. All these evil things come from within, and they defile a person." (Mark 7:20-23)

Quotation
"My memory is nearly gone, but I remember two things: That I am a great sinner, and that Christ is a great Saviour." (John Newton)

Key terms
- Humanity
- Image of God (*Imago Dei*)
- Anthropology
- Fall

- Guilt
- Original sin

For further thought
- What does it mean for human beings to be made in the "image of God"?
- Does human accountability depend upon freedom of the will?
- Is the term 'original sin' still useful?
- Should we speak of societal as well as individual sin? Is there a collective responsibility for the sins of our forefathers?
- Why is 'annihilationism' (the idea that those who are not saved will cease to exist) attractive to some? What do we lose by embracing this view?
- If God commands an action, does that mean we necessarily have the strength to obey him?
- If an evil desire arises from within, are we culpable at once, or only if we consciously endorse it and act upon it?

For further reading
- For chapters 10-16 of this book, see Packer, *Concise Theology*, part 2
- Thirty-Nine Articles, articles 9 and 10
- Westminster Confession, chapter 4, section 2
- Bray, chapter 15
- Horton, chapter 5
- Milne: Chapter 9

11

HUMANITY AND THE GOSPEL MESSAGE, PART 2

Key concept: God provides for humanity to be social and to have a future, but we are condemned even in our religiosity.

1. Introduction

I continue in this chapter the themes begun in the last. I have observed the preciousness, the rebelliousness, the enslavement and the corruption of humanity. Human beings are a most ingenious paradox, a source of bewilderment and contradiction. For example, there are those who speak of the balance of nature and complain that human interference destroys this balance. But if there is no God, humankind must itself be part of nature. Why are *we* not balanced? Why is our interference not part of the balance? It seems that we no sooner speak like this than we come across the problem of sin once again—and this time with no story of Adam and Eve to explain it.

A further paradox is the intense morality of our age despite the absence of absolute moral standards. Seldom has sermonizing from the self-appointed guardians of morality been more strident. In earlier decades, guilt ceased to be a theological category and became merely a psychological one, to be dealt with by therapy. Thus criminals needed to be cured, or 'corrected'; the breakdown of marriage became 'no-fault'. But there has been a rediscovery of the guilt of others, as blame is apportioned for participation in a set of contemporary sins such as ill-defined 'hate speech'. In such an atmosphere, it is hard for the gospel to be heard with its ancient power, for everything conspires to silence it and dismiss it. Yet speak it will and must: "the word of God is not bound!" (2 Tim 2:9). And nowhere does it speak more powerfully in confronting modern atheism than in speaking about humanity which has enthroned itself as God.

But who or what is this humanity that the gospel addresses?

2. A condemned humanity

The gospel call for repentance is based on the testimony of both Scripture and experience, which tell us that we are born averted from God, and alienated from him. Paul calls this birth-state "death"; we are "dead in ... trespasses and sins" (Eph 2:1). But he means by this not merely that we have no spiritual sensitivity to God, although that is true enough. Rather, he sees us under the adverse judgement of God, bearing the condemnation of sin.

It is true that Paul allows that we may perhaps argue the case for our own innocence (Rom 2:15-16). But in view of his conclusion that the law speaks so that all may be held accountable before God, and that all have sinned and fallen short of God's glory (3:9-23), the possibility of arguing our case seems to be purely hypothetical.

The Gospels describe our condemnation as indebtedness, picturing us as being indebted to God in such a way that we have no capacity to pay the debt and can only cast ourselves upon him for mercy (Matt 6:12, 18:23-35). Such an image ties in with that concept of justice in which offences incur punishment, as a debt which is owed. Using the language of 'debt' is a vivid way of expressing the truth that we are dealing with a profound relational alienation between sinners and an offended God.

In connection with God being offended and our condemnation, the Bible uses the term "the wrath of God". This is not some impersonal reflex action in the universe, or some exotic way of describing sin as its own reward. It is an expression of the personal antipathy of God to sin, and it reflects his righteousness. John is prepared to speak of the wrath of God abiding on those who will not believe in the Son of God, indeed of it continuing to abide on such people (John 3:36). Paul speaks of God's wrath being already at work in the world on account of idolatry and its attendant moral decay (Rom 1:18-31). But he also speaks of God storing up wrath for "the day of wrath when God's righteous judgement will be revealed" (2:5), when the secrets of all hearts will be disclosed and with perfect and even-handed justice God assigns all to their proper place.

By his very call for repentance in the light of the coming kingdom, Jesus is adopting this same view. He is as stern in his warnings about present condemnation and future judgement as Paul or John (e.g. Matt 5:25-26; 7:2; 10:28, 33; Mark 9:42-50; Luke 6:24-26). As his story of the rich man and Lazarus (Luke 16:19-31) suggests, he held his own people responsible to the standard of the law of God, and found them largely wanting. It was they, rather than the Romans, who were to be punished (Mark 12:1-11).

Some would wish the forensic note of law, judgement and reward to be excised or ignored. Certainly it must be put in its context, for 'law' as we hear the word does not capture exactly what the Old Testament equivalent word, 'Torah', meant. We should also think of wider relational categories such as forgiveness, reconciliation and love. But in the final analysis such categories are not independent of justice, and the forensic aspect must be given its place. Only in this way can we fully appreciate the meaning of the cross.

3. A suffering humanity

It is generally felt that the fact of human and animal suffering is the greatest evidence against the reality of God. What should be noticed as well, however, is that it forms one of the Bible's great themes. Far from ignoring the matter, Scripture grapples with it, and it is the testimony of the ages that sufferers have been upheld by the word of God even when all else has failed.

From the very beginning, Scripture links suffering with moral failure. When Adam rebels, he is cast from the garden into a world where work is painful, where families quarrel, where childbirth is traumatic, where animal and human are at odds, and where death is a reality. At the heart of the physical suffering is the spiritual desolation of being out of relationship with God.

The Bible contains a catalogue of the sins, crimes, follies and disasters of humanity. As the book of Proverbs reveals, the successful person must be shrewd in the face of evil and must recognize the reality of human sin. In the Psalms we have the heart-rending laments of those who know false friendship and treachery, warfare and exile, the ravages of disease.

'Explicable' suffering is one thing, but the most profound depths are experienced when we cannot even begin to see why suffering may have come. The Bible ascribes some pain to human sinfulness, as God disciplines and punishes (e.g. Luke 13:1-5; Heb 12:5-6), but it also asserts that the connection between pain and sin may not be obvious and direct (John 9:1-3). Indeed, one of the greatest of all biblical works is Job, in which the "innocent" suffers without any ultimate explanation apart from the greatness and glory of God.

There is also a theme in the Bible which gives voice to the meaninglessness of life. Nowhere is this clearer than in the book of Ecclesiastes, with its famous refrain, "vanity of vanities! All is vanity" (Eccl 1:2, 12:8). The preacher explores life and the world from the vantage point of a wealthy prince, only to discover that neither toil nor pleasure gives lasting happiness. Over all humanity's efforts hangs the reality of death; human life is fragile: "the silver cord is snapped, or the golden bowl is broken, or the pitcher is shattered at the fountain, or the wheel broken at the cistern, and the dust returns to the earth as it was, and the spirit returns to God who gave it" (12:6-7). But Ecclesiastes is not alone; there is a certain melancholy, too, in Psalm 90: "The years of our life are seventy, or even by reason of strength eighty; yet their span is but toil and trouble; they are soon gone, and we fly away" (v 10).

Christian anthropology must come to terms with humanity's suffering, and never more so than in the 21st century. The human race has not been so miserable, perhaps, since the 14th century, when the bubonic plague cut a devastating swathe through Europe and the East. It is true, of course, that many great advances have been made in education, medicine, transport, communication and personal liberty (for some). But against these advances are the grim, persistent facts of pollution, corruption, greed, famine, war, genocide and pandemic. There is a note of gloom and despair about the revenge that a depleted and despoiled environment will take on the race—if we do not first engage in nuclear warfare or die from the spread of viruses.

The real measure of our times will not be taken by those who live hedonistically without any knowledge or care of what has gone on. The convulsions of the first and second world wars are almost too stupendous for us to contemplate, with their millions upon millions of dead. So, too, the genocides of Hitler, of Stalin, of Pol Pot. We need to personalize it—to see the terror on the face of a child about to be 'treated' by a Nazi doctor; to hear about the experiences of a refugee, and to realize what the loss of home and family mean; to read what the veterans of World War I went through in the hell that was Somme or Passchendaele.

Whatever we say to all this—and in one sense, there is little to say—we have an obligation to trace the moral and spiritual dimensions. When we do, there ought to be discussions of the individualism which has contributed to loneliness and the materialistic secularism which has created a widespread lack of meaning and purpose. Into such fundamental issues, the Bible speaks with extraordinary power, for it gets to the bottom of our problems. Thus we need to enter contemporary debate with the word of God and make some sense of what seems like the most evident non-sense. It is only the real truth about humanity, combined with an eschatology of firm hope, which can minister to the despair which has been generated by our contemporary foolishness.

4. Social humanity

In one of the most telling moments of the Genesis story, God, having set man in the midst of a delightful garden and having surrounded him with animals and clearly proposed to have fellowship with the man, declares nonetheless, "It is not good that the man should be alone; I will make him a helper fit for him" (Gen 2:18). The aloneness of the man, the first thing to be declared "not good" by God, is only ameliorated by the creation of woman, "bone of my bones and flesh of my flesh" (2:23). It may be right to see in this longing for companionship a reflection of God's own triune nature (cf. 1 Cor 11:1-3). While marriage and the fellowship of the sexes is explicitly referred to here, there can be no doubt that, at a more general level, it is human companionship of any sort that is also in mind. Human beings are social, not independent. The generations rely upon each other, men rely on women (and vice versa), language is part of our make-up, and the web of human relationships reflects our basic interdependence. Human friendship is noted and recognized in Scripture (in Proverbs, for example), and the love of man and woman for each other is celebrated in the Song of Solomon.

Scripture also recognizes what may be called the structures of society, and would endorse their beneficial effects when they exist in accordance with God's wisdom. In the first place, there is the family, having its foundation in the leaving of father and mother and cleaving to the husband or wife, with the consequent unity being characterized as "one flesh" (Gen 2:24; Matt 19:4-6). It is the family of Noah and the family of Lot to which salvation comes, and it is through the family of Abraham that God's promises extend to all families on earth. Although today we take a narrow view of what 'family' entails, in the biblical era the family was a kinship system in which there were strong mutually supportive duties and responsibilities. We ought, however, to distinguish between the teaching of the Bible as such and its use of contemporary modes of life. What remains important on the biblical view is that families should reflect those ordered relationships which are appropriate for the members—relationships of care, responsibility, obedience and honour.[23] Our obligations to family members are stronger (1 Tim 5:8), the blessings we receive through families are deeper (1 Cor 7:14), and our identification with our families is of greater significance (e.g. Psalm 127; Prov 11:21, 17:6).

But family life is by no means the only social structure envisaged in the Bible. While Scripture does not lay down the pattern of civil life, it endorses some basic principles of government and citizenship, whether it is to be found in a village, a city, a nation or an empire. As citizens we are first to be good neighbours to those amongst whom we find ourselves, despite any difference of class, race or religion (Luke 10:29-37). When God taught his ancient people how to love their neighbours, he made sure that they gave attention to such things as safe homes (Deut 22:8), returning lost animals (Exod 23:4), protecting the alien (Lev 19:33-34), respecting land boundaries (Deut 27:17) and maintaining sexual purity

---

23   Consider, for example, Exodus 20:8-12, 14; Leviticus 19:3; Deuteronomy 6:4-9, 13:6-10, 21:18-21; Psalm 127; Proverbs 1:8-9, 4:1-6, 17:6, 19:18; Matthew 5:27-32; Mark 7:9-13; Colossians 3:18-4:1.

(Lev 18:19-23). Even though some of these rules reflect the special relationships of the people of God with each other, they also indicate how the law of love may be said to operate.

Citizens also have obligations to the governing authorities. The Christian citizen will recognize God himself as the ultimate source of governmental authority (Rom 13:1-2), and will therefore honour all those who exercise it, whatever the quality of their rule. A Christian's first obligation is to pray for authorities (1 Tim 2:1-2), but they are obligated also to obey the authorities and to pay their taxes (Rom 13:6-7). This responsibility is limited only by the higher obligation to honour God first (Acts 5:29). Behind these injunctions is the recognition that governing structures as such are good for human society, especially given the sinfulness and waywardness of the human heart.

For their part, the authorities' prime duty is to maintain justice. Whatever else a government may do in welfare or defence or education is nullified by injustice. Justice must be a basic commitment to being fair, a refusal to be swayed by extraneous considerations such as the wealth or poverty of the persons seeking justice (Exod 23:3, 6). The outward expression of justice is the treatment of the deserving with either reward or punishment, as God himself does. Only when this fundamental point is thoroughly established can compassion and forgiveness enter the scene. This is not to suggest that justice and compassion are opposites; justice is the first rule of genuine compassion.

There were other human structures (such as clubs, guilds and associations) in the biblical world, but the Scriptures hardly touch on them, apart from the economic and social relationship known as slavery. There we get a clue to the peculiar biblical insight into all social arrangements, whether family, civic or economic: the possession and exercise of authority is legitimate, but it is authority understood as rightful responsibility exercised in the spirit of service. This is as far removed from modern libertarianism as it is from ancient or modern tyranny, domestic or national. In the case of slavery, it transforms the rights of slaves and masters, helping lead in the end to the widespread abolition of slavery; in the case of governments, it leads to a new concept of what government is about, namely the service of the governed. All this may be summed up in the word "love" (Rom 13:8).

5. Religious humanity

The Bible has no complaint about humanity's lack of religion. Secularism, if indeed it involves lack of organized religion, was unknown. The Bible's criticism is of *false* religion.

False religion involves the world as well as God. It is the threat of powerlessness or moral blindness which encourages humanity to create religion in order to cope with life in this world. The answer for many is to take some part of the world and manipulate it in the hope of influencing the powers-that-be in the spirit world. Others seek to bypass the created order as though it is evil in itself and to reach for God through mysticism. The problem with both approaches is that God is sought other than where he declares himself to be found: in Jesus Christ. In Christ, we are free from the twin errors of using the world to influence God on the one hand, and by-passing the world on the other.

Although atheism was known before the 18th century, it was a rare and remarkable phenomenon. It has now become widespread and even enshrined in such a popular creed as Marxism. Much modern atheism can be traced back to Ludwig Feuerbach, a 19th-century German philosopher and anthropologist, who argued that religion was the creation of men, and that God was "man writ large". But there is now a widespread secular spirit in Western culture. Observers are divided in their analysis of this—some asserting that a new phenomenon has emerged, others that humanity remains religious but in different ways. In my opinion it seems unlikely that human beings, who to this point have been incessantly and universally religious, should suddenly change. It may be better to ask what is the *function* of religion, and how those functions may be occurring in today's world.

It may be that when these questions are explored, some of the wellsprings of contemporary culture may become clearer. If we think of culture in the broadest terms—as the activity of human beings in relating to nature, developing nature and ruling over nature—we can see, for example, that there were 'religious' aspects of Scientism in its heyday, and we will not be surprised to find a 'spiritual' basis in some modern ideologies. The triumph of biblical Christianity at the Reformation opened a new era for humanity's dealings with the natural world. But, paradoxically, it has also given an impetus to the development of a culture which acknowledges no God at all.

In Psalm 8, humanity is described as being "a little lower than the heavenly beings", yet "crowned ... with glory and honour", possessing dominance over the works of God's hands, with all things under our feet (Ps 8:5-6). Hebrews 2 points out how untrue this picture is in the post-fall world, and yet sees its fulfilment in one man: Jesus Christ (Heb 2:6-9). Human culture is not evil *per se*, but is corrupted and tainted by the fall; it has become again and again the vehicle for evil, although it is sufficiently impressive to remind us of the grandeur that was Adam. We must be careful neither to sanctify it, nor dismiss it. Like the world, it is passing away, but it reminds us of a Lord under whose reign all things work together for good, and in whose kingdom all things can be ours (1 Cor 3:22).

6. Future humanity

In an illuminating phrase, Paul speaks of "the man of heaven" who is "the second man". We have all, he tells us, "borne the image of the man of dust"; so shall we "also bear the image of the man of heaven" (1 Cor 15:47-49). Jesus Christ, who is, of course, this "man of heaven", is also described as "the firstfruits", and his ministry is elucidated in terms of Psalm 8 and the rule of humanity over the earth (1 Cor 15:23-28; cf. Heb 2:5-18).

In short, we see in Jesus Christ what humanity should be and what our future as the Lord's people is to be. If we are to understand humanity, we must understand this man who is in himself the gospel.

Consider the light this observation throws on the categories I have already used:

- Humanity is precious, as we know from the work of Christ, past, present and future.
- Humanity is rebellious, in contrast with this man who lived in perfect obedience to his Father.
- Humanity is enslaved, in contrast to this man who is king and Lord, and who rules until all his enemies, including death, are destroyed.
- Humanity is corrupt, in contrast to Jesus Christ, who lives as we should do in perfect purity and uprightness.
- Humanity is condemned, just as this perfect man too is condemned and dies the death we should incur.
- Humanity suffers, and this man suffers hurt, rejection, scorn, torture and death.
- Humanity is social, and this man is in himself "the firstborn among many brothers" (Rom 8:29), the foundation and chief cornerstone of the people of God.
- Humanity is religious, and this man reveals the emptiness of human religion, while restoring the balance between God, the world and humanity.

This man is the man from heaven, the man who is the gospel. No true estimate of human beings can omit him from its reckoning.

———

Key verse
The first man was from the earth, a man of dust; the second man is from heaven. As was the man of dust, so also are those who are of the dust, and as is the man of heaven, so also are those who are of heaven. Just as we have borne the image of the man of dust, we shall also bear the image of the man of heaven. (1 Cor 15:47-49)

Quotation
"To love oneself is the beginning of a lifelong romance." (Oscar Wilde)

Key terms
- Sin
- Wrath
- Pelagianism
- Semi-Pelagianism
- Conscience
- Condemnation
- The man of heaven

For further thought
- Where do you see signs of human religiosity still emerging in today's secularized society?
- "Justice is the first rule of genuine compassion." Do you agree?
- Biblically, from what does God save us?
- Much Christian thought about relationships focuses on marriage or familial relationships, but there is little talk of friendship. What place should friendship have in the Christian life? In your life?

For further reading
- Westminster Confession, chapters 6 and 9
- Bray, chapter 18
- Horton, chapter 6
- Milne, chapter 10

12

THE COVENANTAL NATION

Key concept: In saving the human world, God first created a nation to live under his rule and provide the pattern for salvation.

1. Introduction

In the previous chapter, I briefly raised the subject of how a religion functions, and what it does (or is alleged to do) for its adherents. It is notoriously difficult to define what religion is, but the question of function helps provide an analysis. Without suggesting that I am speaking as an expert on religion (which I am not), I would suggest that we could imagine several functions performed by religion or religions.

A religion may be used primarily to guard and sustain the worshipper in *this* world. The world is a threatening place, and there is much to emphasize the fragility of life. Religion can help regulate nature so that it does our will rather than overwhelming us.

Or a religion may be used primarily to give moral guidance and to help make sense of life, to provide meaning. We find it very difficult if not impossible to live with absolute freedom; we need standards by which to judge things and to which we can endeavour to conform. A sort of spiritual vertigo develops without such standards, and religion may offer help here. Religion can also function to sustain a whole society in much the same way.

Or a religion may be more interested in personal salvation, especially salvation from death. Of all the threatening forces which assail us, death is the worst. Human beings long for permanence and eternity. Religion may function to provide us with assurance of eternity now and an entrance to life eternal in due course. We may be able to sever ourselves from the cycle of existence and gain a sort of immortality free from pain by what we do (or don't do) now.

Clearly, Christianity has functioned in all three of these ways during its history, sometimes emphasizing one element and sometimes another. The mere fact that it purports to achieve the same goals as a similar religion does not validate either; it simply testifies to the existence of certain universal and perennial human problems.

Nonetheless, it is right to enquire whether any of these three functions (and this is not an exhaustive list) does justice to the significance of Christianity. In particular, the Christian doctrine of sin and its consequences determines the nature of the redemption which is the good news (the 'gospel') of Christ. As human beings are both precious and corrupt, as they are both loved and rebellious, so God's action will be addressed to that problem.

That being so, it is not surprising that in contrast to the emphases mentioned above, the Christian gospel moves on a historical level, from the creation "with time" and the fall "in time" to the final new heavens and new earth in the age to come. It is true that the gospel offers the individual the protection of God, that it gives a framework for life, and that it promises personal immortality. But these are not the central focus. At the centre, we have the story which is the history of God's work with a people, culminating in a redeemed and blessed community in a renewed environment. It is his kingdom which has been challenged, and it is his kingdom that is restored, with profound consequences for his glory and our good.

Therefore, given that recorded history begins with the overthrow of God's word, salvation involves the re-assertion of that kingdom word through the formal instrument of the covenant. The notion of 'covenant' was discussed at some length in chapter 3. In this chapter, our focus shifts to the necessary implicate of covenant: the person or people who are the covenant partners. What did a covenantal community look like, and how did God use the covenant in relation to the great saving event of the cross and resurrection? What is continuous between the Testaments, and where do they contrast?

2. The creation of a people of God

A covenant, being at heart promises, presupposes a covenant partner. Having transgressed their original covenant with God (Hos 6:7), Adam and Eve were expelled from the garden with words of promise—a covenant, at heart—which extend to their descendants. As the history of the world began to unfold, it was clear that God had made a choice between people, choosing for himself such persons as Abel, Seth, and finally Noah. With Noah there is a formal covenant, and the line of God's choice extends to Abraham, through whom all the families of the earth are to be blessed (Gen 12:1-3). These important verses enshrine the foundational covenant of God, from which all else flows in due time. The later covenants reflect different political and social organization within God's people, but the essence of God's determination to bless through Abraham and his family remains the same.

At each point where the covenant is established or re-established, we see the elements that Abraham exemplifies so well. By covenant, God intends his blessing upon his people, a blessing in the land and in numbers and in protection, a blessing that is received by faith alone (Gen 15:6), and a blessing which binds the recipients to the rule of God as Adam should have been bound. We also remember that Abraham was blessed for us all, that the form of the promise was universal—including a blessing on all who blessed Abraham, and the extension of Abraham's blessedness to every family on earth (cf. Gal 3:1-18).

As we look at the life of God's people in its national form, when Israel was Israel, we may detect the following features.

a. Redemption history

Certain historical experiences bound the people together, gave them their identity, and set the movement of this national life. The best word to describe these experiences is 'salvation', for they had in common the impotence of the people before a superior enemy, their suffering, their appeal to God and, finally, an act or acts of his mighty, redeeming power on their behalf. Although there were many such moments in the national history of Israel, the one that set the pattern for all the rest was the exodus from Egypt. That event established the language and experience of salvation, and various structures of the national life were set up to remind the people of it. Prior to that salvation, of course, was the covenant, freely entered into by the Lord God (Exod 2:23-25).

When God saved his people, it was with the purpose that they should live together in peace and joy in the promised land. This was their inheritance and their hope. It was described as "a land flowing with milk and honey" (e.g. Exod 3:8), an Eden-like "rest", the consummation of their desires. In the event, the land is an arena both for blessing and cursing, for disobedience is met with the punishment of God upon the people through the land. In the first place, they could not reach it until the disobedient generation had died. Then, when they reached it, it became the scene of earthquake and famine, of disease, wild animals and marauding soldiers, all bringing death and destruction. Finally, in his justice, God removes his people from the land in a devastating exile, and their continued occupancy of the land up to the fall of Jerusalem in 70 AD is at the mercy of imperial powers. As a hope, it was anything but secure and incorruptible.

A third element in the creation of God's people is the part played by human leadership. God allowed a long list of prophets, judges, priests and kings to be his human agents in ruling. They were intended to acknowledge the prior claims of God and to serve the people in humility, but the reality was often far different. Nonetheless, starting with Moses, many important leaders were endowed by the Spirit of God to save and to rule, and something of the blessing of God's rule flowed through them, however inadequately. Even the best of such ones, however, was flawed by sin and faithlessness, and the story of others like Saul is tragic. From time to time we have the promise expressed that genuine and flawless, Spirit-endowed leadership may emerge in God's people (e.g. Deut 18:15-22; Isa 11:1-10; Mic 5:2-6; Psalm 110). But this hope remains unrealized as the Old Testament closes.

b. Redemption structures

When Israel was saved from Egypt, the advent of the national life was marked by the gift of the Torah. God has always expected obedience in his covenant partners, but the details of this obedience were now spelled out in a form suitable for this stage of the people's existence. The fact that it was intended for this nation at this time gives it certain features which it would now be impossible to reproduce even if the element in question had not been repealed in the New Testament. Nonetheless, the fact that the author is God and that he is consistent and truthful means that the *principles* of the Torah remain valid and significant and that the individual enactments retain an illustrative force of what the principles mean.

Thus the food laws of the Pentateuch have now been repealed by New Testament enactment. But it would be most improper to omit them from Scripture, because they had the important effect of isolating God's people from their pagan neighbours, and they therefore continue to point to the holiness which is always the calling of God's people. So, too, the various capital crimes of disobedience in the Old Testament are today punished differently or not at all. The sin remains, but our response may be altered due to changed circumstances. So, too, although few of us own oxen or sheep, the Old Testament pronouncements about how such animals are to be treated can also be regarded as having force in analogous situations (cf. 1 Cor 9:9).

A major part of the law is given over to establishing the 'cult', in the sense of the rituals and ceremonies of worship. When Israel inhabited her land, she had a specially appointed temple, with a priesthood, calendar, altars and a sacrificial system. The whole was carefully set forth by the Lord, intent that he should only be worshipped in the way in which he had ordained. This cultic worship kept the people in touch with their history through the commemoration of various events, and it was a vehicle for praise, for confession and for fellowship. The priests were teachers as well as sacrificial officials.

God also raised up prophets whose task was to speak his word, taking the covenantal stipulations and applying them to the present in such a way as to speak to the future. There were many times when the prophetic word stood in judgement on the people of God, and many times when the prophets were threatened, abused and even killed. Israel's relationship with the word of God was always an uneasy one.

c. Limitations

God-ordained though these structures were, they were manifestly inadequate if we have in mind the final result that God intended. The very suitability of the law as an instrument of national obedience made it inadequate as a final statement of man's obedience to God in all situations. Indeed, Paul saw that the law as given through Moses (especially as interpreted in his own day) held the people of God in bondage, from which release into the liberty of being God's child was both necessary and possible (Gal 3:1-4:10). This was not an overturning of the essence of the law, but a recognition of its limitations and of the abuse of the law by sinful people.

In particular, the New Testament regards the cultic provisions of the law as "a shadow of the things to come" (Col 2:17; cf. Hebrews 9-10). The very repetitiveness of the sacrifices and the frailty of the priests bore testimony to the fact that the cultic system could not do what it pointed to: "For it is impossible for the blood of bulls and goats to take away sins" (Heb 10:4). The problem did not lie in the concept of offering, but in the thing offered, and in the priest who sacrificed.

Even the history of Israel, wonderful as it was, had little permanent significance in itself. The exodus was a marvellous demonstration of God's power, but it remained the release of slaves from Pharaoh, not a matter of enduring importance in meeting the needs of a corrupt and enslaved race "in Adam". Once again it is a shadow, a pattern of something else that was yet to come.

But the chief limitation of the Old Testament religion was towards its centre. No-one can deny the reality of the relationship with God experienced by the godly Israelites. But it was a matter of shadows, of outward signs, of laws that prepared the way without fulfilment. It was a religion in which the experience of the Spirit was intermittent. The Old Testament record is one of constant failure by the nation and its leaders, with God's judgement being experienced frequently. There is no ultimate solution here to the mystery of sin and wrath, only the constant reminder of the problem. The Old Testament witnesses to the tension between wrath and forgiveness, between transcendence and immanence, between national and universal, between life and death, without being able to resolve them. And yet we can never ignore passages such as Isaiah 53, in which the foreshadowing of an answer may be found.

3. The transformation of the people of God

The promises of God were enough to make clear that some great event would transform the people of God and make them closer to what they should be. The prophetic method was to portray the future largely in terms of the promises of the past and the experience of the present—for example, in the blossoming of nature (Amos 9:15) or the return of the people from exile. Jeremiah went so far as to speak of a new covenant (Jer 31:31f). Ezekiel prophesied that God's salvation would emerge out of a determination to honour his own name, which had been sullied by Israel; there was even talk of the closeness of God's Spirit in this age of renewal (Ezek 36:16-38).

Left on its own, therefore, the language of the Old Testament may suggest a deeper continuity between old and new covenant than in fact occurred. But the New Testament provides the interpretive key for an understanding of the Old Testament. That is why I made the point in chapter 5 that the first rule of biblical hermeneutics is that the Bible interprets the Bible; we must not bypass the New Testament's treatment of the Old. Here the new covenant is said to come in Jesus Christ, "for all the promises of God find their Yes in him" (2 Cor 1:20; cf. Matt 26:26-29). All the earthly blessings of the Old Testament are transformed into their enduring and real spiritual counterpart, whether land (Hebrews 4; 1 Pet 1:4), temple (John 2:19-21; 1 Cor 6:19), priest (Heb 4:14), sacrifice (Rom 3:24-25), law (1 Cor 9:21), renewal of creation (2 Pet 3:13), a new Davidic empire (Acts 15:16-18), the exodus (Col 1:13-14), the Passover (1 Cor 5:7-8), the calendar (Rom 14:5-6), prophecy (Acts 2:17-18), the pattern of salvation (1 Cor 10:1-11), leadership (Acts 3:22) or circumcision (Col 2:11-15).

This is not to say that the Old Testament was 'earthly' and the

New Testament is 'spiritual'. Such a view does justice to neither. But there is an experience of deep and personal fulfilment attached to the revelation of Jesus Christ and his Spirit and his Father, an experience that the Old Testament can never adequately be compared with except as shadow to substance. There is continuity between the Testaments, for it is the same God, and the same grace and the same faith, as we can see in Hebrews 11; but there is also the word at the end of that great chapter: "All these, though commended through their faith, did not receive what was promised, since God had provided something better for us, that apart from us they should not be made perfect" (vv 39-40).[24]

One of the greatest elements of the transformation of God's people is in the inclusion of the Gentiles. Frequently the ministry of the Holy Spirit is seen as setting the seal on this miraculous extension of God's mercies (e.g. Eph 1:13-14; Acts 10:47-48). The relationship between Israel and the church is not easy to define, but account needs to be made of the continuity of the people of God, the newness of the Gentiles being grafted in (cf. Rom 11:11-24), and the language of Paul which seems to indicate a continued life for the people of Israel as we await the end, when, with the Gentiles, "all Israel will be saved" (11:26). The respect we should always have for Jewish people—as those who were first to receive the promises of God and from whose nation came the Christ—cannot be in doubt. But this does not mean that anyone, Jew or Gentile, is saved independent of Christ, nor that the modern state of Israel is somehow the fulfilment of promises which are in fact fulfilled in Christ. And yet we need not doubt that the Lord continues to call his ancient people home through Christ and will keep doing so until Christ comes again.

---

24 cf. John 1:16-17 and the ESV footnote: "grace in place of grace".

4. Conclusion

So great a transformation requires a powerful cause. In no way is Jesus Christ born a Jew by accident: "But when the fullness of time had come, God sent forth his Son, born of woman, born under the law, to redeem those who were under the law, so that we might receive adoption as sons" (Gal 4:4-5). He was born under the old covenant, in the nation that God had prepared to receive him. His mission was first and foremost to this people, for through them would come the blessing of God to the whole world. His mission is interpreted through the categories provided by the old covenant. It fulfils them even as it surpasses them. This nation was the cradle of the Saviour.

To say such a thing is, however, to be conscious of a bitter irony. The nation prepared to receive him was the cradle of his rejection, betrayal and death (John 1:11). In the end, he was completely alone as the one Israelite who truly kept the law for the right reasons— and the one Israelite who therefore could not be allowed to live. But in the providence of God this rejection is precisely the place where salvation is won: "Christ redeemed us from the curse of the law by becoming a curse for us" (Gal 3:13). The identity of the sufferer in Isaiah 53 is mysterious no longer; God hallows his own name and so wins salvation for his people, just as he said he would.

In the introduction to this chapter, I spoke of the functions of religion and indicated that however Christianity may function as guardian, as morality or as individual salvation, its chief focus was on the redemption of a community in a renewed environment, under the triumph of God's kingdom. That situation is pictured at the end of the Bible. To get to that point, the Bible passes through the long history of God's people. In itself such a history, including the beginning of the Christian community in the New Testament, would only be a record of failure. But at the very centre of the picture is one who is no failure, and one who turns out to be the foundation on which the whole enterprise rests. We now examine his person and work.

Key verse

Now the LORD said to Abram, "Go from your country and your kindred and your father's house to the land that I will show you. And I will make of you a great nation, and I will bless you and make your name great, so that you will be a blessing. I will bless those who bless you, and him who dishonours you I will curse, and in you all the families of the earth shall be blessed." (Gen 12:1-3)

Quotation

"The order and sum of the sacred and only method of preaching:

1. To read the text distinctly out of the canonical scriptures.
2. To give the sense and understanding of it being read, by the scripture itself.
3. To collect a few and profitable points of doctrine out of the natural sense.
4. To apply, if he have the gift, the doctrines rightly collected to the life and manners of men in a simple and plain speech.

The sum of the sum: Preach one Christ by Christ to the praise of Christ." (William Perkins, *The Art of Prophesying*)

Key terms

- Covenant theology
- Continuity/discontinuity
- Redemption history
- Biblical theology
- People of God

- Jew/Gentile
- Cultic worship

For further thought
- "What is the greatest problem in the world today?" What various answers might you expect people to give? What worldview lies behind each of these answers?
- Many today describe themselves as "spiritual but not religious". Why the dislike for one but the respect for the other? What is such a person trying to say about himself or herself?
- How well did the Old Testament believers know God?
- What difference has Pentecost made to our knowledge of God?
- Is the use of such terminology as 'priest' and 'altar' a danger for the Christian church? If so, why?
- Since the Reformation, many theologians have said that Israel's 'ceremonial' and 'national' laws are done away with under the new covenant, but that the 'moral law' remains. Should this distinction be maintained? Can we preach the Old Testament food laws, for example?

For further reading
- Thirty-Nine Articles, article 7
- Bray, chapter 25

13

THE HUMBLE LORD

Key concept: Into the chosen and covenanted nation is born the Saviour of the world.

1. Introduction

Christianity is Christ. Without him it has nothing to offer to the world. He is its foundation and its touchstone. He is its gospel. There can be no more important question, therefore, than to ask what we think of him. The question, as it confronted the first disciples, is not just "Who do people say that I am?", but rather, "Who do *you* say that I am?" (Mark 8:27-29).

Sometimes there is a discussion about whether we start such an enquiry 'from above' (Christ as divine) or 'from below' (Christ as human). One can point to the opening of Mark's Gospel for the human Christ, and to the opening of John for the divine one. And yet even Mark suggests that Christ is "the Lord" (Mark 1:3), and even John confesses that "the Word became flesh and dwelt among us ... full of grace and truth" (John 1:14).

The supposed tension seems to be misconceived. The New

Testament itself does not give us that polarity, although it bears witness to the historical Jesus of Nazareth who to his contemporaries was clearly all too human. But the readers of the Gospels from that day to this have been members of the post-resurrection generation, and the Gospel writers are not embarrassed in revealing the truth about Jesus from the beginning.

Rather than try to categorize Jesus as from above or from below, it may be better to follow the lead of the Gospels themselves and see him first and foremost as 'from within'—that is, as from within the covenantal nation especially prepared by God to be the cultural and religious cradle of the Saviour (see chapter 12). Hence Matthew begins with the genealogy of Jesus, locating him in the timeline of God's history, and giving him the name of Jesus as the one who "will save his people from their sins" (Matt 1:21), as well as the name Immanuel, "God with us" (1:23). Mark, as we have noted, links Jesus with John the Baptist and hence with Isaiah's prophecy about the coming of the Lord (Mark 1:2-3; cf. Isa 40:3). Luke exhibits Christ in the midst of pious Israelites who are waiting for the one who will redeem Israel. John begins with the Word, but records that when the Word became flesh, and dwelt among us, "He came to his own [people], and his own people did not receive him" (John 1:11).

All this—and it is only the beginning of the evidence—illustrates the way in which the New Testament invites us to assess Jesus in terms of the Old Testament. It is because the Jews rejected his claim to fulfil the Scriptures that he was rejected. To accept that claim is to accept him and to discover the proper categories for understanding his person.

2. The Son

The son of David

Both Matthew and Luke trace the genealogy of Jesus through the royal line, back to David. In several places he is addressed as the Son of David (e.g. Mark 10:48; Luke 18:38; cf. Rom 1:3), and in one place he argues with the Pharisees about his title:

> "What do you think about the Christ? Whose son is he?" They said to him, "The son of David." He said to them, "How is it then that David, in the Spirit, calls him Lord, saying,
>
>> "'The Lord said to my Lord,
>> "Sit at my right hand,
>>   until I put your enemies under your feet"'?
>
> If then David calls him Lord, how is he his son?" (Matt 22:42-45)

In his usual way, Jesus is not claiming the title "Christ" outright, but we know already from Matthew 16 that he accepted it, and hence, too, the titles 'David's Son' and 'David's Lord', paradoxical though this may seem.

The claim to be Christ is, therefore, the claim to rule over Israel as David had done, but as one greater than David. It gathers to itself the great covenantal promises of God to David as given in 2 Samuel 7: "your house and your kingdom shall be made sure forever before me. Your throne shall be established forever" (v 16). Other passages, too, such as Isaiah 11:1-10 and Amos 9:11-15, find their fulfilment in the one who claims to be of Jesse's line.

The Son and Israel

The discretion of Jesus concerning his messianic status can be explained in terms of the misunderstanding that such claims would be sure to arouse (e.g. Mark 1:24-25). Nonetheless, there is no doubt that Jesus saw himself as the king towards whom his preaching of the kingdom pointed. In no other way can we understand the deliberate act of fulfilling Zechariah 9:9 in his entry into Jerusalem (Matt 21:1-11). It is not surprising that the crowd shouted "Hosanna to the Son of David!" (21:9) as they accompanied him.

Nor is it accidental that he died having been mocked as a king and with the superscription "This is the king of the Jews" attached by the Romans to the cross. The Jewish authorities demurred because they themselves understood only too well what he was claiming to be (John 19:21). It is true that Christ portrays the Son of Man as king over the nations (Matt 25:31), but he is first the king of the Jews (cf. 19:28), and even as "the Son of Man" there is a connection with Israel itself (see Daniel 7).

The Son of Man

It is an error to think that this phrase is the equivalent of 'man' or 'human being'. It seems to belong to the portrait in Daniel 7 of the thrones placed at the last day, and to one "like a son of man" being awarded "dominion and glory and a kingdom, that all peoples, nations, and languages should serve him; his dominion is an everlasting dominion, which shall not pass away, and his kingdom one that shall not be destroyed" (v 14). It is therefore an elevated royal title, perhaps meant to incorporate the whole people of God; after all, Israel is also called the "son" (e.g. Exod 4:22; Hos 11:1). It is, at any rate, the title assumed most regularly by Jesus himself, and suggests that his ministry will be both identified with Israel and global in its scope.

The Son and man

Nonetheless, despite this elevated language used of Jesus, there is no doubt that he was regarded both by his immediate contemporaries and by the authors of the New Testament writings as identified with the human race—in short, as man. Interestingly, they left no pen-portrait of his physical appearance, but nothing can be clearer than the humanity of Jesus in the way they described him. He was born (Matt 1:21), he slept (Mark 4:38), he wept (John 11:35), he hungered (Matt 21:18), he loved (Mark 10:21), he prayed (John 12:27-28), he thirsted (John 19:28), he had faith in God (1 Pet 2:23), he grew in wisdom and stature (Luke 2:40, 52), he learned (Heb 5:8), he did not know everything (Mark 13:32), he bled (John 19:34), he was tempted (Matt 4:1-11), he was beaten (Mark 15:15), he was unsure (Mark 14:36), he died (Mark 15:37) and he was resurrected (Luke 24:39).

The New Testament everywhere presupposes and argues from this massively important fact of the real humanity of Jesus, "born of woman, born under the law" (Gal 4:4). We may think of the Pauline arguments in 1 Corinthians 15 or Romans 5 referring to Adam. But the epistle to the Hebrews depends upon the true humanity of Jesus in a unique way. It dwells on the teaching of Psalm 8, where man is seen as "a little lower than the heavenly beings" and as ruling the world, and contrasts this with the fallenness and incapacity of our race. It sees in Jesus the one man, "crowned ... with glory and honour" for the sake of all, and insists, necessarily, that he shares "one source" with those he saves; "Since therefore the children share in flesh and blood, he himself likewise partook of the same things ..." (Heb 2:7-14).

Indeed, the humanity of Jesus is also the foundation of his right to be the priest, in fact the high priest, of God's people: "Therefore he had to be made like his brothers in every respect, so that he might become a merciful and faithful high priest in the service of God, to make propitiation for the sins of the people" (Heb 2:17).

In short, the real humanity of Jesus is not merely an observed and reputed fact; it is a necessary theological basis for the Christian gospel. If he was not truly man, he is not our Saviour, for his manner of saving depends upon that humanity. This is true not merely of what he has done, but what he is doing and is yet to do. He is the "firstfruits" of the race, the first of a mighty resurrected harvest of mankind, and is the man from heaven in whose image we are all being formed (1 Cor 15:20-23, 48). If he is not man now and in the future, our salvation is lost—we are still in our sins (cf. Rom 8:3-4).

In confessing the true humanity of Jesus, the New Testament makes abundantly clear that his identity with us is complete except in the matter of sin. Paul says that Christ was sent "in the *likeness* of sinful flesh" (Rom 8:3). Matthew (4:1-11) and Luke (4:1-13) report him repulsing the temptations of the evil one. Peter remembers vividly how "He committed no sin, neither was deceit found in his mouth. When he was reviled, he did not revile in return; when he suffered, he did not threaten, but continued entrusting himself to him who judges justly" (1 Pet 2:22-23). On the same subject of the cross, Paul (2 Cor 5:21), John (1 John 3:5) and the writer to the Hebrews (4:15) all make the same point in their own way. Finally, Jesus himself challenged his adversaries: "Which one of you convicts me of sin?" (John 8:46). To ask whether Christ can be both truly human and truly sinless is to betray a low estimate of the Christian hope, for we trust that we will one day be like him in this respect especially. It is no accident that the character of Jesus has impressed people in every age and place.

It is tragic that in recent times there has been an attempt to drive a wedge between Jesus and many who would belong to him on the grounds that a masculine person can only represent half the human race. No-one has ever suggested that the identification of Jesus with the race extends to passing through every experience of which human beings are capable. There are many temptations, many situations, many states in life of which Jesus had no experience whatever. He was (as far as we know) unmarried; he never flew in a plane; he never fought in a war; he never ate at McDonald's. Indeed, if he passed through every experience possible, even a large range of them, he would cease to be a representative at all. He would be totally unrepresentative, for part of being human is to be a *particular* human—male or female, Jew or Gentile, tall or short, married or single. It is the particularity which is essential to us. A Jesus half-male and half-female would represent no-one.

Furthermore, the ideology in question has driven an unfortunate and untrue wedge between male and female, who share far, far more than what distinguishes us. We are first of all human beings before we are men or women. It is the grace, joy, peace, love and obedience of Jesus which we imitate, each in our own way, but without the slightest fear that our particularity is to be subsumed into some gigantic 'super-Jesus' transcending sexuality.

3. David's Lord

Our starting point has been to consider Jesus from within the covenantal nation of Israel, noting that Jesus is both David's son and David's Lord. Even in thinking of Jesus as the king of Israel and the Son of man, there is a sense in which he is distinctly from within Israel, connected to her by descent and culture, and representative of her. But the idea that the Christ is also David's Lord takes us to a further development, in which Christ stands apart from Israel and is unique, transcending all the kings in David's line. This is demonstrated by his relationship to Israel, to the nations, to the Spirit and finally to the Father. It is in studying these relationships that we see that he is not only truly man. He is also truly God.

The Lord and Israel

In the parable of the vineyard (Mark 12:1-12), Jesus sees himself in continuity with the prophets of God who have pleaded with Israel over the years. But the continuity is not complete. He is no mere prophet; he is the Son (cf. Heb 1:1-3). The same distinction is present at the baptism and the transfiguration (Mark 1:9-11, 9:2-8). In the latter, Jesus is deliberately identified as the "Son" in contrast with the two greatest figures of the Old Testament, Moses and Elijah (cf. Heb 3:1-6). It is remarkable, given the Old Testament history, that Jesus should be superior to them, and to John the Baptist also (Matt 11:2-15). Indeed, in his ministry Jesus assumes a proprietorial right over the people of God (e.g. Matt 21:12-13,

23:29-39; note especially the extraordinary words of 23:34: "*I send you prophets and wise men and scribes ...*").

The Lord and the nations

Psalm 110 has a universal scope, with the Messiah seated at the right hand of God as God defeats his foes "among the nations" and "over the wide earth" (v 6). Jesus envisages the Son of Man judging the nations (Matt 25:31f). But, more significantly, Matthew (28:16-20), Luke (24:44-47) and John (12:20-32) all portray Christ as having a mission to the nations and drawing them in under his rule. Jesus' claim at the close of Matthew's Gospel cannot be more imperious: "All authority in heaven and on earth has been given to me" (28:18). And he makes good this claim with an extraordinary promise to transcend time and space: "I am with you always, to the end of the age" (28:20). No wonder such a one is seeking disciples in all nations. He is the Lord.

The Lord of the Spirit

In the story of Israel, the Spirit-filled man was raised up by God to save his people. There are some elements reminiscent of this in the ministry of Jesus, not least the way the Spirit drives him out into the wilderness (Mark 1:12) after descending on him "like a dove" (1:10). But when the totality of the New Testament picture is surveyed, there can be no doubt that Christ the Lord joins the Father in sending the Spirit (e.g. John 15:26; Acts 2:33) and that the Spirit can be known as "the Spirit of [God's] Son" (Gal 4:6) or "the Spirit of Christ" (Rom 8:9; 1 Pet 1:11). Jesus is definitely not depicted simply as a Spirit-filled man, such as a prophet, able to do his mighty works and sustain his sinless life merely by the Spirit's power. He has such power in himself. Speaking of his life he says, "I lay it down of my own accord. I have authority to lay it down, and I have authority to take it up again" (John 10:18).

It is clear that we have now passed well beyond the point at which "David's Lord" could simply be regarded as "David's superior" or some similar expression. As the term "Son" in the parable of the vineyard indicates, there is a uniqueness about Christ which demands further explanation. Finally, through an exploration of the relationship with the Father, we can understand what we need to say about his status.

The Lord and the Father

Since Jesus encouraged his disciples to call God "Father", a superficial reading of the New Testament may suggest that the name "Son" was shared with them. But such a thesis will not hold. Believers are indeed the children of God, but only by adoption (Gal 4:1-7; Rom 8:15). As in the parable of the vineyard, Jesus contrasts his sonship with the standing of the disciples. Indeed, we have the voice from heaven which distinguishes him from all others: "This is my beloved Son; listen to him" (Mark 9:7; cf. 1:11).

The 'sonship' of Jesus definitely accords a priority of order to the Father. But it also implies the eternal pre-existence of the Son. John describes the unique relationship thus: "we have seen his glory, glory as of the only Son from the Father, full of grace and truth" (John 1:14). Intimations of such a relationship can be found in the other Gospels too, such as in Matthew 11:25-30, where the Son is uniquely related to the Father and invites a response to himself which assumes that he will be at the centre of piety.

Indeed, when the Jews regarded Jesus' claim to be the Son of God as being a claim to equality with God, they were not wrong (John 5:18); the relationship between Father and Son is such that no other conclusion can follow. Thus he is treated as God with divine honours in such passages as Romans 10:9-13 and Philippians 2:1-11; other passages confess that Jesus is God (e.g. John 1:1, 8:58, 20:28; Acts 20:28; Rom 9:5; Titus 2:13; Heb 1:8).

What such a teaching means for the doctrine of God has already been outlined (in chapter 6). But it raises the equally massive problem of how we think and talk about the person of Jesus Christ. How can he be both God and man? He is like us in every respect except sin; but he is totally unlike us as the unique Son of God, the Word become flesh (John 1:14). It may be that faith will simply need to confess the reality of both truths about one who is God and man, and acknowledge that such a union is beyond our capacity to understand or explain. After all, human psychology is scarcely able to explain human nature (let alone sinless human nature), and our knowledge of what it is to be God is a thousand times more limited still. It is hardly surprising that we are at a loss to say much about the miracle of the incarnation.

On the other hand, we should explore Scripture (and its interpretation in history) for anything further that it may have to teach us.

4. The humble Lord

John's Gospel begins with the *Logos*, a term that would have been familiar to his first readers, whether Greek or Jew. But both sets of readers would have been shocked beyond measure by his statement "The Word became flesh" (1:14)—the Jew because God's Word was not personal and could not be incarnate, and the Greek because spirit and matter could not combine in this way. Nonetheless, this is the bold claim of the Christian message, a claim which evidence for both the humanity and the deity of Jesus forced it to advance. But how did the two natures of Christ, human and divine, relate to each other?

This is where it is very useful to examine how our Christian ancestors have read the Bible and taught its truths. For it was not long before wrong deductions were being drawn from Scripture, and it was such controversy that led, in the end, to clarity. The classic theological formulation of this was given at the Council of

Chalcedon in 451 AD and is reflected in article 2 of the Thirty-Nine Articles:

> The Son, which is the Word of the Father, begotten from everlasting of the Father, the very and eternal God, and of one substance with the Father, took Man's nature in the womb of the Blessed Virgin, of her substance: so that two whole and perfect Natures, that is to say, the Godhead and Manhood, were joined together in one Person, never to be divided, whereof is one Christ, very God, and very Man …

Neither Chalcedon nor the article tell us how such a union of natures can take place, but they assert on the basis of Scripture that such a union did not mingle the two natures, nor did it divide them, but that they are united (in the words of Chalcedon) "unconfusedly, unchangeably, indivisibly, inseparably". This language provides the boundaries within which the truth may be found, but it must not be regarded as an explanation as such, as though by a feat of the imagination we can picture what it would be like to be such a person. The emphasis must rightly fall on the unity of the person of Jesus Christ as he is presented to us in Scripture. In Chalcedon's theology, the attributes of either nature may be assigned to the one person, as in the biblical phrase "they … crucified the Lord of glory" (1 Cor 2:8). The Lord of Glory is God; you cannot crucify God. You can crucify a man. But because Christ is both God and man in one person, you can use the language of either nature for the one.

Various other attempts have been made to do justice to the New Testament data, but the thinking of most Christians over the years has dismissed them from contention as not satisfying the conditions of the Bible. Some such attempts are:

a. Docetism: that Christ was God appearing in the guise of a human being.
b. Adoptionism: that Christ was a man inspired by God.

c. Nestorianism: that the human and divine in Christ are associated rather than united.
d. Apollinarianism: that the human spirit of Christ is replaced by the Divine *Logos*, thus producing a God-man who is a mixture.
e. Kenoticism: that the Word "emptied himself" of his divine attributes and became man, resuming his attributes at his ascension.

It is true, of course, that various texts of the New Testament will mention one side or another of the person of Jesus. He has power and yet is impotent; he sees into the heart and yet he is ignorant; he is the Lord of glory but he is crucified; he is God but he prays. The possibility for unbalanced speculation about the psychology of Jesus is present. But the unity of his person is the overwhelming impression from the Gospel accounts; it seems that human and divine are not so opposed that they cannot be united in him.

Nowhere is this clearer than in the account of the crucifixion. His naked weakness is there for all to see. His pretensions to kingship are destroyed: "he had no form or majesty that we should look at him, and no beauty that we should desire him" (Isa 53:2). But the cross is both the shame and the glory of the Son of God: "he was pierced for our transgressions; he was crushed for our iniquities ... with his wounds we are healed" (53:5). He is never so god-like as on the cross. This is the hour of his glorification. This is his throne, and through it he draws all people to himself and defeats Satan (John 12:31-32).

Perhaps the most compelling title for Jesus is "the Servant of the Lord" (see Mark 10:45), with its background in Isaiah 53. The servant comes into the world deliberately in order to save. His service is his death. The personal union between manhood and Godhead is easiest to perceive from the servant vantage point, for our ideas about God are properly drawn from this source (see also 2 Cor 8:9). There is more than one way of being God-like and showing absolute power (1 Cor 1:18f).

5. Conclusion

Jesus must be understood from within the covenant people of God. It is by these categories that he can be best assessed. When we use the clues provided for us in Old Testament and New Testament, we see only that he is both God and man; no other description will suit the facts about him.

The servant of the Lord came, however, to serve. Already we have begun to see how. But in the next chapter we study his life of service and its implications in more detail.

———

Key verse

But when the fullness of time had come, God sent forth his Son, born of woman, born under the law, to redeem those who were under the law, so that we might receive adoption as sons. (Gal 4:4-5)

Quotation

"In times past, He convinced us that our human nature by itself lacked the power of attaining to life; today, He reveals to us a Saviour who has power to save even the powerless." (*The Epistle to Diognetus*)

Key terms

- Christology
- Incarnation
- Lord
- Sonship
- Docetism
- Sinlessness
- Adoptionism
- Nestorianism
- Kenosis

For further thought
- What are the similarities and differences between Christ the "great high priest" and Israel's priests?
- What is lost if Jesus was not fully human? If he was not fully divine?
- Some would regard the doctrine of the incarnation as logically absurd, like a square circle. How would you respond?
- Given what we have seen about sinful humanity and the holiness of God, how is it possible that Jesus can be fully man and fully God? Does this tell us anything about the nature of humanity?
- Can God be crucified?
- How can Jesus be divine if he did not know the date of his own return?
- Theologians debate whether Christology should begin 'from above' or 'from below'. How does the approach taken here differ? Which approach do you prefer?

For further reading
- Thirty-Nine Articles, article 2
- Westminster Confession, chapter 8, sections 1-3
- Bray, chapter 26
- Horton, chapter 7
- Milne, chapters 13-15

14

THE CRUCIFIED LORD

Key concept: The humble Lord, rejected by his own people, lays down his life for the world.

1. Introduction

Samuel Zwemer, a famous missionary to the Muslims, wrote:

> If the Cross of Christ is anything to the mind, it is surely everything—the most profound reality and the sublimest mystery. One comes to realize that literally all the wealth and glory of the gospel centres here. The Cross is the pivot as well as the centre of New Testament thought. It is the exclusive mark of the Christian faith, the symbol of Christianity and its cynosure.[25]

Zwemer's estimate is undoubtedly correct, and it is a measure of the appalling weakness of some of what passes for Christianity, including evangelical Christianity, that for so many the cross is not "everything".

---

25 SM Zwemer, *The Glory of the Cross*, Marshall, Morgan & Scott, 2014, p 4.

The weakening of the centrality of the cross in Christianity has much to do with the refusal to understand human problems in a scriptural way. God is holy and righteous; we have suppressed the knowledge of God, rejected his rule, and have lived lives of pollution and disobedience. Sin has stained our whole personality and earned the rejection and wrath of God. We are guilty sinners, and even our righteousness is offensive to the Lord (cf. Isa 64:6). Whatever else are the problems of the race—and they are profound and heart-rending—they cannot be compared to our moral and spiritual corruption. The other problems are the result of this corruption; in the end they will pass away, and we will be left with our accountability to God. It is this fundamental misery which the cross addresses: "If the Cross of Christ is anything to the mind, it is surely everything …" When we think that humans are not as sinful as the Bible says, the cross ceases to be at the centre.

In order to consider the meaning of the cross, we will first examine Mark's Gospel, where we see the words and works of Christ and then the testimony of Peter as one of the apostles. Then we will summarize the New Testament preaching of the cross so that we can hear the original message of "Jesus Christ and him crucified" (1 Cor 2:2).

2. The mystery of the cross in Mark's Gospel

Mark begins with Jesus preaching the gospel of the kingdom and calling for repentance (Mark 1:14-15). The original hearers would undoubtedly have regarded such an announcement as momentous and confronting, but they would not automatically connect the person and work of the prophet himself with the announcement.

As the Gospel unfolds, however, it becomes clear that Jesus is more than a prophet, that the coming of the kingdom is bound up with what he says and what he does. He has come to preach (1:38), but his preaching is accompanied by miracles reminiscent of God's great redemption from Egypt. And just as Pharaoh was God's adversary, so Jesus is involved in a conflict with Satan through his trials, through demon-possessed persons, and through those who would divert him from his ministry. Unlike Israel and the prophets (but like God), he is victorious in these trials and never fails to exhibit an obedience, love and faithfulness of a quality not seen before.

In short, his whole life is indivisible from what he came to accomplish. By his preaching and miracles he declared God's word; by his life of obedience he fulfilled that word and equipped himself to be the deliverer.

Almost from the beginning of Mark, his death is also being foreshadowed (see, for example, 2:20 and 3:6). Mostly the coming death of Christ is factually referred to, without apparent meaning being assigned to it. There is a growing precision about the nature of his death, and a theme of misunderstanding and rejection by the disciples (e.g. 8:31-33). But it would be inadequate to accept this at face value; the Gospel is, at the same time, recording the revelation made to the disciples that he is the Christ and is the Son of God. Such a reference as 2:20 is indicative of what is at issue, since it assumes that Jesus is the bridegroom. The rejection and murder of the Christ, the Son of God, the Bridegroom, in the midst of Israel cannot be without profound meaning, however much it was initially a mystery to those who witnessed it. At the very least, the judgement of Israel and the beginning of blessing for the Gentiles is being foretold (12:1-12).

At two significant points in the Gospel, particular light is shed on the meaning of this death.

a. Mark 10:45

In Mark 10:35-45, the apparent clash between the kingly, powerful Messiah of the kingdom and the suffering Messiah is brought to the surface. The sons of Zebedee regard Jesus as the future and glorious king (v 37). In this they are right (v 40), but they have not begun to understand that the path of glory is through suffering service, for them and for Jesus. In particular, Jesus has come "not to be served but to serve, and to give his life as a ransom for many" (v 45).

The saying culminates a section that runs from 8:27. The question of what a man can use to ransom himself is raised at this point: "For what does it profit a man to gain the whole world and forfeit his soul? For what can a man give in return for his soul?" (8:36-37). Nothing, not even the world itself, is sufficient to pay for a life. It is only by losing a life that saving it can occur (8:35). On the other hand, the life of the Son of Man is given, and this proves to be a ransom sufficient for many (as opposed to few; cf. Ps 49:7-9).

It is important to see in this passage the vital element of *substitution*. The ransom is substituted for the life of the captive; it is a compensation or exchange. In this case the ransom is not money, but the life of Jesus Christ; the life substitutes for the life of "the many", which is what the Greek preposition *anti* indicates.[26] As Michael Horton observes, it is impossible to understand the Greek term "as intending anything other than substitution".[27] Although the whole of Jesus' life was service, it is, of course, his death specifically which provides the ransom: the cross is crucial. As to why this man could claim to be the ransom, far from needing to be ransomed himself, there is a hint in the strange form of the saying: "For even the Son of Man came not to be served but to serve" (Mark 10:45). Here was one who *chose* to come, who *chose* the path of the cross.

Further light is shed on the passage if, as is likely, Isaiah 53 should be understood as its background. Here, too, we have the suffering servant, giving himself for us in a vicarious (i.e. substitu-

---

26 "For even the Son of Man came not to be served but to serve, and to give his life as a ransom *anti* [for, in the place of] many."

27 M Horton, *The Christian Faith: A systematic theology for pilgrims on the way*, Zondervan Academic, 2011, p 498.

tionary) way. In particular, Isaiah 53:10 seems to be making the same point as Mark 10:45, where the "offering for guilt" is a ransom for those who are to be saved: "Jesus, as the messianic Servant, offers himself as a guilt-offering (Lev 5:14-6:7, 7:1-7; Num 5:5-8) in compensation for the sins of the people".[28]

b. Mark 14:24

"And he said to them, 'This is my blood of the [new] covenant, which is poured out for many.'"[29] These words are, of course, part of the symbolic words and actions of the last supper. Jesus had performed a number of such symbolic acts, but this one was the most significant since it related his death unambiguously to the great redemption of the exodus, as well as to the promise of the new covenant in Jeremiah. The phrase "blood of the covenant" is reminiscent of Exodus 24:8, where the blood of burnt offerings and peace offerings was thrown on the people to formalize their pact with God. In Jeremiah 31 the theme is forgiveness, and we may see here the promise of a new relationship based on sacrificial death (blood) and issuing in forgiveness. Thus, if the motif in Mark 10:45 is substitution, the motif here is sacrificial death: "As the Old Covenant had been ratified by the sprinkling of sacrificial blood, so God's New Covenant with men is about to be established by Jesus's death, and the cup ... makes those who share it partakers of the benefits and obligations of this New Covenant".[30]

The story of the death of Jesus is given a great deal of space in Mark and the other Gospels because of its significance. Mark's appears a straightforward account, devoid of theological interpretation. This is not the case; witness, for example, the links between

---

28 WL Lane, *The Gospel of Mark*, NICNT, Eerdmans, 1974, p 384.
29 On the possible inclusion of the word 'new', see the ESV footnote.
30 CEB Cranfield, *The Gospel According to St Mark*, CGTC, Cambridge University Press, 1959, p 427.

the end of all things described in chapter 13, and chapters 14-16, where the end of all things is inaugurated in the death and resurrection of Jesus.

But at the heart of Mark's story two things stand out. The first is the declared innocence of Jesus. Pilate, the judge in this case, clearly believes him to be without guilt (15:10, 14-15). Guilt is attributed to him, imputed to him, without good cause. The second is that at the same time God, the supreme judge in this case, also imputes guilt to him, but with the intention of saving the world. The curse of God falls upon him as he hangs on a tree, and he cries out in God-forsakenness (15:34). But, as Mark is also careful to point out, the centurion saw the truth (15:39), and God both destroyed the temple veil (15:38) and raised the innocent to life (16:6). Whatever is happening in the death of Jesus, it is not merely a martyrdom, the death of a freedom fighter, or a political assassination. It has cosmic significance and bears on the whole relationship between God and man. It is a ransom.

3. Peter interprets the cross

Before widening the scope of the investigation, we will now take one of the smaller New Testament books, 1 Peter, and see how this apostle assesses the significance of the death of Jesus, of which he was an eyewitness.

The first thing to notice is that he affirms the central importance of the cross, in common with the other New Testament writers. He is not writing specifically about the death of Jesus, but references to it can be found throughout the letter (1:2, 11, 18-21; 2:4, 7, 21-25; 3:18; 4:1, 13; 5:1). I do not intend to expound these passages in order, but to summarize Peter's approach. He sees the death of Jesus as:

a. **an example (2:21):** Christ's submission to his enemies provides a pattern for the life of faith and obedience despite provocation. The thought of Christ's sufferings sustains the believer (e.g. 4:1, 13), and he or she can even be said to share in them.

b. **a sacrifice (1:2, 18-21):** We are sprinkled with the blood of Christ, as the worshippers were in Exodus 24, as a sign of the participation in the covenant. We are ransomed not through the death of the blameless animal but through the death of Christ.

c. **a victor (2:4, 8; 3:18-20):** Christ was rejected by his people, but as the elect one of God now stands as the "stone of stumbling". He preached his victory on the cross to "the spirits in prison". The cross is the triumph of Christ, for through it he secures a people for God who are "a chosen race, a royal priesthood, a holy nation" (2:9-10; cf. John 12:31-32).

d. **a substitute (2:24, 3:18):** This idea may already be found in the ransom (or redemption) language of 1:18-19. But it is clearly the meaning of 2:24, where Isaiah 53 is invoked. Furthermore, Peter says specifically that Jesus "bore our sins in his body on the tree". To "bear sin" is an Old Testament phrase used to indicate bearing the penalty of sin (e.g. Num 18:1, 22, 32). In speaking thus of the death of Jesus, Peter is bringing it into the realm of the substitution of one who is judged or penalized for the many with the consequent healing that comes from his suffering. This is called 'penal substitutionary atonement'. The same thought is present, though not as explicitly, in 3:18, where it is said that Christ has "suffered once for sins". This does not mean that he died in place of or on behalf of sins, but rather that he died *on account of* or *with respect to* sins. That his bearing of sin's punishment is in view is shown by what follows: "the righteous for the unrighteous"—that is, as a substitute for the unrighteous, with the aim "that he might bring us to God". Peter's use of the word "once" testifies to the total sufficiency of what Christ has accomplished: no further blood needs to be shed; the once-for-all sacrifice has been offered (cf. Heb 10:11-14).

4. The apostolic preaching of the cross

The preaching of the cross both depends upon and reveals the doctrine of God. If God is as he has been described in chapters 6-9, and if human beings are hopelessly ensnared in sin and guilt as described in chapters 10-11, much of our doctrine of the atonement (i.e. how God and man are reconciled) is determined already. We can therefore penetrate to the meaning of the cross (as far as is possible) by bringing together what we know about God and the apostolic words about the death of Jesus.

The cross and the power of God

At first sight, it may seem that the cross is the abnegation of the power of God. It seems like his defeat. The New Testament has an entirely different perspective. Peter declared: "this Jesus, delivered up according to the definite plan and foreknowledge of God, you crucified and killed by the hands of lawless men" (Acts 2:23). Again and again, the apostles appealed to Scripture to show that God had foreordained the death of Jesus—that the cross was a fulfilment, not a failure.

Indeed, the doctrine of the cross is a constant reminder to us that God's ways are not our ways (cf. Isa 55:8). If we ruled the world, our methods would be very different. But God has appointed weak and foolish things to display his power. In an eloquent passage near the beginning of 1 Corinthians, Paul contrasts the preferred religion of his Jewish contemporaries (the power of "signs" and wonders) and the preferred philosophy of the ancient Greeks ("wisdom") with the actuality of power. This is the foolishness of God, and it consists of the cross and the preaching of "Christ crucified" (1 Cor 1:18-2:6). Here is focused the energy of God. It conforms to the graciousness of the one who serves (Mark 10:45), and is matched both by the lack of nobility in his chosen people (1 Cor 1:26-31) and the weakness of those who preach the gospel (1 Cor 3:5-9; 2 Corinthians 10-13).

There is a great lesson here for gospel ministry, since our prevailing temptation is to embark on "the quest for power", given the state of the church and our weakness compared with society. What we must learn is that the gospel of the cross is the power of God for salvation; we must be willing to trust it, and to let God's word do its work. We must share Paul's declaration: "For I am not ashamed of the gospel, for it is the power of God for salvation to everyone who believes ..." (Rom 1:16).

The cross and the work of God

The way of the cross should not have come as a surprise to those conversant with the Old Testament. God had often revealed himself as the gracious Saviour of a sinful people. That he did so by using men filled with the Spirit has been noted before. But in the Word become flesh we have a Saviour who is not merely inspired by God, but one who is God himself. In Paul's words, "All this is from God, who through Christ reconciled us to himself ... in Christ God was reconciling the world to himself ..." (2 Cor 5:18-19).

It is essential to grasp this point, lest the doctrine of the substitution of Christ be allowed to drive a wedge between Father and Son, with the 'angry Father' being appeased by the offering of the 'loving Son'. The work of atonement was the work of God, Father, Son and Holy Spirit, one in love and righteousness, one in the determination to save the world. In the words of Jesus:

> "For this reason the Father loves me, because I lay down my life that I may take it up again. No-one takes it from me, but I lay it down of my own accord. I have authority to lay it down, and I have authority to take it up again. This charge I have received from my Father." (John 10:17-18)

If we are to speak of a sacrifice to God in the Lamb of God, it is a sacrifice without parallel at this crucial point: the victim is both God and man. The very thing that gives it its unconquerable value is the identity of the one who is the sacrifice, and that he comes from the side of God. The atonement is a work of the Trinity: "the blood of Christ ... through the eternal Spirit offered himself without blemish to God" (Heb 9:14).

The problem that some see in penal substitution, as being the conflict of Father and Son, is in fact a 'problem' of God's attributes and the difficulty which we human beings experience in reconciling God's love with his wrath. If it seems that the offended party (God) punishes an innocent party (Christ) for the sins of an offending party (us), there is some ground for complaint. But once it is recognized that in the cross the offended party bore the punishment due to the offending ones, the difficulty turns into the most wonderful of all demonstrations of the love of God, Father, Son and Holy Spirit.

The cross and the love of God

It is tragic that the love of God is so taken for granted on the one hand and so little experienced on the other. A great gulf is fixed between God's love and his justice. The consequence is that when we speak of God's unconditional love, the picture is of one who bathes the universe with the warm glow of his undiscriminating pleasure: 'God will love all equally, come what may'. Such a view is very far removed from the Bible. In Scripture, God's unconditional love is called "grace"; it is love for the unlovely and sinful. But it is certainly not undiscriminating. It is fully cognisant of the sinfulness of sin and never wavers in its condemnation of it. The love of God does not compromise his holiness; nor, however, does it conflict with his holiness. God loves in a thoroughly good and righteous way.

When this is accepted, we are in a position to understand the words of John: "In this is love, not that we have loved God but that he loved us and sent his Son to be the propitiation for our sins"

(1 John 4:10). The demonstration of his love was in the sending of his Son to be a sacrifice. Modern misunderstanding of God's love would be content that he sent his Son, although the reason for so doing may be thoroughly obscure. In fact, it is the atoning sacrifice which is the chief demonstration of the intensity of God's love. God's attributes are never in conflict with each other.

The cross and the wrath of God

God's wrath is his righteous hostility to sin, expressed in the punishment of offenders (e.g. Rom 1:18, 27, 32; 2:3, 5). His punishment is both experienced now and stored up for the day of judgement. The law of God imposes penalties, whether that law is known in its Israelite embodiment or merely written on the heart (Rom 2:12-16). The law is absolutely just and holy and good, but its adverse judgement is without mercy, "so that every mouth may be stopped, and the whole world may be held accountable to God" (3:19).

At the very heart of several key treatments of the cross is the thought that Jesus Christ, the Son of God, bore the penalty of sin. Thus in 2 Corinthians 5:18-21, God's reconciling work is described as "not counting [the world's] trespasses against them" (v 19). This he does not, as some would say, by a divine word of forgiveness without penalty; rather, "For our sake he made him to be sin who knew no sin, so that in him we might become the righteousness of God" (v 21). This cannot mean that God made Christ *into* a sinful person (for then he would need to be saved himself), but only that he *treated* him as a sinful person. That is, he punished him for our sake, so that he may treat us as righteous, not counting our trespasses and sins against us.

The same idea is present in Galatians 3, where we are told that "Christ redeemed us from the curse of the law by becoming a curse for us—for it is written, 'Cursed is everyone who is hanged on a tree'" (v 13). Christ's becoming a curse means that he was the object of punishment even though he was without sin, never having offended the law.

The same thought is present in texts such as Hebrews 2:17, 1 John 2:2 and Romans 3:25, where the thought is that of "propitiation": God's wrath being averted or turned aside. The death of Christ is the atoning sacrifice which accomplishes this, and we are invited to approach God solely on the ground of what he has done for us in his death.

The idea of propitiation would be unworthy if it were presented as God somehow being satisfied by the death of a human victim. But Scripture does not let us forget that God is himself the Saviour, and that he propitiates himself at enormous cost to himself. This so transforms the concept of propitiation that it becomes almost unrecognizable. The reason for keeping it is as a reminder that, in justifying the ungodly, God himself remains just: "It was to show his righteousness at the present time, so that he might be just and the justifier of the one who has faith in Jesus" (Rom 3:26). Forgiveness is free to us but costly to God. The cost of bearing our sin is certainly no 'legal fiction', as though God were simply pretending that sin had been dealt with. Even in our own experience, the restoration of relationships in a way which does justice is painful. Thus it is typical of the love of the Son of God that he should choose to become one with us and undergo the judgement of our sin, a cost which we could not meet ourselves. Love does not ignore sin, but overcomes it. And this is the love of God for us (cf. 1 John 4:8-10).

The cross and the enemies of God

Satan is defeated at the cross. In particular, his hold over the human race is broken and God begins the great work of bringing Jew and Gentile to himself (see John 12:31-32). Paul has another way of putting this: he portrays Satan as a spiritual Pharaoh and sees God in Christ releasing the captives and transferring them to the Son's kingdom (Col 1:13-14). This is achieved by the liberation which is forgiveness (2:13-15). Forgiveness is the victory of the cross by which Satan is forced to flee.

But the Bible speaks, too, of human beings as the enemies of God. In a moving passage, Paul exhibits the love of God by describing the enemies of God being won even while they were yet sinners (Rom 5:5-11). In the cross, God's enemies are reconciled and saved from the wrath to come. In all his thinking the apostle always moves back to the great historical event of the cross, by which he is thoroughly assured that God loves not just his people in a general sense, but Paul himself as an individual (Rom 8:31-39; Gal 2:20).

5. Conclusion

We can never feel that we have done justice to so great a theme as this. It is not surprising that the health of a church can be measured by its devotion to Christ and him crucified. It shows how seriously we take sin and its effects, and how seriously we cling to God's grace. The cross is the source of our justification and the pattern of our sanctification, as we take up our cross to follow the Saviour. In the words of Charles Wesley's hymn:

> Happy, if with my latest breath
> I might but gasp his name;
> preach him to all, and cry in death:
> behold, behold the Lamb!

Of course, the death of Christ is not the whole of the gospel. For the gospel attests also that God raised him from the dead, and he now reigns as the king in God's kingdom. To these truths we now turn.

―――

Key verse
He himself bore our sins in his body on the tree, that we might die to sin and live to righteousness. By his wounds you have been healed. (1 Pet 2:24)

Quotation

"As there is only One God, so there can be only one gospel. If God has really done something in Christ on which the salvation of the world depends, and if He has made it known, then it is a Christian duty to be intolerant of everything which ignores, denies, or explains it away ... Intolerance in this sense has its counterpart in comprehension; it is when we have the only gospel, and not until then, that we have the gospel for all." (James Denney, *The Death of Christ*)

Key terms
- Atonement
- Propitiation
- Ransom
- Penal substitution
- Sacrifice
- Forgiveness
- Redemption
- Victory

For further thought
- How was sin dealt with under the old covenant? What were the defects of these methods?
- Why could God not merely forgive, without the death of Jesus?
- Could Jesus have died as an infant and been the Saviour of the world?
- How do you respond to the charge that penal substitution is 'cosmic child abuse'?
- In what way was Satan defeated at the cross?
- Are you aware of any type of personal ambition that plays a part in your own life? How does the cross address this?

- This chapter concentrates on "the death of Christ". It may be that the category of "the work of Christ" would be better, because it is wider and includes more of what Christ has done. Which term do you prefer?

For further reading
- Thirty-Nine Articles, articles 15 and 18
- Westminster Confession, chapter 8, sections 4-8
- Milne, chapters 16-17

15

THE EXALTED LORD

Key concept: The humble Lord is exalted to the right hand of God, from where he rules over all things.

1. Introduction

Many years ago, Dr David Jenkins, then the Bishop of Durham, became famous (or notorious) for his denial of the resurrection of Jesus. But did he really make such a denial? Two letters to the *Church Times* in Britain illustrated the problem neatly.

The first author wrote:

> Sir, Thomas doubted, but Dr Jenkins rejects the physical proofs Jesus gave Thomas to resolve his doubts. If his fellow bishops are not ready to dismiss him, it is time for believing Christian lay-folk and priests to oust Jenkins and his ilk from positions of leadership in *our* Church. The "Jenkins show" is a great Easter story for the media, maybe, but for Christ it is a new wound in his body.

The second author wrote:

> Sir, In the present uproar concerning the Bishop of Durham's recent remarks it seems to me that only two questions and their answers are of any significance:
>
> 1. Does the Bishop of Durham believe that God raised Jesus from the dead?
> *Answer:* Yes
>
> 2. Does the Bishop of Durham believe that Jesus Christ is alive now?
> *Answer:* Yes
>
> Will someone please tell me what all the fuss is about?

What was happening? Who was right, and does it matter?

It is not all bad that these questions are vexing modern Christians, since it is a reminder of the importance of the resurrection for our faith. As Paul put it: "if Christ has not been raised, then our preaching is in vain and your faith is in vain ... your faith is futile and you are still in your sins" (1 Cor 15:14, 17).

What is most interesting in theological debate, however, is the inability of some theologians (including evangelical ones) to incorporate the resurrection in their systematic approach. They find it easier to answer the question "What does the death of Jesus mean?" than "What does the resurrection of Jesus mean?"

The problem of the resurrection is not exhausted by its historicity, vital though that is. We must go further and examine the theological significance of the resurrection. Failure here means that we cannot understand the whole work of Christ, which is described by such words as the ascension, the session and the *parousia*.

2. The resurrection of Jesus Christ

Historicity

It is only natural that our first instinct should be to enquire whether such an event occurred. When asked "What event?", we could reply impatiently that we are speaking of the genuine death and burial of Jesus Christ, and of the claim that on the third day he came alive again bodily and left the tomb. He was then seen over a 40-day period by several hundred people, and he mixed with, spoke with and ate with many of them.

The New Testament itself invites us to take the historical question seriously. Its view of causation (in which God's power is appealed to directly and without any embarrassment) is not the same as that of the secular historian. But it clearly suggests that on the one hand something happened in time and space to a human being called Jesus of Nazareth, and on the other hand that this was witnessed and reported in such a way that we can call the witnesses right or wrong, but not right *and* wrong: "For we did not follow cleverly devised myths when we made known to you the power and coming of our Lord Jesus Christ, but we were eyewitnesses of his majesty" (2 Pet 1:16); "he has fixed a day on which he will judge the world in righteousness by a man whom he has appointed; and of this he has given assurance to all by raising him from the dead" (Acts 17:31).

Historical research can comment on the resurrection of Jesus Christ; in theory, it can provide evidence which suggests that it did or did not occur. But on its own terms it cannot 'explain' it or comprehensively account for it. There are some things about the past that historians as such are the last to know or understand, unless they are prepared to agree that God may do miracles as he sees fit.

When the historicity of the resurrection is examined, a number of factors should be considered. In general terms, however, the Bible itself invites us to examine the credibility of witnesses such as John, Matthew, Peter and Paul. If we believe that their writings overall are credible, it will suggest that credence should be extended to the resurrection. We will note that the apostles were willing to die for their "witness".[31] There is the obvious failure of the authorities to refute the preaching of the resurrection by producing a body and a tomb. There is the existence of the church itself, with its appeal to a widespread experience of the resurrected Christ (1 Cor 15:6).

Those who seek to refute the evidence do so in two main ways:

a. They discredit the witnesses by pointing to what they believe are contradictions in their accounts of the events. To this one may argue that the apparent discrepancies demonstrate the lack of collusion among the witnesses, are consistent with most other reports of singular events from different points of view, and are in principle capable of resolution.

b. They accept the sincerity of the witnesses but conclude that, consciously or unconsciously, they are describing their own subjective experience of the risen Christ by imagining external and historical forms. This they were prone to do because in ancient times people were more credulous and superstitious and therefore more prone to believe the impossible. Often, although not always, such critiques stem from an unwarranted scepticism about the possibility of the miraculous. To this one may reply that the actual accounts that we rely on (e.g. Luke 23-24) seem to go out of their way to claim the validity of the historical and the truth of the bodily resurrection. It is extremely ironic, after all, that one of the most famous men in history is Thomas, who has lent his name to the expression 'doubting Thomas' precisely because he would not believe the truth of the resurrection without the evidence of his own eyes, ears and hands. We can overstate the alleged credulity of our ancestors.

---

31 The Greek word *martureō* means 'to testify' and 'to bear witness', but also gives us our English word 'martyr', which is tied specifically to the function of those whose witness to the truth is tested to the point of death.

We also need to note that in the ancient world the question was not whether there is life after death. It was generally believed that the soul or spirit lived on. The issue was the resurrection *of the body*, a belief that was scorned by the intellectuals. We know that the idea of a crucified Saviour was hard to preach; but so too was the idea of a resurrected man. It would have been far easier simply to say that he was alive and with God. That the apostles stuck to their story is further evidence that this is what they had experienced (see 1 Corinthians 15, where this was the point at issue).

Nature of resurrection

I would argue, then, for a *bodily* resurrection. I am especially unimpressed with the argument which relies on the fact that Paul fails to mention the empty tomb in 1 Corinthians 15, which is sometimes taken to suggest that Christ's resurrection was "spiritual" as opposed to "bodily". This seems to be an attempt to soften the scandal of the resurrection, to make it more palatable to a secular world. But all it accomplishes is the making of a vacuous Saviour and a half-salvation. According to the Bible, we are saved in the arena of the body as well as the spirit. As I have noted, Paul's opponents in 1 Corinthians 15 doubtless believed in life after death; what they objected to strenuously was a resurrection of the body. Thus the suggestion made in the letter I quoted in the introduction—that the bodily resurrection simply does not matter as long as we say that Christ is still alive—is exactly what Paul and the other apostles repudiated.

At the same time, at every point the New Testament also witnesses to a transformation in the body of Christ. His victory over death took him into a new sphere of bodily existence. While he assured his disciples that he was not a ghost, and he ate and drank with them, he also appeared to move mysteriously and to be recognized only when he wished. Whether in the 40-day interim the body of Christ was in its final glorious form, or whether it was to undergo further transformation, we do not know. Paul, in speaking of the resurrection body which we will all share, refers to a "spiritual body" (1 Cor 15:44), by which he means a body which is controlled by the Spirit. He denies that flesh and blood inherits the kingdom and contrasts the old body to the new by use of the analogy of seed and full-grown plant. These clues would suggest that we do not yet know what awaits us in the glory of being conformed to the resurrected and glorified Christ, and that it would be better to be very cautious about speculating concerning the precise mode of his resurrection. We look with eager expectation for the manifestation of "the man of heaven", knowing that we will bear his image in our resurrection from the dead (15:48-49).

Significance of the resurrection

When Peter spoke on the day of Pentecost, he gave voice to the fundamental truth about the resurrection: that it is God's positive verdict on the rejected and crucified Saviour—a direct reversal of the human verdict. "This Jesus ... you crucified and killed by the hands of lawless men. God raised him up, loosing the pangs of death, because it was not possible for him to be held by it" (Acts 2:23-24). Peter immediately links the resurrection to prophecy. The deliberate plan and foreknowledge of God that led to the death of Jesus was also the ultimate cause of his resurrection; and this plan was expressed through the prophets, notably through David: "For you will not abandon my soul to Hades, or let your Holy One see corruption" (2:27, citing Psalm 16). If God had not kept his word, one could only conclude that Jesus was not the Holy One and thus not the Saviour. The fact that he paid in full for our sins on the cross meant that he must be raised again; less than full payment would mean that he would remain condemned, for that is what he undertook to achieve.

The resurrection is, therefore, God's vindication of the person and work of the "Son of God in power according to the Spirit of holiness by his resurrection from the dead, Jesus Christ our Lord ..."

(Rom 1:4). Paul also writes that Jesus was "delivered up for our trespasses and raised for our justification" (4:25). Hence Paul concludes that, "If Christ has not been raised, your faith is futile and you are still in your sins" (1 Cor 15:17). It is, of course, not merely sin which is defeated in the work of Christ, but the consequence of sin, namely death: "The sting of death is sin, and the power of sin is the law" (15:56). In defeating sin, Christ overcomes death, and it is therefore no accident whatever that the cross is followed by the resurrection as the mighty reversal of the punishment laid down in the garden of Eden.

But there is even more involved. The resurrection is the inbreaking of the new age. Peter quotes Joel: *"in the last days it shall be ..."* (Acts 2:17). The day of fulfilment has arrived: "we bring you the good news that what God promised to the fathers, this he has fulfilled to us their children by raising Jesus ..." (13:32-33). The "age to come", "eternal life", has dawned in Jesus Christ. That age will be the age of a general resurrection (Dan 12:2). Although the general resurrection has yet to occur, the one specific, greatest instance has arrived as the harbinger of the rest: "Christ the firstfruits ..." (1 Cor 15:23).

The resurrection, then, is the foundation of the Christian hope (e.g. 1 Pet 1:3-5). Like the death of Jesus, it reaches back from the future and helps shape the pattern of the life of faith in the present age. The experience of regeneration can also be described as a death/resurrection, as in Romans 6:1-11. In this passage, we "walk in newness of life" now (v 4), yet we also wait for our future resurrection in union with him: "we *shall* certainly be united with him in a resurrection like his ... we *will* also live with him" (vv 5, 8). In Colossians, we are told that, raised with Christ as we are, we should "seek the things that are above", putting evil to death, putting on the good, conscious that we have "put on the new self, which is being renewed in knowledge after the image of its creator" (Col 3:1, 10).

The resurrection is also the basis of our present experience of God. The declaration that Jesus Christ is Lord is also a command that we should turn from sin to him, that we should enthrone him as Lord in our lives in true repentance. From this flows our forgiveness, the very essence of salvation. Without a doubt, Christian piety is trinitarian; we pray to the Father in the name of the Son and in the power of the Spirit. But from another point of view it is Christ-centred, and the Christ whom we worship is not a figure from the past, but is our contemporary and living Lord who will one day come again. The Lord Jesus is absent from us; but he is also present (as is his Father) in the coming of the Spirit (John 14). Hence he promises always to be with us, even to the end of the age (Matt 28:16-20).

But a consideration of this subject leads to the further stages in Christ's glory, namely his ascension and enthronement.

3. The ascension of Jesus Christ

Once again this doctrine is based on an event, recorded by Luke in Acts 1. The 40 days of appearances come to a decisive end with the withdrawal of Jesus and the angelic promise, "This Jesus, who was taken up from you into heaven, will come in the same way as you saw him go into heaven" (v 11). The reference to the cloud (v 9) and the angels' words remind us that his departure is a prelude to his return, that the ascension sets a clock going that will cease only at the end. We are living in that special time between his two appearings and should be careful to behave appropriately in that time. Part of that appropriate behaviour consists, of course, in our walking "by faith, not by sight" (2 Cor 5:7), in this way contrasting favourably with those who saw and talked with Jesus on earth (John 20:29; 1 Pet 1:8).

It may be thought that the ascension is not worthy of particular attention in a doctrinal summary, being simply the necessary interlude between resurrection and 'session' (see below). It is at the intersection between two states and two ages. But it is worth noting that the ascension reminds us of the separation of Jesus from his disciples in his bodily state, and his spiritual presence with them: "A little while, and you will see me no longer; and again a little while, and you will see me" (John 16:16); "I tell you the truth: it is to your advantage that I go away, for if I do not go away, the Helper will not come to you. But if I go, I will send him to you" (16:7). But at the same time it tells us clearly that Jesus remains both true man and true God, and his withdrawal is not to be regarded as the loss of his true humanity, but its transference to another plane of existence, in glory, to his Father (20:17; 1 Tim 3:16). It speaks also of his continued triumph (Eph 4:8-10) and reminds us that Jesus is Lord of this present age.

4. The session of Jesus Christ

'Session' is a technical word for the judge or ruler who is seated to exercise his or her official prerogatives. Even today, we may speak of a court or a parliament as being 'seated' or 'in session'. In Old Testament times, we think of the elders seated at the gate, or of monarchs like David and Solomon seated on the throne. In the messianic Psalm 110, we have the oft-quoted words: "The LORD says to my Lord: 'Sit at my right hand, until I make your enemies your footstool'" (v 1). In the concepts of the time, the right-hand seat was given as a mark of honour to the one with executive power, like Joseph or Daniel in the royal court (see also Mark 10:37).

In the New Testament, Jesus is depicted as having ascended to glory and taken the right hand seat (e.g. Acts 2:33). By such a position he is called Lord and is regarded as reigning over this present age, so that it may even be called "the kingdom of Christ and God" (Eph 5:5). This may not be thought to prejudice either the divine status of the Son on the one hand or the power of the Father on the other, but to indicate something of how God has chosen to rule in this present age:

> For he must reign until he has put all his enemies under his feet. The last enemy to be destroyed is death. For "God has put all things in subjection under his feet." But when it says, "all things are put in subjection," it is plain that he is excepted who put all things in subjection under him. When all things are subjected to him, then the Son himself will also be subjected to him who put all things in subjection under him, that God may be all in all. (1 Cor 15:25-28)

The rule of Jesus is related not only to his divine status, but his representative role as the fulfilment of Psalm 8 (see 1 Corinthians 15; Hebrews 2). He fulfils and surpasses the task given to Adam in the garden. In doing so he is "bringing many sons to glory" (Heb 2:10). As their representative, he is also praying for them—or, better, he is the one who has earned the right to be the intercessor for them at God's right hand (Rom 8:34; Heb 7:25). Christ's intercession, manifested in John 17, is in the first place for apostolic fidelity and truth in his original followers and in all who believe through their word (v 20); it then widens to include his desire that they should share his Father's love with him. He is not praying for all the world, but for those from the world who are to believe (v 9). In short, his prayers are the comfort of his people as he focuses on their salvation.

The lordship of Christ is not only expressed in the gospel; it is also the very power by which the gospel advances in this present age. In sending his disciples on their universal mission, and in promising his unfailing presence, Christ asserts that all authority in heaven and on earth had been given to him; he now exercises that authority by being with his disciples as they make more disciples of all nations (Matt 28:16-20). The outpouring of the Spirit on the day of Pentecost is the work of Christ (Acts 2:33), and the work of evangelism, preaching, pastoring and prophecy is his work (Eph 4:11), in which human beings are his agents and ambassadors. At the end of the age, the lordship of Christ will be especially expressed in his judgement, in the submission of every creature to him, and in the summing up of all things in him (Phil 2:1-11; Eph 1:9-10; Acts 10:42).

5. Conclusion

The glory of Christ is manifested in the bodily resurrection. But the unity between the humbled and the exalted Lord, between Christ in his humility and Christ in his glory, is first and foremost seen at the cross. It is there in particular that he conquers Satan and the world and is exalted, or "lifted up" on high (John 3:14). His great work is finished in the sense that it has fully paid for our sins. But his ruling work continues. The salvation he accomplished at the cross is now being realized in the lives of the ones for whom he died. We now examine what the Bible says about the work that he is doing by his word and the Holy Spirit.

———

Key verse

"Let all the house of Israel therefore know for certain that God has made him both Lord and Christ, this Jesus whom you crucified." (Acts 2:36)

Quotation

"For man is by nature afraid of death and the dissolution of the body; but there is this most startling fact, that he who has put his faith in the cross despises even what is naturally fearful, and for Christ's sake is not afraid of death." (Athanasius, *On the Incarnation of the Word*)

Key terms
- Bodily
- Resurrection
- Ascension
- Session
- Intercession
- Immortality

For further thought
- Can we regard the resurrection of Jesus as historically proved?
- What is the connection between Christ's resurrection and our own?
- What is the relationship between "immortality" and "resurrection"?
- What does it mean to have the risen Christ interceding for us (Rom 8:34; Heb 7:25)?
- Which is more important: the death of Jesus, or the resurrection of Jesus? Can they, or should they, be separated?
- Why do some theologians appear to have so much trouble fitting the resurrection into their systematic theologies?
- In what ways does the resurrection of Jesus make Christianity unique among world religions?

For further reading
- Thirty-Nine Articles, articles 3 and 4
- Horton, chapter 8
- Milne, chapter 18

16

THE LORD WHO IS SPIRIT

Key concept: The exalted Lord sends his Spirit as the one who will bring us to salvation through union with him.

1. Introduction

A friend of mine once heard an evangelistic talk to teenagers in which the cross was portrayed on a blackboard as bridging the awful gap between God and man caused by sin. But the bridge was shown to be inadequate. It did not quite reach over the chasm. What was required, according to the speaker, was the human hand reaching out and grasping the cross. Our response was described as being vital for salvation.

In the same spirit, a well-known evangelist was once heard to say words to this effect at a mission where response was indicated by "coming forward": "I can't get you out of that chair. Your best friend cannot get you out of that chair. God himself cannot get you out of that chair. Only you can move your will and come to the front."

We can sympathize with both evangelists. After all, the Bible unambiguously calls for human response. Peter did on the day of

Pentecost, for example. There is nothing particularly saving about the spiritual passivity engendered by a social "doctrine" of infant baptism, religious respectability and human sin.

Nonetheless, though we may sympathize with both evangelists, we must question whether they have fully understood the gospel they proclaim. The gospel, as we have seen, is a work of grace. God's love to the disobedient and sinful is one of the most striking features of what he has done in Jesus Christ. But in each of the illustrations used above, it is as if God's work ceases with the cross and resurrection. Having come this far towards us, he stops and invites us to come the rest of the way toward him. He has come, let us say, 95 percent of the distance, but there remains the vital element of human response, without which 5 percent remains undone and all is lost.

But think of the Bible's teaching about sin (see chapters 10, 11). Sin brings death more than sickness (Eph 2:1-3). It is incapacitating and disabling: "I have the desire to do what is right, but not the ability to carry it out" (Rom 7:18). If God's work of salvation ceased with the resurrection of Jesus, and all he does now is to offer the gospel in the hope that we may respond, none would be saved. But in fact his work of grace continues until it is thoroughly finished. It is this work of his that we now turn to study.

As before, salvation is the work of the Triune God, but we follow the lead of Scripture in associating this work particularly, but not completely, with the Holy Spirit.

2. The person of the Spirit of God

In chapter 6, I made the point that the Spirit of God is presented to us in the Old Testament as the personal presence and power of God and that in the New Testament his unique and personal attributes become more closely defined. It is not surprising that he is regarded as a person of the Trinity. Yet the evidence of his personhood—in such things as his interceding and his grieving—is apparent throughout the New Testament.

Just as important is what the New Testament reveals about the relationship of Father, Son and Spirit. It is fundamental to our view of God that what the New Testament reveals about these relations is not just "economic" (i.e. set up for the purposes of salvation and revelation) but "essential" (i.e. revealing something of the very nature of God in its permanence). Thus the name of "Son" is not merely a convenient expression for Jesus Christ, but is a revelation of the essential relationship that has always existed, and will always exist, in God. He is eternally the "only-begotten" of the Father.[32]

In this light we can also explore the relationships of the Spirit. In this case, Christian thinkers have favoured the word "proceed"—particularly in the Nicene Creed—in the sense of being "sent" or given.[33] The Spirit proceeds from the Father, or is sent by the Father: "And I will ask the Father, and he will give you another Helper, to be with you forever, even the Spirit of truth …" (John 14:16-17).

In this passage, Jesus prays to the Father, who "sends". But in other passages, such as John 15:26, it is Jesus who also sends: "But when the Helper comes, whom I will send to you from the Father, the Spirit of truth, who proceeds from the Father …" In Peter's great speech on the day of Pentecost, he also identifies both Father and Son as sending the Spirit: "Being therefore exalted at the right hand of God, and having received from the Father the promise of the Holy Spirit, he [Jesus] has poured out this that you yourselves are seeing and hearing" (Acts 2:33; see also John 20:22-23).

It is undoubtedly the case, then, that the Father "sends" the Spirit. But how is it best to think of the Son? Here Christians are divided. Some would say that the Spirit is sent "from the Father *through* the Son"; others would say that he is sent "from the Father

---

32 See the Thirty-Nine Articles, article 17.
33 See the Nicene Creed in the appendices to this book.

and the Son ..." Reformed confessions such as the Thirty-Nine Articles and Westminster Confession adopt the second view;[34] the Eastern Orthodox churches are strongly for the first option. Much of the argument between Orthodox and other churches is based on this distinction. In the case of the original wording of the Creed, the Orthodox seem to be right; but that does not solve the problem of which form of words is more scriptural.

The debate may seem quite trivial, but, as with many such matters, important consequences may flow from the different emphases, especially in the areas of Christology, ecclesiology and piety. It is important to note two further things. First, the Spirit's presence brings with it the presence of both Father and Son: "If anyone loves me, he will keep my word, and my Father will love him, and we will come to him and make our home with him" (John 14:23). In other words, the provision of the Spirit does not distance us from Father and Son, but does the opposite. Second, the Spirit is also regarded as the Spirit of the Son: "God has sent the Spirit of his Son into our hearts, crying, 'Abba! Father!'" (Gal 4:6; cf. Rom 8:9; Acts 16:7). This emphasis on Christ should warn us against the tendency to focus too much on the Spirit, since the Spirit's own focus is on Christ and the Father. Indeed, it is right to detect the presence of the Spirit when the Father and the Son are exalted (see John 16:12-15).

The equality of the Spirit within the Trinity is not compromised by his 'procession' any more than the Son's equality suffers from the fact that "the head of Christ is God" (1 Cor 11:3). Indeed, the Spirit's special work, as the one who proceeds from the Father and the Son, is to unite us with God, to be the presence of God abiding in his people. At the same time, the Scriptures also speak of our "abiding" in Christ. We receive the blessings of redemption through being united with Christ by the Spirit. While this retains

---

34 See the Thirty-Nine Articles, article 4; and Westminster Confession, chapter 2, section 3.

the characteristic focus of the Bible on Christ, the Spirit's indispensable role is clear.

We turn now, therefore, to the subject of union with Christ, which is the way by which God through his Spirit draws us to himself and makes us the recipients of all his blessings. In so doing, attention is given pre-eminently to the apostle Paul, although passages such as John 15:1-11 bear on the subject.

3. Union with Christ

The great Reformer John Calvin puts a fine emphasis on our union with Christ. He begins Book 3 of the *Institutes* by posing and answering this question:

> How do we receive those benefits which the Father bestowed on his only-begotten Son—not for Christ's private use, but that he might enrich poor and needy men? First, we must understand that as long as Christ remains outside of us, we are separated from him, all that he has suffered and done for the salvation of the human race remains useless and of no value for us.[35]

Paul's teaching is too subtle for easy classification, but if we approach it through the question of the *use* to which the fact of union with Christ is put in his argument, something of its significance becomes clear. Here are five categories of thought that will open up the topic for us.

Being "in Christ" distinguishes me from unbelievers

The unbeliever is outside of or "separated from" Christ (Eph 2:12). Paul says that the non-Christian is "in Adam" (1 Cor 15:22); the

---

35 J Calvin, *Institutes of the Christian Religion* (FL Battles trans), Library of Christian Classics, vol 1, JT McNeill (ed), Westminster John Knox Press, 1960, p 537.

descendants of Adam are all marked for death through their connection with him. They bear his image and thus suffer his fate (15:22, 49). In Romans, the focus is on the sinfulness of Adam's descendants (5:19). Here, too, Paul notes that sin leads to death (5:17).

In each case, there is an explicit contrast with Christ. Through Christ's obedience, there comes acquittal and life (Rom 5:18); those who are in Christ will also bear the image of "the man of heaven", "the last Adam" (1 Cor 15:45-49). In short, there are two regimes, two ages, two men; we are either in one or in the other. Our destiny is determined by that connection. To be in the sphere of Christ is to have entered the future (2 Cor 5:17). Those in Christ are therefore not to have fellowship with the unbelievers (2 Cor 6:14-16; 1 Cor 7:39).

Being "in Christ" includes me in God's plans

The chief thing we need to know about the future is that all things are to be summed up in Christ (Eph 1:10). He is the future, and our supreme hope is to be with him and in him and like him forever (Phil 3:20-21).

In fact, Christ sums up our personal history as believers and includes it in the whole sweep of God's work in saving the world. Ephesians 1:4 speaks of pre-time; Ephesians 2:5-6 speaks of our salvation in time, while verse 6 also speaks of our salvation applied; 2:10 speaks of our life in time; 2:7 speaks of the future. All are "in Christ". So, too, is creation, which is through, in and by Christ.

The implications of all this are threefold. First, Jews and Gentiles are now on an equal footing. Both are "sealed with the promised Holy Spirit" (Eph 1:13), and both "have access in one Spirit to the Father" (2:18). The legal requirements of the Old Testament, which once created a barrier between Gentile and Jew (and hence between Gentile and God's blessing), are abolished in Christ (2:14-15). We thus belong to one another in a way that transcends all human distinctions.

Second, salvation is completely of God. It is no accident that the word "grace" becomes prominent in Ephesians 2:4-10, nor that the legal requirements are abolished in 2:14f. We are God's creation in Christ for good works, not our own creation by good works. Hence Paul refers to our election "before the foundation of the world" (1:4).

Third, we are reminded once more that the Christian hope is not an escape from creation, but a participation in God's renewed creation. Christ is the heir of all things, and by being in him we are joint heirs (Rom 8:17; 1 Cor 3:21-23).

Being "in Christ" identifies me completely with Christ's death

In a number of places, Paul mentions our union with Christ in his death and hence his resurrection (e.g. Rom 6:1-11; Gal 2:20). Vivid expressions such as those in Galatians 2:20 have led to the view that Paul was speaking of a form of mystical experience. A closer examination of context, however, reveals that his interest was otherwise. The chief point is his concern to safeguard justification by faith alone. It is only because we are in union with Christ through his death that we have any standing before God. This explains, too, his harsh words about certain people being "severed from Christ" (5:4). Apostasy in this case is not immorality or blasphemy; it is a repudiation of Christ's atoning death through the addition of our good works to his atoning death. Christ's justification and human justification were being mixed. That is why the Reformers spoke so strongly of "faith *alone*". We cannot add to the gospel without subtracting from it.

Being "in Christ" secures my completeness

The letter to the Colossians witnesses to another variation of the temptation to add to Christ. The danger here was adding a mixture of other spiritual practices in order to attain a higher spirituality. Paul's answer is the same: we are "in Christ".

He begins by expounding the majesty of Christ in the cosmos

and in redemption (Col 1:15-20). He insists that in Christ are hidden "all the treasures of wisdom and knowledge" (2:3), and, in words that could scarcely be grander, "in him the whole fullness of deity dwells bodily" (2:9). Christians, therefore, "have been filled in him" (2:10), and thus they have every spiritual blessing. You cannot have more than Christ; to attempt to have more is to endanger what you have. The Christian duty is to abide in Christ: "Therefore, as you received Christ Jesus the Lord, so walk in him, rooted and built up in him and established in the faith, just as you were taught, abounding in thanksgiving" (2:6-7). The great temptation to go 'beyond' Christ into a spirituality which seems attractive, with its ascetic disciplines and visions, is to be resisted. The old way of faith in Christ with thanksgiving remains the only way of Christian spirituality. Our devotion is faith and thanksgiving.

This completeness includes, of course, the gift of the Holy Spirit. Paul speaks of being "sealed with the promised Holy Spirit" (Eph 1:13), given to the Gentiles when they believe in Christ. Hence our access is "in one Spirit to the Father" (2:18). Not to have the Spirit of Christ is to be an unbeliever (Rom 8:9); to believe in Christ is to receive the Spirit (Gal 3:1-2).

All this lays the foundation for a proper understanding of good works in the Christian life. It would be impossible to be in Christ without good works as a result. That would be a denial of the Spirit. It is because our lives are "hidden with Christ in God" (Col 3:3) that we are to put to death the earthly and put on the garments of righteousness. To be in Christ is to be under his lordship, and his Spirit is at work in us to produce the fruit of obedience. Indeed, "godliness", rather than spirituality, is the genuine Christian piety. We are liberated from the cultivation of private spiritual ascetic exercises, including such things as flagellation, to engage in the task of being what Christ has made us in the world. The good works mentioned in Colossians 3, for example, are blessedly other-person-centred.

Being "in Christ" unites me with others

Our baptism in the Spirit unites us into the body of Christ (1 Cor 12:12-13). Being in Christ is a position of privilege because it unites me with those from whom I would be otherwise divided by class, race or sex, and enables me to bless them and to receive blessing from them through the service we render to one another. Not only does being in Christ divide me from those in Adam; it also unites me in sympathy and love with my fellow believers: "If one member suffers, all suffer together; if one member is honoured, all rejoice together" (12:26). It is our duty to maintain this unity which is given, since "There is one body, and one Spirit—just as you were called to the one hope that belongs to your call—one Lord, one faith, one baptism, one God and Father of all, who is over all and through all and in all" (Eph 4:4-6).

4. Conclusion

Our union with Christ, according to John Murray, "is really the central truth of the whole doctrine of salvation not only in its application but also in its once-for-all accomplishment in the finished work of Christ".[36] Certainly it focuses our whole attention on Christ and emphasizes the sheer graciousness of salvation. It teaches us, therefore, that God reaches out for us and draws us to himself, overcoming our all-too-natural sloth, indifference and hostility. His salvation does not stop short with the cross. He then proceeds to draw us to himself, unite us with our Saviour, and prepare us for our glorious future. In a sense, the rest of the subjects that we are now to study flow from this basic perspective.

---

36   J Murray, *Redemption Accomplished and Applied*, Banner of Truth Trust, 1979, p 161.

Key verse
For all who are led by the Spirit of God are sons of God. For you did not receive the spirit of slavery to fall back into fear, but you have received the Spirit of adoption as sons, by whom we cry, "Abba! Father!" (Rom 8:14-15)

Quotation
"Wherever God erects a house of prayer
The Devil always builds a chapel there:
And 'twill be found upon examination
The latter has the largest congregation." (Daniel Defoe [1661-1731])

Key terms
- Holy Spirit
- *Filioque*
- Economic Trinity
- Essential Trinity
- Union with Christ

For further thought
- What is the Holy Spirit's part in our salvation?
- "God himself cannot get you out of that chair. Only you can move your will and come to the front." Is this kind of evangelistic appeal appropriate? What would an alternative approach look like?
- What, if anything, is wrong with the idea that we must choose God if he is going to save us?
- Based on this chapter, is it possible for a church or ministry to place too much focus on the Spirit? What might this look like?
- What are the implications of being in union with Christ for our relationship with God? For our relationships with other believers?

- The '*filioque* clause' in the Nicene Creed says that the Spirit "proceeds from the Father and the Son". Are we diminishing the Spirit when we speak about him in this way?

For further reading
- Thirty-Nine Articles, article 5
- Bray, chapter 27
- Horton, chapters 9 and 11
- Milne, chapters 18-20

PART THREE

KNOWING THE SAVIOUR WHO IS LORD

- The exalted Lord summons his elect to faith and salvation through his word and Spirit.
- The saving response to the gospel word involves both faith and repentance.
- The exalted Lord by his grace justifies those who have faith in him alone.
- Salvation belongs to the Lord alone as he calls those whom he chooses.
- The life of faith is lived in the context of the world, the flesh and the devil, and under the cross of Christ.
- Christ is the Lord of the life of faith, as we follow him and keep his commandments.
- The life of faith is lived by the power of the Spirit of God and through faith in God.
- The life of faith is lived in the fellowship of the church of God.
- The life of faith is lived with the help of the ministry of the word of God.
- The life of faith is lived by hope in the coming of Christ the Lord.
- In the end, all will be raised, all will be judged, and God will be glorified.

17
—

THE LORD WHO SUMMONS

Key concept: The exalted Lord summons his elect to faith and salvation through his word and Spirit.

1. Introduction

If the initiative in salvation belongs to God, all the more so because we are "dead in ... trespasses and sins" (Eph 2:1), how does his work of uniting us to the Saviour proceed? We have seen that it is linked in some way to the Holy Spirit, and we have seen that our union with Christ exhibits the impact of death and resurrection which we see in Jesus. But we are left with the difficulty of how this relates to our humanity, and whether God's grace is so irresistible that it simply turns us inside out without our having the slightest clue as to how it has happened.

Let us begin to think about these issues by considering again the nature of God's saving word.

We have already noted that, alongside the Bible's strong emphasis on God's grace, there exists a powerful emphasis on human responsiveness. In particular we observe that, just as in the relationships between people, language plays an indispensable role, so too in God's relationship with us he does not bypass language, but uses it as his medium of communication. Indeed, in the word of God itself, we can see a wonderful variety and beauty of words, and we can take pleasure from the way God relates to us so appropriately. It seems that he fits his gracious approach to our capacity to respond.

It is not surprising, then, to discover that the way God chooses to save us is through his word and the power of his Spirit. In older literature this was described as his 'effectual calling':

Q: What is effectual calling?

A: Effectual calling is the work of God's almighty power and grace, whereby (out of his free and special love to his elect, and from nothing in them moving him thereunto) he doth, in his accepted time, invite and draw them to Jesus Christ, by his word and Spirit; savingly enlightening their minds, renewing and powerfully determining their wills, so as they (although in themselves dead to sin) are hereby made willing and able freely to answer his call, and to accept and embrace the grace offered and conveyed therein.[37]

Our responses are shaped by the impact of God's word and God's Spirit. So, too, the nature of the Christian life—including the church, the sacraments and the ministry. What is this 'effectual call' of God? It has to do not with such ideas as being called into a particular job or opportunity, but with the way in which God calls us to himself through the power of his word blessed by his Spirit.

---

37 The Westminster Larger Catechism, question 67. The Westminster Larger Catechism is widely available online, including at the Christian Classics Ethereal Library website (ccel.org/ccel/anonymous/westminster2.html).

2. The powerful word

We first come across the concept of God's word in creation, where in Genesis 1 all things come to life from his speech. This is taken to be a sign of his power, since it is by speech alone that he accomplishes all things. The creation is sustained by the word of God (Ps 119:89-91; Heb 1:3), and his word sanctifies creation to our use by declaring it to be good (1 Tim 4:4-5). The same word which created and sustains the universe has promised a new creation and holds back the future judgement so that people may be saved (2 Pet 3:5-9).

The garden of Eden was also the scene of God's word directed to Adam and Eve, under which rule they were intended to live out their lives. But doubt was cast on God's word, and by the same word they were expelled. In re-asserting his rule by redemption, God chose to use the instrument of the covenant: a word of promise. Kingdom is exercised through covenant, and the original pattern restored, in part at least. The law also expressed God's covenant rule over his wayward people, as did the prophets and writings.

It was the prophetic teaching—thoroughly endorsed by the mass of Old Testament thought—that God's word, unlike human speech, is infallibly powerful in its effects:

> "For as the rain and the snow come down from heaven
>   and do not return there but water the earth,
> making it bring forth and sprout,
>   giving seed to the sower and bread to the eater,
> so shall my word be that goes out from my mouth;
>   it shall not return to me empty,
> but it shall accomplish that which I purpose,
>   and shall succeed in the thing for which I sent it."
> (Isa 55:10-11)

Against this background, John identifies the Son of God as the Word of God through whom all things were made (John 1:3). In so doing, he not only throws light on the status of the Son, but binds creation and redemption together—the Redeemer is the Creator—and makes the same point as Paul in 2 Corinthians 1:20: "For all the promises of God find their Yes in him". Christ is the power and the content of the word of God. He *is* the Word whom God now and always directs to the human race.

3. The gospel word

The gospel of God was promised beforehand in the Scriptures and committed to the apostles. Its content concerns "[God's] Son, who was descended from David according to the flesh and was declared to be the Son of God in power according to the Spirit of holiness by his resurrection from the dead, Jesus Christ our Lord" (Rom 1:3-4). In accordance with all we have noted about God's word, Paul goes on to assert that the gospel is "the *power* of God for salvation to everyone who believes, to the Jew first and also to the Greek" (1:16).

The gospel as Jesus preached it contained the same inherent claim. In proclaiming the kingdom (Mark 1:15), he was re-asserting the sovereignty of God's word and inviting his hearers to place themselves under God's rule through repentance and faith. It was clearly through the instrumentality of the word that God's blessing came upon those to whom Christ ministered. In the parable of the sower, the seed scattered abroad is identified as the word of God, and the various soils respond in accordance with how the word takes root (or fails to do so). In the good soil, the word brings forth a hundredfold yield, having been received with "an honest and good heart" (Luke 8:8, 15).

In biblical terms, nothing can replace the word as a source of gospel blessing. It is interesting to note Paul's specific disclaimer in 1 Corinthians 1:17: "For Christ did not send me to baptize but to preach the gospel …" Churches or evangelists that fail to note the significance of God's word in his work of salvation will be a curse rather than a blessing, because they will intrude other methods of salvation into the process by which we come to know God and leave many religious people in complete darkness:

> How then will they call on him in whom they have not believed? And how are they to believe in him of whom they have never heard? And how are they to hear without someone preaching? And how are they to preach unless they are sent? ... So faith comes from hearing, and hearing through the word of Christ. (Rom 10:14-15, 17)

The so-called 'mainline' churches of the West were, and in some places still are, especially prone to mistakes in this area, since they have had (until recently) a large nominal population, and have rested content on the normal rites of admission. For them, "preaching the gospel" has sounded somewhat disreputable, like "conversion" and being "born again". But the same problem can also afflict an upfront growth-oriented church, where the word of God can be supplanted by programs, events, spectaculars and insidious perversions which stroke the ego rather than save the person.

The content of the word of God is the kingdom; it is also Christ as Lord. But because the offer of the gospel at its very centre is forgiveness, it is possible also to define the gospel as Paul does by calling it "Christ crucified" (1 Cor 1:23). Christ casts out the ruler of the world by his death (John 12:31) and so he is Lord through the cross.

Many would place the emphasis of the gospel offer elsewhere than on forgiveness—for example, on abundant life, or the Holy Spirit, or health, peace, good family relations, or being born again. And indeed the New Testament writers used different expressions: for example, John speaks often of "eternal life"; Paul is more likely to refer to "righteousness" or "reconciliation". But if the apostolic preaching in Acts offers any clue, *forgiveness* is the essence, for each of these other ways of putting things also rests upon the turning away of God's wrath and the receiving of his acceptance and mercy.

Nonetheless, the gospel does more than merely declare God's forgiveness. It invades a person's life and brings them to new birth, new life, a new era of existence, a new way of seeing reality. If we are to be saved, it will have to be through the revolution of moving from being in Adam to being in Christ—from the old to the new. We must be moved from the old age of sin and death to the new age of abundant life and the Spirit of God. We must be transferred from the kingdom of darkness to the kingdom of God's beloved Son. We must become a new creation. We must cease to be dead in sins and become alive together with Christ. We must enter the age to come and find our lives hidden with Christ in God.

You will recognize the expressions in the last paragraph as being some of the ways that the New Testament speaks of the impact of becoming a child of God. The general name for this in theology is 'regeneration' (or 'new birth'). The word reminds us of the total renewal of all things (Matt 19:28),[38] as well as the individual's passage from death to life (Titus 3:5). The two are connected, for what happens to the individual here and now is a prelude to and preparation for the renewal of all things at the end: it is the future invading the present. It is obvious that without regeneration a person is not saved, for he or she would be unfit for the future:

> "Truly, truly, I say to you, unless one is born of water and the Spirit, he cannot enter the kingdom of God. That which is born of the flesh is flesh, and that which is born of the Spirit is spirit." (John 3:5-6)

If we observe the richness of the biblical presentation (such as putting off "the old self" and putting on "the new self" in Colossians 3), we can speak of regeneration as being a process rather than an event. Calvin seems to have used the word thus. But in subsequent

---

38 The Greek word *palingenesia*, translated in the ESV as "new world", literally means 'regeneration' or 'renewal'.

use the word has been restricted to refer to the point at which a person passes from the old to the new. This is legitimate, as there is a need to focus on that moment so that we can appreciate the contrast between old and new: "Therefore, if anyone is in Christ, he is a new creation. The old has passed away; behold, the new has come. All this is from God ..." (2 Cor 5:17-18).

It is for this reason that we need to remind ourselves again of the spiritual danger posed by much church life. Where the need for regeneration is not understood, or the means which God characteristically employs are not appreciated, the church has no interest in distinguishing between 'nice people' and 'new people' (to modify CS Lewis's distinction).[39] Indeed, since the new people are not necessarily 'nice', there is sometimes a tendency in churches to ignore them, or worse. We are certainly capable of judging people by the wrong criteria (1 Cor 11:17-22; Jas 2:1-7).

Another common misunderstanding (with consequent errors) is to forget that regeneration is God's work; "all this is from God" (2 Cor 5:18). It is true that he uses human ambassadors, and that he seeks repentance and faith. But the ambassadors are simply his instruments, and the repentance and faith arise from the work of his word and Spirit. It is all of him. If we fail to recognize this, we confuse regeneration with conversion, the divine work with the human response. The consequence is that we exalt human activity and open the way to psychological manipulation in evangelism and too intense an introspection in spiritual life. God is free to bring an infant to new birth (and I believe he frequently does); that child will then respond to the word of God as it progressively grows old enough to do so. Sometimes the child will even have a conversion experience of conscious repentance and faith; but although this experience may be of great significance, it will not be the same as

---

39 See CS Lewis, *Mere Christianity*, HarperCollins, 2018. Book 4, chapter 10 is titled 'Nice people or new men'.

regeneration or be the point of salvation.

If God does bring an infant to new birth by his Spirit (and see Luke 1:15, concerning John the Baptist), that is not his stated and ordinary means, for in normal terms regeneration is attributed both to his Spirit and his word: "You have been born again, not of perishable seed but of imperishable, through the living and abiding word of God ... this word is the good news that was preached to you" (1 Pet 1:23, 25; cf. Jas 1:21).

In John 3, Jesus delineates the work of the Spirit in bringing new birth.[40] Furthermore, Paul attributes enlightenment and new life to the Spirit of God. According to him, we have come to life by the Spirit (Gal 5:25). He describes the Spirit as being given "that we might understand the things freely given us by God"; he goes on: "And we impart this in words not taught by human wisdom but taught by the Spirit, interpreting spiritual truths to those who are spiritual" (1 Cor 2:12-13; cf. 2 Cor 3:1-6).

Some have concluded from the New Testament emphasis that there is a special ministry of revelation given to the Spirit in the new era of Christ. This ministry supplements or bypasses the Scriptures and some (or all) Christians receive messages from God in appropriately spiritual ways—through leadings, dreams, visions, voices and so on. It is often thought that this is what Paul means when he speaks of being led by the Spirit.

In making such a point, however, two highly significant factors are overlooked:

a. In a number of places in Scripture, the word of God is described in such a way as to remind us that it is *God's* word, and therefore powerful and self-fulfilling in its own right. I have already mentioned Isaiah 55:11, but we should also consider Hebrews 4:12-13: "For the word of God is living and

---

[40] It is extremely doubtful that by "water" in this passage he means Christian baptism as such (see Ezek 36:25-27).

    active, sharper than any two-edged sword ..." Whatever view we take of the relationship between word and Spirit, it must not result in us despising the word as impotent or lifeless. We should also notice the seamless transition between verse 12, where God's word is described, and verse 13, where God himself is described. Whatever God's word does, God does.

  b. There is in any case the strongest of connections between word and Spirit in the Bible. The Holy Spirit inspires Scripture. Prophets speak by the inspiration of the Spirit. Jesus speaks of God's word thus: "For he whom God has sent utters the words of God, for he gives the Spirit without measure" (John 3:34). In another place Jesus puts the relationship even more closely: "It is the Spirit who gives life; the flesh is no help at all. The words that I have spoken to you are spirit and life" (6:63). In Paul's vivid metaphor, "the sword of the Spirit ... is the word of God" (Eph 6:17).

In sum, it is a serious mistake to sever word and Spirit; to be led by the Spirit is to be led by the word, which is the product of the Spirit's work. When Paul describes the Spirit's illuminating work in 1 Corinthians 2, he does so without doubt in the context of the ministry of God's word: "my speech and my message were not in plausible words of wisdom, but in demonstration of the Spirit and of power, so that your faith might not rest in the wisdom of men but in the power of God" (vv 4-5).

4. The preaching of the word

The new creation is from God, but he commits the reconciling word through which it comes to his human ambassadors. It is their task to preach or herald the word. Preaching is not so much a method as a reminder that the word is a declaration of news and a summons to repentance. It does not require a 20-minute monologue from a carved pulpit; the word can be preached in far less formal ways.

But the idea of preaching preserves the nature of the communication—namely, that it is a message, not a discussion; a declaration, not a question; a summons, not a debate. That is not to downplay the importance and usefulness of discussion, question and debate in Christian communication, but to remind us of its essence.

Preaching is a human activity, but even here we have not reached a peculiarly 'human' side of the process of salvation. It is an activity carried out at the behest of God, with the message of God, in the strength of God, and looking for results from God:

> What then is Apollos? What is Paul? Servants through whom you believed, as the Lord assigned to each. I planted, Apollos watered, but God gave the growth ... For we are God's fellow workers. You are God's field, God's building. (1 Cor 3:5-6, 9)

The ambassador is accountable to God, as is the listener. But it is God's work. Not surprisingly, the New Testament reminds us that it is carried on with prayer (e.g. Acts 6:4).

The ambassador is accountable both for content and method. The content must be Jesus Christ (1 Cor 1:23, 3:11), and this means none other than the scriptural Christ. Hence the chief business of the teacher is to expound the Scriptures which enshrine the Saviour. But the method must accurately reflect the one who said, "I am the way, and the truth, and the life" (John 14:6). It must honour the truth; it may not pervert it, add to it, or subtract from it. It must honour its audience by eschewing manipulation or trickery:

> We have renounced disgraceful, underhanded ways. We refuse to practice cunning or to tamper with God's word, but by the open statement of the truth we would commend ourselves to everyone's conscience in the sight of God. (2 Cor 4:2)

Indeed, the preacher's business is to centre on Jesus Christ, "with ourselves as your servants" (2 Cor 4:5).

Preaching is a spiritual task, to be conducted with spiritual means. It is the way in which God releases those who are captive to the evil one and enlightens the blind, and it must not be imagined that the power resides in rhetorical skill or personality. And yet God sees fit to use the personality which he has created. Therefore, the preacher's business involves such things as careful preparation and delivery.

How does the preacher know who to address? How can he tell whom God intends to call through his words? There is no real problem here. God has issued a general call to the whole race: "he commands all people everywhere to repent" (Acts 17:30). Jesus said to go into all the world. It is our task to publish his word abroad; it is his to bless as he sees fit, with his 'effectual call'. This means that we can be armed with great confidence: we do not have to make converts; we need only to preach, pray and trust in God.

5. Conclusion

We have begun to see more clearly the way in which the foundational doctrines of God and salvation impinge on the way we relate and behave. Clearly our methods ought to reflect the truth about God and his gospel, but often they fail as we are simply instinctive or pragmatic in our responses. Here is where the continued reformation of the church must begin!

———

Key verse

"For as the rain and the snow come down from heaven
    and do not return there but water the earth,
making it bring forth and sprout,
    giving seed to the sower and bread to the eater,

so shall my word be that goes out from my mouth;
   it shall not return to me empty,
but it shall accomplish that which I purpose,
   and shall succeed in the thing for which I sent it." (Isa 55:10-11)

Quotation

"The only promise I try to make to my readers, however inadequately carried out, is that of unoriginality. I hope to present nothing whatever original in these pages. This is not an effort at comedy." (Thomas C Oden, *Systematic Theology*)

Key terms

- Effectual calling
- Regeneration
- Conversion
- Rebirth
- Evangelism
- New life

For further thought

- Describe some of the dangers involved in separating Spirit and word.
- How does the New Testament use the concept of 'calling'? How should this shape our use of the word to speak of God's work in our lives?
- Where do we see the power of words at work in human affairs and relationships? How is God's word like ours? How is it different?
- Can a child be born regenerate? What might we expect such a child's experience of faith and conversion to look like?
- Why is preaching important to Christianity? How does an awareness that regeneration is God's work coexist with a commitment to careful preparation for Bible teaching?

- Think about your church or sphere of ministry. How might the principles outlined in this chapter bring continued reformation to these ministries?

For further reading
- For chapters 17-25 of this book, see *Concise Theology*, part 3
- Westminster Confession, chapter 10
- Horton, chapter 10

18

THE LORD WHO SUMMONS: OUR RESPONSE

Key concept: The saving response to the gospel word involves both faith and repentance.

1. Introduction

Christ Jesus saves us once for all by his death for us on the cross. But the saving work of God includes the application of that redemption to the individual. As we have seen in the previous chapter, this involves his summons to us through his gospel word, blessed by his Spirit to bring us regeneration or new life. Our salvation is all of grace.

But the word of God also calls us to repentance and faith. We cannot respond without regeneration, but by the power of the Spirit we are able to exercise repentance and faith. This moment is often called 'conversion', although for many people they may not be aware of any specific time when they came to know the Lord. The key question is not "When were you converted?" but "Are you now converted?" That is, are you now living in a relationship with the

Lord in which you experience repentance and faith? Are you living the life of faith?

2. Responsibility

When we study the subject of the human response to the word of God, there is scope for two broad failures.

In the first place, we may over-emphasize the power of God at the expense of the reality of the human personality. The approach adopted in this book—with its method of beginning with God and his work—must guard against this error. It may easily be assumed that, so all-encompassing is God's work, there is nothing left for human responsibility or action. Such a view can even lead to universalism, in which we are saved without knowing it—conversion is simply the discovery of our already-saved condition.

But the more usual error is to seek to overestimate the spiritual capacity of the person at the expense of God's power. To this way of thought, sovereignty resides in the human will, and the best work of God cannot change the will to make it conform with his. Through our prayer and God's work, circumstances may conspire to allow the gospel to lay siege on the sinner's heart; but the citadel cannot be taken unless its ruler voluntarily surrenders. The question is then raised whether anyone will be saved, for which human will is good enough to choose God?

The Bible adopts a different course. It endorses divine sovereignty *and* human responsibility: "work out your own salvation with fear and trembling, for it is God who works in you, both to will and to work for his good pleasure" (Phil 2:12-13). Just as God rules the world by using the capacity and nature of the things he has created, but remains nonetheless intimately involved with creation at every point, so he rules us. He does not bypass the will; he renews it and so enables it to choose aright. He respects his creation while righting it.

Just as a strong doctrine of God's sovereignty over nature can be abused and become a reductionist scientific atheism, so this doctrine of the human person can be abused in a secularizing psychology. It is true that psychology may give a very full account of conversion. It can examine the mindset of the convert, it can analyse the circumstances, it can show why one speaker was powerful and another weak; it can even discuss the effects of massed choirs. There is no need whatever to dispute any of this—God is not absent from his world, and he uses the ordinary to achieve the extraordinary. And yet problems arise when such descriptions are thought to 'explain' what has happened. Even concerning non-Christian conversions of various kinds, we may object to this inadequate approach; where Christian conversion is concerned, it seems blatantly reductionist. It leaves God out, and it presupposes that God is thought of as merely one cause among many rather than the Lord of all the factors involved. It is as if a chemical analysis of paper was thought sufficient to explain a message printed on the paper.

In fact, as we know, God did not choose to convert everyone mystically and spontaneously. The incarnation is testimony to his determination to save the world in accordance with the way in which he created it. So, too, is the fact that Jesus preached: God approaches us in human language (indeed in a specific, time-determined human language) and thereby obliges us to listen and to respond as human beings, in line with our own nature and capacity. He took the steps involved in this exercise, including that of committing the message to the uncertainties of writing and transmission. His chief messengers were not angelic spirits but men of flesh and blood.

Not only was the method used to bring us to know God appropriate to our humanity; so was the response sought: "Jesus came into Galilee, preaching the gospel of God, and saying, 'The time is fulfilled, and the kingdom of God is at hand; repent and believe in the gospel'" (Mark 1:14-15). From the human side, the gospel is to be received by repentance and faith. Indeed, such a gospel could only be responded to in this way. Sometimes Scripture mentions one of these, at other times the other; but it consistently seeks for these as the crucial elements in response: together they make up 'conversion', and, so close is the relationship between them that one may stand for both: faith involves repentance, and repentance involves faith. Much more needs to be said about our response to God, but repentance and faith lie at the centre of it, and we must begin by closely examining the summons to such a conversion.

3. Repentance

As we have been reminded, the ministry of Jesus began with the call to repentance (Mark 1:15). This was also the substance of the message of his predecessor, John the Baptist (1:4). When Peter preached on the day of Pentecost, his sermon issued in a call to repentance (Acts 2:38). Paul summarized his teaching in Ephesus like this:

> "I did not shrink from declaring to you anything that was profitable, and teaching you in public and from house to house, testifying both to Jews and to Greeks of repentance toward God and of faith in our Lord Jesus Christ." (Acts 20:20-21)

What is 'repentance'? Why is it so important? Clearly such a central idea must be carefully understood, and the Christian preacher today is in dereliction of his duty if he fails to teach his flock what it means and to exhort their compliance. Yet there are false and inadequate views as to its meaning, and much preaching which lacks this note of summons and challenge.

The word itself

The Greek word *metanoia* originally meant 'later knowledge'. In due course, it began to bear the meaning of 'change of mind', 'change of feelings'; in cases where the earlier view was foolish or improper, the idea of 'regret' or 'remorse' came in. But this was not necessarily about a change of ethics or behaviour; "the reference is always to an individual instance of change of judgement or remorse in respect of a specific act which is now no longer approved".[41] There is, therefore, no suggestion of "an alteration in total moral attitude"; the Greek language "has no knowledge of *metanoia* as repentance or conversion in the sense found in the OT and NT".[42]

The biblical development

In the great covenant-speech at the end of Deuteronomy, Moses warned the people of the anger of the Lord and the consequences to them of disobedience. Yet the way of blessing is also open if they "return to the LORD your God, you and your children, and obey his voice in all that I command you today, with all your heart and with all your soul …" (Deut 30:2). Here are various characteristics of the scriptural approach, namely the idea that people must "return" or "turn again" (cf. 1 Kgs 8:33) from that which makes repentance necessary, and also the central place of the Lord himself. The essence of biblical repentance is not remorse or regret for specific deeds as much as re-orientation of the whole of life toward God himself. Naturally, this involves confession and repudiation of specific offences, but there is much more to it than that. Indeed repentance is nothing else than faith from another point of view, in that it casts itself on Christ for mercy.

In Old Testament times, external forms, days and liturgies were vehicles of public repentance. There was a fierce prophetic attack on these forms, but not on the grounds that the external forms were themselves pernicious. Rather, the point of attack was that they

---

41 G Kittel (ed), *Theological Dictionary of the New Testament* (G Friedrich trans), vol 4, Eerdmans, 1976, p 973.
42 Kittel, *Theological Dictionary of the New Testament*, p 973.

were effectively cloaking unrepentant hearts (e.g. Isa 1:11-17). The outward display of religion is always good camouflage for impenitence (but so, too, is a self-righteous attack on the outward forms!).

Even in Deuteronomy, however, the need for sincerity was made clear. Moses affirms that "the LORD your God will circumcise your heart and the heart of your offspring, so that you will love the LORD your God with all your heart and with all your soul, that you may live" (Deut 30:6). Here the sign of circumcision is given its true meaning as a reference to a personality filled with love for God and desire to do his will. Here, too, repentance is spoken of as God's work and God's gift. This is the basis of that great Old Testament hope of renovation for God's people (see Jer 31:31f; Ezek 11:17-20, 36:26-27).

The teaching of the Old Testament adds nothing in essence. Repentance is not a feeling of sorrow, it is not a change of mind, and it is not a series of expiatory actions (although it may well contain all these); it is a radical turning of the whole person to God in submission. There is now a fresh urgency, however, imparted by the announcement of the coming kingdom (Mark 1:15; cf. Acts 17:30-31), and, most important of all, there is the presence of the new age in the death and resurrection of Jesus. In this action, and by the Holy Spirit, God fulfils his promise of the "circumcision ... of the heart" (Rom 2:29; cf. 8:3-4). Thus Peter and his colleagues understand that the experience of being baptized with the Holy Spirit is the demonstration of Christ's lordship and the gift of "repentance that leads to life" (Acts 11:18).

Paul draws these elements together in Romans 6:1-11, and shows how the fact of union with Christ in death and resurrection is the foundation of the Christian life:

> How can we who died to sin still live in it? Do you not know that all of us who have been baptized into Christ Jesus were baptized into his death? We were buried therefore with him

by baptism into death, in order that, just as Christ was raised from the dead by the glory of the Father, we too might walk in newness of life. (vv 2-4)

Note the twofold ways in which the doctrine of repentance proceeds:

a. Repentance is the gift of God (Acts 11:18); but it is also the obligation of all people (17:30-31).
b. Repentance is a unique event (Acts 2:38); but it is also the ongoing path of Christian obedience (Col 3:5f, 3:12f).
c. Repentance is the death of the old nature; but it is also the life of the new nature "being renewed in knowledge after the image of its creator" (Col 3:10); this is what some theologians refer to as 'mortification' and 'vivification'.

4. Faith

Biblical 'faith' is essentially the notion of reliance, dependence, trust. It includes, of course, 'belief' in the sense of the conviction that something or someone is true. But the concept involves necessarily the element of personal commitment which a word like 'trust' captures. It has been suggested, too, that a word like 'persuasion' may best be used, since we are talking of a great fact or a divine person persuading us of the truth in a way that claims our commitment and allegiance. Thus faith may be thought of as the persuasion, based on the evidence of the gospel of Jesus, that God is our Father and that he lovingly accepts us for Jesus' sake. Such a persuasion or conviction or knowledge is, indeed, 'faith'.

Just as repentance is both a gift and an obligation, so too is faith: "For by grace you have been saved through faith. And this is not your own doing; it is the gift of God ..." (Eph 2:8). Elsewhere, Paul thinks of our relationship with God as knowing God, and puts the gift/obligation aspect like this: "But now that you have come to know God, or rather to be known by God ..." (Gal 4:9).

Faith is accorded great power in Scripture: by faith, mountains may be moved (Mark 11:23); by faith, the mouths of lions may be stopped and great journeys undertaken (Heb 11:8, 33); by faith, even the ungodly may be justified (Rom 4:5). And yet, from another point of view, faith is weak. It is, after all, trust in (or on) another, and it is contrasted with works or deeds. The secret is, of course, that faith is only as powerful as the object of faith. The very reason for the choice of faith as our key response to the gospel is faith's weakness. Faith is humility. But its strength is immense *if* it depends on the immensely strong.

It follows from this observation that there is a necessary connection between faith and truth. Faith is only as good as its object. If we have faith in the wrong thing, it will harm us. Thus, for example, some people have faith in the stars, while others have faith in lucky charms or special numbers. Such faith may be much stronger, inwardly speaking, than many a Christian's faith. But because faith takes its strength from its object, even the most powerful confidence in something false is ultimately empty superstition. Indeed, the difference between faith and superstition is not in the person who exercises the trust but in the authenticity of what they have trust in.

This is what makes the current tendency to oppose faith and reason, or faith and science, so absurd. There is no moment in the day when we are not exercising faith (for example, in the person to whom I am married, or in the bank which holds my money, or in the chair on which I am sitting, or in the textbook I am reading). Sometimes our faith is misplaced; often faith has to go beyond immediately demonstrable evidence; sometimes faith is foolish. But, in the end, it can only succeed if it is well placed. And when it is, it is immensely fruitful.

A particularly common but damaging form of false faith or superstition is the idolatrous religious idea. The human mind is capable of many wrong notions about God; for example, the view that he does not punish. If one's trust is founded on such a God, it cannot amount to the saving faith of the gospel. This demonstrates the need for sound teaching in churches, for, although sound teaching cannot in itself create faith, saving faith cannot be enjoyed without the truth. Faith will always be stunted and ill-motivated where knowledge is lacking (cf. Col 1:9-10; 1 Cor 14:20). The same thing applies to the ill-informed idea of faith which dominates the 'prosperity gospel'. It is not based on the truth of God's word.

An illustration of this principle may be found in the experience of those who give up work to 'live by faith'—that is, without any obvious means of support. Apart from the drain on the Christian community that such persons must represent, their 'life of faith' is not godly because it is at odds with Scripture (2 Thess 3:6-13). The true life of faith is a life of obedience to the word of God. We live by faith at all times, in paid employment or not, because the whole of the Christian life should be the life of faith. It is focused on Jesus, but it is shaped by Scripture as the word of God. God will bless the life of faith that trusts his true revelation in Scripture.

Because the strength of faith arises from its object, Scripture puts little emphasis on the quantity of faith. Indeed, Jesus points out how little faith is required to do great things (Luke 17:5-6). The man of divided faith was fully blessed (Mark 9:24). This is not, of course, an excuse for weakness of faith or slackness in believing, for doubt is the source of sin (Gen 3:1).

At the heart of faith is assurance. Some would separate the two and describe a journey undertaken between faith and assurance, the initial movement toward God and the full rest of the person in the knowledge of his love. Such a movement may well be the testimony of many, and weakness of faith condemns others to stay in the shallows of Christian experience. Nonetheless, it is difficult to chart such a two-stage experience in Scripture, and it may reflect an initially faulty apprehension of the gospel. After all, Hebrews 11:1 defines faith as "the assurance of things hoped for, the conviction of things not seen".

If by assurance we mean the knowledge of God's fatherly love and forgiveness, there is one thing in particular which hinders a person from coming to this knowledge immediately on receiving the gospel: any remaining belief in the necessity of good works to save. As long as the person retains some degree of profound dependence on self, or alternatively some proud despair at the evil of one's own self (and hence an impossibility of salvation), assurance is not possible. True assurance, the birthright of every Christian, can only arise when it is recognized that God in Christ is our only hope in life and in death. We may claim the wonderful liberty of the children of God when we realize that all is from him and that the gospel is forgiveness, not achievement. That is assurance; but that, too, is saving faith.

I have intentionally introduced the idea of Christian liberty at this point, for we must now note the crucial, pivotal role played by faith in the doctrine of good works. Christian liberty is, first and foremost, forgiveness; that is the blessed, wonderful freedom from sin's penalty. We are now relieved from any necessity of keeping the law to achieve salvation. We are set free, instead, to do good works for the right reasons—for the love of God and of others, without any thought of reward. The greater our assurance of God's forgiveness, the greater our motive for pleasing God (Luke 7:47-50). Faith gladly believes the word of God, and believing fulfils its commandments. Only faith can be the source of true obedience.

It is not surprising, then, that faith and repentance are so closely allied in Scripture. In a real sense they are the same. Repentance contains an emphasis on turning away from sin, faith an emphasis on turning to the Saviour. But to turn from sin is useless without faith, and faith is useless without a radical repentance of heart and mind. A response to the gospel which does not conclude with a person fully committed to Christ—trusting him as Saviour and ready to obey him as Lord—is not a saving response. The suggestion of an older and defective piety that we could make Christ Saviour in the first instance and Lord second is totally erroneous.

Repentance and faith amount to conversion. There are, of course, different conversions open to the human personality, of which Christian conversion is but one. It is worth noting that a spiritual experience labelled 'conversion' and given a Christian gloss does not necessarily entail salvation. Conversion and regeneration are not identical, although they may occur together; or, more precisely, regeneration will bear fruit in conversion (Titus 3:3-7). Conversion to Christ is essential as the start of the Christian life, but it is the product of regeneration and must be made of true repentance and faith. The real question is not whether and when we were 'converted' but whether we are now trusting Christ.

Baptism is related to repentance as an outward sign. But it is a sign of the gospel before it is a sign of repentance. In short, it 'preaches' the gospel with its action of washing in God's threefold name, and submitting to baptism is the mark of submission to God. As such, it is edifying; when baptism becomes the gospel rather than a sign of the gospel, it becomes a superstition, and instead of preaching the gospel it obscures the gospel.

5. Conclusion

This chapter began by raising the question of divine sovereignty and human responsibility. Neither should be denied; both must be affirmed strongly, although the sovereign grace of God must be firmly protected. Once we have understood this, we can move on to the first blessing of faith and repentance—namely, justification, the subject to which we now turn.

Key verse

"The times of ignorance God overlooked, but now he commands all people everywhere to repent, because he has fixed a day on which he will judge the world in righteousness by a man whom he has appointed; and of this he has given assurance to all by raising him from the dead." (Acts 17:30-31)

Quotation
"The cross is laid on every Christian ...When Christ calls a man, he bids him come and die." (Dietrich Bonhoeffer, *The Cost of Discipleship*)

Key terms
- Repentance
- Divine sovereignty
- Human responsibility
- Mortification
- Vivification
- Assurance
- Liberty
- Baptism

For further thought
- What is the difference between regeneration and conversion?
- How do God's works in salvation show "his determination to save the world in accordance with the way in which he created it"?
- How would you strengthen faith?
- How should the Christian respond to the comment, "I wish I had your faith"?
- Describe the connection between faith and knowledge.
- How would you respond to the claim that a person may have Christ as Saviour without having him as Lord?

For further reading
- Westminster Confession, chapters 14-15
- Bray, chapter 28

19

THE SAVING LORD WHO JUSTIFIES

Key concept: The exalted Lord by his grace justifies those who have faith in him alone.

1. Introduction

"The saying is trustworthy and deserving of full acceptance, that Christ Jesus came into the world to save sinners" (1 Tim 1:15). With this simple sentence, Paul gets to the heart of what Christianity is all about. Despite the complexities of theology, ethics, apologetics and so on, it is a religion of salvation—the salvation of sinners, saved by Jesus Christ. Not long after, Paul adds, "For there is one God, and there is one mediator between God and men, the man Christ Jesus, who gave himself as a ransom for all, which is the testimony given at the proper time" (2:5-6).

We have seen that God graciously saves sinners by regenerating them and uniting them with his Son, Jesus. We have seen that he does this through his forgiveness-offering word blessed by his Spirit. But this still leaves unanswered questions about how this is consistent with his righteousness and how it ties in with the death of Jesus on the cross. We may indeed be saved from sin by the loving Father, but in some sense our conscience remains uneasy. Is there not more for us to do? In other ways, our conscience may deceptively start to commend us: Can we not approach God with our consecrated lives and so pacify both him and our conscience? Will this not be the meaning of our lives from now on?

2. The judgement seat

It is easy to lose sight of the basic facts of our existence and hence to miss the heart of the gospel. Almost from the beginning, the human race has launched itself into history alienated from God and dead in trespasses and sins. But history is purposeful; it is moving towards God's appointed end, and part of that end is the judgement of God. Of course it is true that we live beneath that judgement now, and that it is adverse already (e.g. John 3:36). But God's great patience is awaiting the end, the final judgement at which the secrets of people's hearts will be disclosed, and he will deliver his ultimate verdict on each individual. Paul calls this part of his gospel (Rom 1:16-18), and he extends its effects to the Jew and the Gentile—that is, to the whole world.

Paul uses the phrase "the wrath of God". This wrath is operative now in the course of history, as was made clear when the Lord banished Adam and Eve from Eden into a life of struggle, pain and death (Gen 3:14-19). In Romans 1, we learn that God's wrath has been revealed in the present age as he "gave [people] up" to their idolatry and suppression of the truth about him (vv 24, 26, 28). But it is also "the wrath to come", which is stored up for the final judgement (1 Thess 1:10). There are those who wish to distance God from wrath as though anger is unworthy of him, but to do so they must expunge whole sections of the Old Testament and overlook the argument of the epistle to the Romans. The Bible unashamedly speaks of hell as the destination of sinners who are under the wrath of God (e.g. Matt 25:41-46; 2 Thess 1:8-9); if we find this to be a problem, it is because our own perceptions are shaped by sinful human ideas rather than by Scripture.

When we turn to the question of the standard of judgement, there is some confusion about the purpose of God's law. It is true that the law was given through Moses to the children of Israel after they were saved from Egypt. Thus we see that a leading purpose of the law of Moses was that God's saved people should live and prosper in accordance with its teaching.

Nonetheless, at its heart the law also embodies God's standard for all people everywhere. Murder, theft, idolatry, adultery and covetousness have always offended God, whether practised by those who knew the Mosaic law or not (e.g. Gen 9:6, 20:3-7). We can hardly explain the catalogue of sins in Romans 1:18-32 otherwise, especially with its conclusion: "Though they knew God's righteous decree that those who practice such things deserve to die, they not only do them but give approval to those who practice them" (v 32). These are pagan sins in the first instance; they would not be sins, however, if they were not transgressions of the will of God for humankind.

Thus the law given through Moses accomplishes four things (but does not alter the basic fact of sin and condemnation):

a. It brings precision to the definition of God's will, and hence to the definition of human sinfulness (5:13).
b. It inspires sinful human beings to greater depths of sin, even though it is in itself "holy and righteous and good" (7:7-12).
c. It reveals explicitly that the consequence of sin is condemnation, or death, a fact to which conscience had always borne witness (2:12-16).
d. It demonstrates the holiness of God, who is the author of such a perfect and righteous standard (3:2-6).

Paul argues, then, that all people, Jew and Gentile alike, "are under sin" (3:9), and he concludes that "whatever the law says it speaks to those who are under the law, so that every mouth may be stopped, and the whole world may be held accountable to God. For by works of the law no human being will be justified in his sight, since through the law comes knowledge of sin" (3:19-20). He has already quoted the psalmist on the point of human righteousness: "None is righteous, no, not one; no-one understands, no-one seeks for God" (3:10-11). When Paul is addressing the reality of human death, he does not cloak the bitterness involved: "The sting of death is sin, and the power of sin is the law" (1 Cor 15:56). We would not have much to fear from death, he says, were it not for the fact that we die as sinners; we would not have anything to fear from dying as sinners were it not for the power of the law—that is, the law's condemnation of sin.

3. Our appearance before the judgement seat

The Bible can speak so boldly of "the wrath to come" because it has so clear a picture of human hopelessness. We are ensnared by transgression. Not only have we offended God once or twice, though that is enough; not only have we engaged in evil deeds, though that is bad enough; not only have we had evil thoughts and spoken evil words, though that is bad enough; we have in fact become the slaves of sin and the enemies of our Creator, and we are quite incapable of saving ourselves. The disease has gone too long unchecked and every aspect of our personality is affected. We sin spontaneously and frequently.

That is why Scripture speaks in two ways about "good works". Of course, the Lord delights in goodness and requires of us works of goodness. But if they are done in order to make up for our failings, or presented to him in order to appease his wrath, or done while separate from him, they earn only his renewed condemnation and anger. Works done for the wrong motive, or out of alienation from God, are worse than useless. They compound the problems of being human: "If anyone else thinks he has reason for confidence in the flesh, I have more ... but whatever gain I had, I counted as loss for the sake of Christ" (Phil 3:4, 7); salvation is "not a result of works, so that no-one may boast" (Eph 2:9).

The perspective that "works of the law" are useless, or worse than useless, in commending us before God's judgement seat is deeply offensive to the human spirit. It speaks clearly of our weakness, which is not a pleasant thought for those nurtured to believe in personal superiority and effectiveness. It also exposes us to sharp moral critique, and we do not easily cope with the shame this engenders. Many are the ways, therefore, that human beings use to argue their own virtue; one of the most dangerous is the abuse of biblical religion (Luke 18:9-14).

But if Christianity is not moralism, neither is it a message of condemnation: "Christ Jesus came into the world to save sinners" (1 Tim 1:15). How do we have hope in the face of the righteous judgement of God?

4. Hope through judgement

It is notable that God's grace in the Old Testament provides a model for his salvation in the New Testament. He can be seen reaching out with salvation to the helpless and unlovely, the lost and hopeless. In case after case the arm of the Lord is extended in favour of the foolish and weak, and in ways which demonstrate that salvation belongs to the Lord alone. Gideon's success is founded on a tiny army which does not fight; Jericho is taken by distinctly unmilitary methods; David defeats Goliath; the blinded Samson defeats more enemies in his death than in his life; the children of Israel stand still by the sea to observes the destruction of their enemies—the Egyptian dead washed up on the seaside. Again and again, the same message is clear: God and God alone is Saviour.

All this is, of course, a prelude to the cross. It is impossible to imagine beforehand (or without the revelatory word of God) that such a foul method of execution would become the means of salvation of the world. Yet such is the case, and by the substitutionary death of the innocent victim on the cross, God brings salvation. At the heart of the cross is the issue of God's righteousness. It is undoubtedly true that "in his divine forbearance he had passed over former sins" (Rom 3:25), but the consistency of such forbearance with his justice still posed a problem. The Bible does not suggest that it is the way of God to forgive without a ground in his justice. But to demand justice of human beings is to demand what they cannot supply. The cross is God's answer: "It was to show his righteousness at the present time, so that he might be just and the justifier of the one who has faith in Jesus" (3:26).

But how is the achievement of the cross to be applied for the benefit of sinners? Two opposing ways have been suggested, a contrast which was at the heart of the Reformation.

In one, as the *Catechism of the Catholic Church* says, quoting the Council of Trent, justification "is not only the remission of sins, but also the sanctification and renewal of the interior man".[43] This righteousness, stemming from God and imparted to the sinner, now becomes the ground on which forgiveness continues.

In contrast, Reformation theology teaches that the benefit of the cross is applied by 'reckoning' or 'imputing' it (not by imparting it) to the sinner. The righteousness of God is given as a free gift to the sinful person and itself becomes the only true and proper ground on which forgiveness may occur.

In such a case, the way in which the gift is received becomes highly important. If the gift is conferred on those who deserve it, through good works, it loses its gift quality. The Bible declares,

---

43 Catholic Church, *Catechism of the Catholic Church*, paragraph 1989.

therefore, that such works, even ones inspired by God, have nothing to do with receiving the gift. Indeed they would distort the whole situation. On the contrary, the gift is to be received by faith, and by faith alone:

> If Abraham was justified by works, he has something to boast about, but not before God. For what does the Scripture say? "Abraham believed God, and it was counted to him as righteousness." Now to the one who works, his wages are not counted as a gift but as his due. And to one who does not work but believes in him who justifies the ungodly, his faith is counted as righteousness ... (Rom 4:2-5)

As we can see here, faith is the issue both in the Old and New Testaments. Abraham—together with all God's people who came before Christ—was justified by trusting in the promises of God, which pointed to Christ. We are justified by believing in the gospel word, which also points to Christ.

Since so much depends on faith, it is vital to understand what the Bible means by the faith which saves. We have already discussed the nature of faith at some length, but the following points will help to complete the picture:

a. Faith is not itself a good work substituted for all other good works because of our incapacity.
b. Faith is the opposite of a good work in this respect: it receives, it holds, it comes empty-handed. It is the quality which Jesus saw and valued in the people who had nothing. It is the one quality which gives God the glory. It is true worship.
c. Faith is the basic *relational* attitude; without it, no communion can take place. You must trust the one who speaks and promises.
d. Faith is not mere 'belief', although it certainly involves that. It is trust, confidence, assurance, even boldness.

e. Faith is isolated in this context. The emphasis must fall on faith *alone*, because to place the emphasis on, say, "faith working through love" is to reintroduce good works at precisely the most dangerous point. As far as salvation is concerned, we are saved by faith alone.
f. But faith is never alone. True faith grasps hold of the word of God with its promises and commands and fulfils them. Faith that is genuine is always accompanied by good works. This is why much of the remainder of this book looks at the good works that must form part of the Christian life. Indeed, it is why this entire project is called "the *life* of faith".

5. Justification by faith

In short, when we are faced with the problem of the judgement seat of God and our own standing in his sight, we find that acquittal is possible despite our guilt. The God who says "I will not acquit the wicked" (Exod 23:7) is the very one who, Paul says, "justifies the ungodly" (Rom 4:5).

Between these two contradictory statements is the cross.

It is on the grounds of the death of Christ that God remains just *and* gives his acquittal verdict to the unjust. The very form of the Greek word *dikaioō* ('to justify') joins in the testimony, since it reveals that God's action is indeed a declarative one. He does not create moral transformation before he can forgive; he forgives, and this leads to transformation.

Some draw a distinction between "forgiveness" as a negative, washing-away-sin type of thing, and "justification", which is the cloak of righteousness. There is, of course, a distinction, for one speaks of the personal and the other the public. But forgiveness is positive and joyful as is justification, and there is no need to contrast them in the way suggested. Both are powerful words for the brokenhearted and the sin-sick of heart. Both constitute the healing power of the gospel. If for me, sinful as I am, insignificant as I am, lost and lonely as I am, condemned as I am, there is at the very heart of the universe a word of forgiveness, a cloak of righteousness, I am the happiest of all persons.

As part of such wonderful, life-changing news, "justification by faith" may sound rather formal and stilted. But it is embodied to perfection in Jesus himself, who only sought for faith in those who came to him, and specifically and fervently welcomed "all who labour and are heavy laden" (Matt 11:28), declared God's blessing on the poor in spirit, and was himself known as "a friend of tax collectors and sinners" (11:19). What Paul taught, Jesus was. Even in his dying moment, he asked for forgiveness for his enemies and gave assurance to the dying thief (Luke 23:34, 43). In seeking justification, one seeks Jesus, for it is in him that all its riches may be found. He is the one "who became to us wisdom from God, righteousness and sanctification and redemption, so that, as it is written, 'Let the one who boasts, boast inf the Lord'" (1 Cor 1:30-31).

Discussion sometimes occurs on the topic of whether justification by faith is central to the gospel. The word 'central' is something of a trap, but as long as we begin our thinking with the judgement seat of God and perceive that everything for us depends upon a favourable verdict from God, we can scarcely be indifferent to the question of how this can occur. The doctrine of justification by faith exalts Christ, the cross, God's grace and his Spirit, and it attacks human pride and self-sufficiency. It is foundational for Christian obedience and it determines how we approach God personally and corporately. The Christ who is the gospel is the Christ of justification by faith and no other.

6. Conclusion

John Bunyan knew the wonder and joy of justification imputed to us through the death of Christ received by faith alone and not by good works. He describes his hero Christian thus:

> Now I saw in my dream, that the highway up which Christian was to go, was fenced on either side with a wall, and that wall was called *Salvation*. Up this way, therefore, did burdened Christian run, but not without great difficulty, because of the load on his back.
>
> He ran thus till he came at a place somewhat ascending; and upon that place stood a Cross, and a little below, in the bottom, a sepulchre. So I saw in my dream, that just as Christian came up with the Cross, his burden loosed from off his shoulders, and fell from off his back, and began to tumble, and so continued to do till it came to the mouth of the sepulchre, where it fell in, and I saw it no more.
>
> Then was Christian glad and lightsome, and said with a merry heart, 'He hath given me rest by his sorrow, and life by his death!' Then he stood still a while, to look and wonder, for it was very surprising to him that the sight of the Cross should thus ease him of his burden. He looked, therefore, and looked again, even till the Springs that were in his head sent the waters down his cheeks. Now as he stood looking and weeping, behold, three shining ones came to him, and saluted him with, 'Peace be to thee:' so the first said to him, 'Thy sins be forgiven thee;' the second stripped him of his rags, and clothed him with change of raiment; the third also set a mark on his forehead, and gave him a roll with a seal upon it, which he bid him look on as he ran, and that he should give it in at the celestial gate: so they went their way. Then Christian gave three leaps of joy, and went on singing ...[44]

---

[44] J Bunyan, *The Pilgrim's Progress*, Element Classics of World Spirituality, Element, 1997, pp 38-39.

Key verse
Now to the one who works, his wages are not counted as a gift but as his due. And to the one who does not work but believes in him who justifies the ungodly, his faith is counted as righteousness. (Rom 4:4-5)

Quotation
"The doctrines of religions are comprised in Jesus Christ and in Adam; and its morals in our native corruption and in grace." (Blaise Pascal)

Key terms
- Judgement
- Justification
- Faith (alone)
- Works of the law
- Imputed righteousness

For further thought
- God says, "I will not acquit the wicked" (Exod 23:7). Does the cross represent a change in God's attitude?
- Is 'justification by faith alone' part of the gospel message?
- What is the difference, if any, between forgiveness and justification?
- Is justification by works the Old Testament way and justification by faith the revelation of the New Testament? How were the Old Testament people of God saved?
- Consider the five 'solas' of the Reformation: Scripture alone, grace alone, faith alone, Christ alone, to the glory of God alone. How are these five elements related to each other?
- What is the relationship between our understanding of sin and our 'self-esteem'?

For further reading
- Thirty-Nine Articles, articles 11-14
- Westminster Confession, chapter 11
- Horton, chapter 12

20

THE SAVING LORD: HIS CHOICE

Key concept: Salvation belongs to the Lord alone as he calls those whom he chooses.

1. Introduction

I have already spoken of the joy of discovering that, insignificant, lost, lonely and sinful as we are, there is a true word that at the very heart of the universe forgiveness and reconciliation may be found, even for us. This true word comes from God and assures us that he is the Father who makes peace. We may experience the prodigal's delight in encountering as a Father the one who was for him, not against him, when he returned from the far country.

To what extent, however, is this great truth 'discovered'? Such a word suggests that the truth is hidden and that we voyage in search of it until we find it. The name of a 1977 television program on man's religious quest suggests the same thing: *The Long Search*. This attitude has continued to characterize many modern approaches to religion and spirituality in the decades since.

But the sort of Christianity which I have been describing is not a human search for God, but a response to God's initiative. He is the one who reveals himself, rather than being the one who is discovered at the end of a long search. That is not to deny the reality of the human search for God, or the fact that people come to him after longing to meet him. But the moment of encounter is shaped by circumstances of time, place and person which are of God's choosing rather than ours. Lydia met Paul at the place of prayer in Philippi, but they were there because of a vision from God (Acts 16:9), and Lydia's faith was God's gift: "The Lord opened her heart to pay attention to what was said by Paul" (16:14).

We have seen in the discussion of God's call (chapter 17) that although the initiative must belong to God, the human response of faith and obedience is not bypassed. The doctrine of grace, and, in particular, justification by faith, demonstrates the same truth. If God is to be exalted as the Saviour and human pride brought low, priority must be given to his work of acquitting the guilty; the human response of faith is the trust which draws its effectiveness and power from Christ himself.

All this, however, brings us to the question of choice: do we choose God, or does he choose us? In technical terms, we now turn to the doctrine of 'election'. In order to see it more clearly, our first study will be the preaching of the gospel as disclosed in 1 and 2 Thessalonians. In this we will see that we choose God because he first chooses us (cf. Gal 4:9; 1 John 4:19).

2. The preaching and reception of the gospel

The letters to the Thessalonians make a useful study for several reasons: they are brief; they are relatively simple; they reflect Paul's teaching and concerns for fairly recent converts; they contain important material on the subject. If we ask the question, "Who is regarded as being responsible for the gospel being received by the

Thessalonian Christians?", light is thrown on the problem of divine and human choice.

Broadly speaking, the material contains three answers.

a. Paul and his fellow workers are responsible

The gospel they brought was "our gospel" (1 Thess 1:5); the Thessalonians imitated the evangelists (1:6); the evangelists "had boldness ... to declare to you the gospel of God in the midst of much conflict" (2:2); they spoke "not to please man, but to please God" (2:4); they were "gentle" and "ready to share" with the Thessalonians (2:7-8); they toiled and laboured (2:9); they exhorted, encouraged and charged (2:11); salvation itself hangs on the evangelist's word (2:16); the work of the evangelist establishes the converts and supplies "what is lacking in [their] faith" (3:2, 10). Paul sees himself as instructing the converts and identifies his word with the word of God (4:2, 8; 2 Thess 2:15, 3:14-15).

There is no doubt that Paul worked very hard to evangelize the Thessalonians. He suffered persecution yet persevered with his ministry, and he ensured that the message he gave was pure and accurate. The mere fact of election did not prevent him from labouring with all his might to see that the gospel was preached.

b. The Thessalonians themselves are responsible

Paul praises his readers for the example they set when they "received the word in much affliction", which resulted in them becoming an example to believers in the region and their faith in God going forth everywhere (1 Thess 1:6-8). When the message came, they "turned to God from idols to serve the living and true God" (1:9); they "accepted it not as the word of men but as what it really is, the word of God" (2:13). Paul was so concerned lest they be tempted to fall away that he "sent to learn about [their] faith" (3:5); he exhorts them to love the brethren "more and more", and to work with their hands (4:10-11). Those who did not believe were those who "refused to love the truth and so be saved" (2 Thess 2:10).

The very fact of Paul's letters, with their exhortations, warnings, reminders and rebukes, is a testimony to the responsibility of his converts. Christianity depends upon the word and the response it generates in precisely this way, and neither believers nor unbelievers can blame God for failure in themselves.

c. God is responsible

Notwithstanding (a) and (b), however, there is no doubt whatever about the proven and substantial responsibility of God in the preaching and reception of the word. Even the passages given above are frequently to be found in a wider context which attributes the salvation of the Thessalonians to God.

Thus, the faith, love and hope of the Thessalonians provoke Paul to thank God (1 Thess 1:2-3). The gospel came to them in word, "but also in power and in the Holy Spirit and with full conviction" (1:5); the joy of the Thessalonians was inspired by the Holy Spirit (1:6); the courage of the evangelists was "in our God", and the gospel itself is not a human invention but is "of God" (2:2, etc.), indeed, it was accepted "not as the word of men but as what it really is, the word of God", an active word that is "at work in you believers" (2:13). The love that the Christians show to one another has been taught to them by God (4:9).

There are three noteworthy features of these and other passages from within the two epistles.

First, there is a sense of God's control of history. The response of the Thessalonians is merely part of the wider flow of God's dealings with the world. There is nothing like a complete exposition of "salvation history" here, but the Jewish response to Jesus and the prophets, and their opposition to gospel preaching, is "so as always to fill up the measure of their sins"; to this Paul adds, "But God's wrath has come upon them at last!" (2:16). Furthermore, "the day of the

Lord" is to be preceded by "the rebellion" and by the coming of a mysterious figure known as "the man of lawlessness"; there is a restraint working in history "so that he may be revealed in his time" (2 Thess 2:2-6).

Second, there is the fact of prayer. Again and again, by petition and by thanksgiving, Paul roots the attitudes and behaviour of the Thessalonians to God's work in them by praying that they will exhibit certain traits or by expressing gratitude for what he sees. There is no doubt that he believes in the efficacy of prayer, and that he believes fully that God overrules, changes and even sends "a strong delusion" (2 Thess 2:11) on the human heart. Yes, prayer is a human activity; but the power of prayer is God, and so we are necessarily involving his control.

Third, there is the fact of election. If the success of the gospel is ascribed so strongly to God, what does this say about the source of human salvation? Paul has no hesitation in ascribing the application of salvation to God: "For we know, brothers loved by God, that he has *chosen* you"—and the evidence for this is the power, the Holy Spirit and the full conviction that accompanied the word (1 Thess 1:4-5). The Thessalonians, Paul believes, are not going to fall, but why? "For God has not destined us for wrath, but to obtain salvation through our Lord Jesus Christ" (5:9). Clearest of all, however, are Paul's words in 2 Thessalonians 2:13-15, where God's choice that they may be saved issues in the call of God through the gospel, and hence their response. No wonder Paul immediately prays for them and refers to them as "beloved by the Lord" (v 13). In contrast, upon those who "refused to love the truth and so be saved", God sends "a strong delusion, so that they may believe what is false, in order that all may be condemned who did not believe the truth but had pleasure in unrighteousness" (vv 10-12).

3. God and his history

Paul's letters to the Thessalonians give an indication of how we should describe the work of God. If we change the focus to the whole of Scripture again, the story remains identical. God is seen as the Lord of history, one who organizes the affairs of humanity both on a large scale (e.g. Amos 9:7) and on an individual one (Prov 16:1, 4; 19:21).

It is fitting that Israel be reminded of the width of God's work, as in Amos 9:7, but the reminder is needed precisely because of the consistent focus on God's people. Israel is not the people of God by accident or by her own choice; she is the one God specifically chose for this role. Abraham the patriarch is chosen; so, too, individuals amongst his descendants, even surprisingly so (e.g. Gen 25:23). When succour was needed in time of famine, God chose the least of the brothers and over-ruled the history of their lives to bring salvation to pass. Human decisions—even *evil* human decisions—were woven into the purposes of God (Gen 45:7-8, 50:18-20). The covenant with Abraham provided the reference point for God's choice when release from Egypt was needed: the choice was in accordance with God's past promise, not in accordance with the virtue, wisdom, size or might of the people to be delivered. Indeed it seems more to have been the helplessness of the people which attracted God's grace (see Deut 7:6-11, 9:4-5; Ezek 16:1-14).

In the outworking of God's purposes, it is his dear Son who is "delivered up according to the definite plan and foreknowledge of God" (Acts 2:23). The crucifixion of Jesus is one of the necessities of history, for God had written it into the covenantal documents (e.g. Luke 24:25-27). Paradoxically, it was the elect people of God who were the instruments in the rejection of the beloved. Even here, however, just as Joseph's rejection led to blessing for all, Egypt and Israel alike, so now the rejection of the Messiah leads to astonishing blessing for the Gentiles, and ultimately, since "the gifts and the calling of God are irrevocable" (Rom 11:29), to the blessing of Israel as well. God's sovereign freedom cannot be controlled or computed—"he has mercy on whomever he wills, and he hardens whomever he wills" (9:18)—but nor will his stated purpose of salvation and blessing for the elect be lost: "a partial hardening has come upon Israel, until the fullness of the Gentiles has come in. And in this way all Israel will be saved …" (11:25-26).

The Bible tells us that God has "a plan for the fullness of time", which is "to unite all things in [Christ], things in heaven and things on earth" (Eph 1:10). The same passage describes God as the one "who works all things according to the counsel of his will" (1:11), and refers specifically to the way in which he has, by his mighty power, incorporated both Jews and Gentiles into salvation (1:12-14). In short, the Christian hope of the fulfilment of all things in Christ rests upon the power and goodwill of God as revealed to us. We believe that he is going to accomplish the glorious climax of all history. But such a climax can only be achieved if he is in fact the one who over-rules human dispositions and plans to achieve his perfect goal. Our hope depends upon his willing capacity to do this.

4. God and his people

All things are to be summed up in Christ; every knee is to bow to him. But the division of humankind—begun even with Abel, Seth, Noah and Abraham, and continued through Isaac and Israel—is permanent. The bounds of his choice are immeasurably widened by the inclusion of the Gentiles, but they are not equivalent to the human race itself (e.g. John 17:9, 20-21).

This is not to deny the universality of God's invitation to salvation. His love is for the world (John 3:16), and he commands "all people everywhere" to repent (Acts 17:30). The words of Jesus are unrestricted: "Come to me, all who labour and are heavy laden, and I will give you rest" (Matt 11:28). Furthermore, God's saving work in the world has had all sorts of positive impacts which have blessed the nations. But, nonetheless, the invitation is scornfully rejected by many, and this is not surprising given the incapacity of the human heart to please God or to want to please him. God will in no way cast out any who may want to come to him; but we are dead in trespasses and sins, and do not wish to come. This is the irony of 'free will'; the will is free when it is unforced by any external influence, but our will is corrupted by its connection with the whole sinful personality, and we are incapable of willing our own salvation (see Rom 7:15-20).

Thus in the very passage in which Jesus warmly invites "all who labour and are heavy laden" to come to him, he also rejoices in the power of God, "Lord of heaven and earth", who has "hidden these things from the wise and understanding and revealed them to little children; yes, Father, for such was your gracious will". He affirms, "All things have been handed over to me by my Father, and no-one knows the Son except the Father, and no-one knows the Father except the Son and anyone to whom the Son chooses to reveal him" (Matt 11:25-27).

In the saving of his people, then, God chooses or elects those who will belong to him. Luke puts it boldly: "And when the Gentiles heard this, they began rejoicing and glorifying the word of the Lord, and as many as were appointed to eternal life believed" (Acts 13:48). John puts it no differently: "All that the Father gives me will come to me, and whoever comes to me I will never cast out" (John 6:37; cf. 1:13). Paul attributes salvation to God's choice "before the foundation of the world" (Eph 1:4).

In a classic passage, Paul says: "For those whom he foreknew he also predestined to be conformed to the image of his Son ..." (Rom 8:29). In an endeavour to forestall what seem to be the harsh implications of this teaching, some have explained that the word "foreknew" in this passage means that God simply had pre-cognition of the future, and could therefore see who would accept or reject the gospel. As well as being at odds with the whole emphasis of Scripture on the sovereignty of God, the suggestion founders on the meaning of the word. In scriptural terms, to foreknow means something like "to have prior relationship with", "to love beforehand", which confirms the predestinarian thrust of the passage. As the very next verse says, "those whom he predestined he also called" (8:30).

The emphasis of Scripture falls very decidedly on God's choice to save his elect. But his choice of less than all means inevitably his non-choice of some (others would say his rejection of some). In the passage which specifically takes up this issue, Romans 9:14-26, Paul deliberately exalts the right of God to make his own choice without being in the slightest unjust. By the use of the question "What if …?" (v 22), Paul diverts our attention from what in any case does not concern us. We would love to have access to God's mind about all this, either in order to gloat or complain. Scripture exonerates God but refuses to encourage speculation. At a more personal level, Jesus did exactly the same (Luke 13:22-30).

Scripture prefers to underscore God's love for his elect. In an eloquent passage Paul asks:

> If God is for us, who can be against us? He who did not spare his own Son but gave him up for us all, how will he not also with him graciously give us all things? Who shall bring any charge against God's elect? It is God who justifies. Who is to condemn? Christ Jesus is the one who died—more than that, who was raised—who is at the right hand of God, who indeed is interceding for us. (Rom 8:31-34)

There are passages like this one which bring the death of Christ into direct connection with the salvation of God's people as such, and in a sense we may think of 'particular redemption' or, in an unfortunate and misleading expression, 'limited atonement'. Christ's death is sufficient for the redemption of any who come for salvation; but he especially laid down his life with the intention of saving his people:

"The good shepherd lays down his life for *the sheep*" (John 10:11); "Christ loved *the church* and gave himself up *for her* ..." (Eph 5:25; cf. 1 Tim 4:10).

There is a great danger here of becoming obsessed with the question of identifying the elect, and even asking "Am I elect?" Such questions presuppose that we have some secret access to God's mind other than Scripture. Jesus Christ is God's great public word, and faith in Christ is the way of salvation. The doctrine of election is useless—and worse—if it does not focus our attention on Christ in whom we are chosen before the foundation of the world. Faith in Christ is the evidence of our election by God.

5. The blessings of election

For those who focus on Christ, the knowledge of God's election is "full of sweet, pleasant, and unspeakable comfort".[45] We may indeed see in it the very gospel itself. The following features are worth noting in particular.

a. Election exalts God and humbles man

It is the constant tendency of both secularism and human religion to give power and status to the human race at the expense of God. Much preaching is simply the glorification of man, and the self-centredness of false piety is something to behold. But the Christian doctrine of salvation displays the power and wonder of God, since it is premised on the impotence and corruption of man. The doctrines of the cross and of justification by faith achieve this end. So, too, does the doctrine of election, which removes our last pretence (that we choose God) in the knowledge that our choice of him arises from his choice of us in Christ before the foundation of the world. This doctrine is highly offensive to the proud human spirit;

---

45 Thirty-Nine Articles, article 17.

yet, paradoxically, it establishes humanity in its only security and freedom: in the hands of the living God (see 1 Cor 1:26-31).

b. Election brings assurance and confidence

When any part of salvation can be thought to depend upon human capacity, there is always room for doubt and for loss of faith. But when we realize that God's salvation involves not only the reconciling death of Jesus but also the application of reconciliation to our lives, we can trust him to keep and guard us. The Lord Jesus referred to this when he spoke of God shortening the days of tribulation "for the sake of the elect" and observed that "false christs and false prophets will arise and perform signs and wonders, to lead astray, if possible, the elect" (Mark 13:20, 22). So did Paul, when he asked rhetorically, "Who shall separate us from the love of Christ?" and continued: "neither death nor life, nor angels nor rulers, nor things present nor things to come, nor powers, nor height nor depth, nor anything else in all creation, will be able to separate us from the love of God in Christ Jesus our Lord" (Rom 8:35, 38-39).

It is not possible that God's purposes for his elect should fail. On the other hand, one of the ways in which he guards his elect is to give them his word of warning and exhortation, by which he keeps them to the end. We persevere because he perseveres with us. Those who are truly regenerate will not turn assurance into presumption. They are right to trust the Lord to keep them until the end, remembering that the Lord as usual works through his word of encouragement and warning (e.g. John 10:27-28; Col 2:6-7; Phil 4:1). We have seen this already in regeneration and conversion, where the human response is called for and expected, although it is God who brings all to pass. Our experience of God as we go on is no different in principle from our initial encounter with him.

c. Election has a goal

Our discussion has been set in the context of God's purposes for all of history (e.g. Eph 1:9-10). As far as the elect are concerned, God's purpose is that they be "conformed to the image of his Son" (Rom 8:29), "holy and blameless before him" (Eph 1:4), living for "the praise of his glory" (1:12). When Paul makes a famous statement about God's sovereignty working all things together "for good" (Rom 8:28), that "good" should be perceived as conformity to Christ, a goal which will involve the difficult and painful as well as the easy and plain (cf. 8:17). Our understanding of election and its purposes will sustain us in such time and help us to remember that election confers no exemption from difficulty.

d. Election, prayer and preaching

It may be thought that the doctrine of election paralyses Christian activity, but such is not the case. On the contrary, the confidence in God that it generates inspires Christian obedience and, in particular, prayer and preaching. Both of these activities rely on God's power, and we are enabled by the knowledge of God's sovereignty to carry them out to the full but leave the results to him. Armed with this confidence, we may preach Christ crucified and obey the scriptural word, "Let the one who boasts, boast in the Lord" (1 Cor 1:31).

6. Conclusion

At first, it is natural to think that the doctrine of election as outlined here cannot be true. We think that human autonomy must be respected and that the decision to be saved must belong to us. But when we understand that our human situation is so bad that we cannot save ourselves and that as sinners we flee from God, we come to see that we choose God because he has first chosen us. We see, too, that this is not because of any goodness or attractiveness in us, but that it is entirely the grace and mercy of God at work. As a result, we are moved to worship our great God and thank him all the more for his compassion.

Key verse
"All things have been handed over to me by my Father, and no-one knows the Son except the Father, and no-one knows the Father except the Son and anyone to whom the Son chooses to reveal him. Come to me, all who labour and are heavy laden, and I will give you rest." (Matt 11:27-28)

Quotation
"The idea (the merely philosophical idea) of God who remains to be reached, whom we need to seek out because he is absent and remote, had no room in Christian theology. In Jesus Christ, God has sought and found us." (Karl Barth, *The Faith of the Church*)

Key terms
- Election
- Free will
- Predestination
- Calvinism
- Arminianism
- Particular redemption

For further thought
- What practical use is the doctrine of election?
- Three sources of responsibility in the Thessalonians' salvation were identified: the evangelists, the recipients and God. How have you seen this threefold responsibility in your own Christian life? In the ministry of your church?

- Can we be "Arminian on our feet and Calvinist on our knees"?
- What types of questions are raised by the idea that God organizes all the affairs of humanity on a large scale and on an individual scale? How does the gospel help us to resolve these issues?
- Is there anything helpful about asking, "Am I one of the elect?" Is there a place for pondering one's status as being "chosen by God"?
- If God knew that sin was going to enter the world, why did he allow it to happen? Why not simply create a world where no sin was possible?

For further reading
- Thirty-Nine Articles, article 17
- Westminster Confession, chapters 3 and 17

21

THE LIFE OF FAITH: ITS CONTEXT

Key concept: The life of faith is lived in the context of the world, the flesh and the devil, and under the cross of Christ.

1. Introduction

Since chapter 16, in which the subject was the Holy Spirit and our union with Christ, I have been expounding various aspects of the Christian life, especially its beginning. The point has now been reached, however, where the focus shifts from what may be called the initiation of the Christian life to its growth and continuance. I have described it as "the life of faith" as a reminder that it never ceases to be what it began as—namely, a life lived by faith in the God who has spoken and acted for us in Jesus Christ:

> I have been crucified with Christ. It is no longer I who live, but Christ who lives in me. And the life I now live in the flesh I live by faith in the Son of God, who loved me and gave himself for me. (Gal 2:20)

God's election of his people in Christ and his purpose that they should be holy and blameless before him reminds us that his kingdom has come into the world to restore what is his, but that it has yet to reach fulfilment. To understand the life of faith correctly, we must properly appreciate where we stand in the processes which God had set in train. The children of God are those "on whom the end of the ages has come" (1 Cor 10:11). We have been rescued "from the present evil age" (Gal 1:4), but it retains its reality for the time being. Death, suffering, sin and evil abound. On the other hand, the "powers of the age to come" (Heb 6:5) are already at work (most notably the Holy Spirit), and Jesus Christ is Lord, "not only in this age but also in the one to come" (Eph 1:21).

The Christian, then, is at the centre of conflict. In order to struggle effectively, we must know both our *enemies* and our *resources*; we must understand the times.

2. The adversaries of the life of faith

The world

The created world is, of course, very good (Gen 1:31), and it remains under the providential care of the good God. But the early chapters of Genesis describe a world in which suffering is the consequence of humanity's rebellion against the Creator (3:17-19), and this observation is endorsed by the New Testament (e.g. Rom 8:20). The environment of affliction and misery is clearly the result of sin and expresses the judgement of God. Sickness (Deut 29:22), drought (Amos 4:7), national disaster (Luke 21:23) and death itself (Acts 5:1-11, 12:23; 1 Cor 11:30) proclaim the verdict of God on the rebellion of humanity. In addition, the world not only delivers the judgement of God; it is under the same judgement and will itself pass away (1 Cor 7:31).

But the pain of the world is not only a reminder of the original fall. Climate change has provoked a widespread consciousness about the environment and in particular the way in which the world has been pillaged by humankind. There is no need to look further for evidence of inveterate sinfulness and the resultant tangle of unfortunate consequences than in our treatment of the natural world. That the biblical text sets us as having dominion over the world is not an excuse for our wastefulness and cruelty. Rather, it challenges us both to care for the world and to use it to the glory of God and to serve human needs (Gen 2:15).

There is, therefore, an ambiguity about the world's relationship to humanity. The world remains our home, and the theatre of God's glory. But it is an uncomfortable and temporary home. The situation is much complicated by the corruption of humanity itself. Such is our nature since the fall that we misunderstand our true position in the world. The creation exercises an enormous fascination for the disordered senses of humanity. Not only do we abuse the creation; we misuse it. In particular, we forget that it is passing away, and put our trust in it rather than God (1 John 2:15-17).

This false trust or worldliness takes several forms. It may consist of the love of wealth (1 Tim 6:6-10, 17-19) or pleasure (Jas 4:4), or it may even be a confidence in outward religious show. In general terms, all trust in human power, wisdom or pomp apart from God is worldliness. Because of our attachment to the creation, humanity can be identified with the world and assume its name. We become the 'worldly' human being, and as such we are joined with others who think like us, forming a 'corporation', a sort of embodiment of worldliness, which impresses by weight of numbers and by the display of human power and wisdom. This is "the world" in the sense of humankind organized apart from God (e.g. 1 John 3:13; John 17:14). The story of the Tower of Babel, right at the start of human history (Genesis 11), stands as a constant reminder that sin always tarnishes brilliant human skills. Short of the coming of God's kingdom, there is no utopianism in the Bible.

One extreme form of worldliness gives every appearance of being the opposite. It is the attempt to combat the fascination of the world by forbidding its use: "Do not handle, Do not taste, Do not touch" (Col 2:21). This asceticism is useless in itself (v 23), and constitutes an assault on the true doctrine of creation: "For everything created by God is good, and nothing is to be rejected if it is received with thanksgiving, for it is made holy by the word of God and prayer" (1 Tim 4:4-5). Indeed, in Christ all things belong to the Christian (1 Cor 3:21-23). Of course, only faith in the word of God can give us a true and balanced approach to the world.

The flesh

In chapter 10, I described human beings as precious, rebellious, enslaved and corrupt. A biblical term for the indwelling power of sin, the enslaving corruption which continuously acts out of rebelliousness against God's kingdom, is "the flesh". That the unregenerate is fleshly is true by definition: "For the mind that is set on the flesh is hostile to God, for it does not submit to God's law; indeed, it cannot. Those who are in the flesh cannot please God" (Rom 8:7-8).

Since the work of Christ is so plainly directed at the defeat of sin, many have concluded that the flesh has completely lost its hold on the Christian, or, with more realism, that the Christian may pass through an experience beyond conversion which will so diminish the power of the flesh that an almost sinless life is possible (a 'second blessing', or 'baptism with the Spirit'). In this way of thought, the Christian, being a "new creation" (2 Cor 5:17) and the dwelling place of God's Spirit, is well able to defeat sin whenever he or she chooses to exercise their will and call on the Spirit's aid to do so. Such Christian utopianism, leading in some cases to the 'perfectionism' movement, is fundamentally either Pelagian or semi-Pelagian, underestimating the power of sin and redefining the law in order to enable us to keep it in this life.[46]

Without a doubt, regeneration is a mighty event, and the power of the indwelling Spirit cannot be negligible. The Christian experiences repentance with the entail of a break from the past and a "walk in newness of life" (Rom 6:4). We are set free from slavery to sin. But Scripture connects such events not with a *second* blessing, but with the initial moment of salvation (e.g. Rom 6:1-4); this fact in itself should make us pause.

Consideration of 1 John throws further light on the situation. In this epistle, it is clear that sin remains a factor in the Christian experience, though without the same unchallenged force that it once had. The denial of sin is a lie (1 John 1:8-9), yet the ongoing practice of sin is inconsistent with the regenerating power of God (3:9). The mere fact of the exhortations and rebukes of the New Testament epistles also demonstrates that sinfulness remains an important reality. It is never suggested that sin is automatically overcome, either once for all or over a period; rather, the stern battle called 'mortification' must be undertaken.

In this connection, the central passages of the New Testament are those in Galatians and Romans. In Galatians Paul writes: "For the desires of the flesh are against the Spirit, and the desires of the Spirit are against the flesh, for these are opposed to each other, to keep you from doing the things you want to do " (5:17). The warfare between Spirit and flesh receives an extended commentary in Romans 7-8. Many would regard Romans 7 as referring to Paul's pre-Christian experience and Romans 8 as a description of life after the coming of the Spirit. Whether this is true or not (and I am convinced that Romans 7 describes something of the experience of the

---

46 Pelagianism takes its name from Pelagius, a 5th-century British monk who emphasized the goodness of humanity and human free will to do good. For more, see the glossary and analysis in Horton's *Pilgrim Theology* or the chapter on 'Inability' in Packer's *Concise Theology* (pp 85-86).

Christian), Romans 8 makes clear that there is no instant and simple conquest of the flesh in regeneration:

> So then, brothers, we are debtors, not to the flesh, to live according to the flesh. For if you live according to the flesh you will die, but if by the Spirit you put to death the deeds of the body, you will live. (vv 12-13)

The Lord's provision of a petition for forgiveness in his model prayer (Matt 6:12-15) is a necessity for the Christian life, and we cannot escape the pull of sin.

The devil

While the Bible is notably reticent about the origin and nature of the evil one, there is no doubt about his reality. Furthermore, although Satan is regarded as being a mighty or supreme adversary, accompanied by many who like him are evil spirits, there is no hint anywhere that he matches God in power or wisdom.

The Old Testament reveals little about him. The identification of "the serpent" of Genesis 3 with Satan awaits the New Testament (Rom 16:20; Rev 20:2). Where Satan (literally 'opponent') appears, as in Job, he is under the rule of God and is sent to test or try God's servants (cf. 2 Sam 24:1 together with 1 Chron 21:1). He is certainly associated with malign intent, and it comes as no surprise when the New Testament describes him as "a roaring lion" (1 Pet 5:8), "the tempter" (Matt 4:3), "a murderer from the beginning, and ... the father of lies" (John 8:44), "the evil one" (1 John 2:13), and "destroyer" (Rev 9:11).[47] He is particularly linked with falsehood, just as he used deception in the garden of Eden. In 2 Corinthians 11, Paul especially locates the demonic activity of our times with the preaching of a false gospel, "another Jesus than the

---

47 'Apollyon' means' destroyer' (see ESV footnote for Revelation 9:11).

one we proclaimed" (v 4). The devil does not need to use the occult as long as he has even more powerful means to distort God's word and bring us undone.

The clearest activity of Satan and his host in the New Testament is to strike out at the plan of God for the redemption of the world. His assault on Jesus (Matt 4:1-11) is not merely a paradigm of temptation for the benefit of Christians, but is more importantly his attempt to divert Christ's mission. He is eventually implicated in the betrayal and death of Jesus itself (John 13:27). In attacking Jesus, Satan may be thought of as defending his own, for the New Testament presents him as having a special sway over unbelievers, even giving him the titles of "the ruler of this world" (12:31), and "the god of this world" (2 Cor 4:4). He is portrayed as being "at work in the sons of disobedience" (Eph 2:2), and as having "blinded the minds of the unbelievers" (2 Cor 4:4). Redemption is spoken of as deliverance "from the domain of darkness" and transfer "to the kingdom of [God's] beloved Son" (Col 1:13-14).

Although this language suggests the clash of two kingdoms in the ministry of Jesus—and indeed there is some truth to this—we need to exercise caution. First, although there are two kingdoms, it is an unequal clash. Christ is stronger than "the strong man" (Mark 3:27), and he binds and plunders him. Second, we need to recollect that sin is the chief enemy, and that death is the last enemy. In other words, the struggle rages on a number of fronts, and there is a very real danger in exalting the importance of the devil. Human responsibility for sin must be recognized.

The cases of demonic possession encountered by Jesus must be seen first of all as part of Satan's general outburst against the Son of God (see again Mark 3:27). That is not to deny the possibility of contemporary occurrences of the same phenomenon; but the chief exorcism, the chief casting out of demons, remains the preaching of the gospel. Not surprisingly, the activity of Satan in the rest of the New Testament is frequently connected with persecution, with anti-Christ and false prophets and with all that will destroy the faith of Christians (e.g. Acts 5:3, 13:8-10; 2 Cor 11:3; Eph 6:10-20; 1 Thess 2:18, 3:5; 2 Thess 2:9-10; 1 Pet 5:8; 1 John 4:1-6). Thus, while there may be some support for the notion of the tempter who is continually inwardly inciting Christians to sin, the emphasis falls elsewhere. We do well, once again, not to exaggerate the independent significance of the devil, as though he is an equal and opposite version of the Holy Spirit.

Finally, it is also worth noting that Satan is linked with false religion through the concept of idolatry being the worship of evil spirits (Gal 4:8-10; 1 Cor 10:20-22). Even here, however, we need to assert a strong doctrine of creation, so that we do not become obsessed with the alleged powers and evil spirits, but remember that God is all powerful and that he has declared that the creation is his: "the earth is the Lord's, and the fullness thereof" (1 Cor 10:26).

Henry Smith, a noted Puritan preacher, once portrayed the plight of man in this fashion:

> Man goeth forth in the morning, weak, naked, and unarmed, to fight with powers and principalities, the devil, the world, and all their adherents; and whom doth he take with him but his flesh, a traitor, ready to yield up at every assault unto the enemy?[48]

This is a sombre and rhetorical view, but not so far removed from that of the Bible. It is far more realistic than the view of those who neglect the Bible's eschatology in favour of such things as prosperity teaching and instant holiness. But even so, it is not complete, for we need to set the whole into the wider context of the status enjoyed by the Christian as one adopted by God, with the suffering that this entails.

---

48 J Brown (ed), *The Sermons of Henry Smith: The silver-tongued preacher*, University Press, 1908, p 139.

3. The suffering of the children of God

There is an unavoidable tension in the Christian life between the experience of suffering and the status of being the children of God that we enjoy. In this respect, Romans 7-8 is the key passage.

In Romans 7, Paul expresses anguish at the continued presence of the flesh, which actually uses the law to stimulate sin (vv 7-12). The flesh continually pulls him into ungodly patterns of thought and behaviour, so that he exclaims in despair, "Wretched man that I am! Who will deliver me from this body of death?" (v 24).

This cry of despair is accompanied by his inward groaning (8:23) at his relationship with the created order. The world is in anguish, having been caught up in human rebellion; it has been "subjected to futility", brought under "bondage to corruption"; "we know", he writes, "that the whole creation has been groaning together in the pains of childbirth until now" (8:20-22). God's children suffer with the world and from the world. We are so powerless that "we do not know what to pray for as we ought" (8:26). Indeed there is a litany of horrors to which even the believer is vulnerable: tribulation, distress, persecution, famine, nakedness, danger, sword, angels, rulers (8:35-38). Finally, we are to be confronted with death itself (8:38).

How can we interpret the presence of such things in the believer's life? They could be thought of as proof of God's disfavour, indications of God's anger, and of his own lack of faithfulness. It is sometimes suggested that the children of God should enjoy physical, spiritual, emotional and financial prosperity, as some in our own day are teaching. Thus it is suggested that a poor or sick or depressed or guilty Christian is a contradiction in terms, and a thoroughgoing self-examination is called for, focusing especially on the faithlessness which has led to this situation.

The apostle's approach is quite different. He accepts the reality of these factors in Christian experience, and, rather than seeing them as disproof of our status with God, he regards them as evidence of it. His approach is marked by the following features.

a. Confidence in the work of Christ

The power of the flesh is not met in the first instance with human effort to improve, but with the gospel of Christ's victory and our part in it: "There is therefore now no condemnation for those who are in Christ Jesus" (8:1). God's forgiveness is the key factor and is not defeated by human sin or overturned by human suffering.

b. Confidence in the work of the Spirit

Those who are "in Christ" have received the blessing of God's gracious presence in his Spirit, and the forgiven, cleansed sinner is now subject to the Spirit's influence in walking worthily of Christ (8:4). We are to put to death the deeds of the body, and this will indeed require every effort, but this happens "by the Spirit" (8:13), who alone makes progress possible, just as it is the Spirit who helps us in the weakness of our prayers (8:26).

c. Confidence in adoption

The Spirit is given because we have been made the adopted sons of God (cf. Gal 4:5-6), and the Spirit witnesses to this fact as we are enabled to call God "Father" (Rom 8:15-16). But there are two special features of this adoption which need to be remembered:

   i. In keeping with the Bible's attitude to time and history, it is an adoption which is true, which is waiting to be revealed, and which has yet to occur: It is *true* because those who possess the Spirit are called sons of God and call him Father now (8:14-16). It is *awaiting revelation* because the whole creation yearns for the moment when the truth will become apparent (8:19). It *has yet to occur* because our bodies remain, and "we wait eagerly for adoption as sons, the redemption of our bodies" (8:23). We are saved in hope rather than full experience (8:24-25). We are creatures of two ages, redeemed and awaiting redemption. It is essential to give both sides of this paradox their due if we are not to misunderstand the nature of our present experience.

ii. Secondly, our adoption makes us "fellow heirs with Christ" (8:17). The word "heir" confirms the first point. Jesus himself is an heir—that is to say, one who is truly a son but waits for the moment of consummation or glory. Choice of the word "heir" is very deliberate: it draws attention to the tension of the 'not yet' status that Christ, the heir, has suffered. To be a fellow heir with Christ is to suffer with him. The pattern of life of the chief heir must also be reproduced in the co-heirs. Already Paul has exhorted us to the ongoing mortification of the deeds of the body (8:13). Now he reveals that none of the sufferings of the present time are outside the will of God—even for the sinless Lord, let alone for his fellow heirs. Those who wish to avoid suffering are those who will not take up the cross.

d. Confidence in the sovereign love of God

Our sufferings are part of God's plans for bringing us to glory (8:17). They serve our salvation. They are like the pain of childbirth, the necessary prelude to future joy. To rob us of our suffering is to rob us of our assurance of sharing in "the freedom of the glory of the children of God" (8:21), the adoption which is yet to come, namely "the redemption of our bodies" (8:23). Had this already occurred—if we are meant to be prosperous, healthy, sinless, happy—there could be no cause for hope. But, heirs as we are, we wait in hope and patience for that which is to come.

The justification for this attitude is what we know of God. He has reversed our condemnation, he has given us his Spirit, and we may address him as Father. Paul also points to the loving sovereignty of God who does all things for good to those who are his chosen heirs (8:28-30). We ought to note that "the good" here is defined as likeness to Christ, and avoid the abuse of the text which suggests that every little detail of life will make us comfortable and happy because God is in charge. The list in verses 29 and 30 is meant to indicate the absolute determination of God to save his sons; the purpose is, of course, that Christ may be "the firstborn among many brothers" (8:29).

By this means we arrive at Paul's grand conclusion: "in all these things we are more than conquerors through him who loved us" (with the word "loved" in the past tense pointing us back to the cross). This means that nothing "will be able to separate us from the love of God in Christ Jesus our Lord" (8:37-39). The Christian life is not one in which we avoid suffering and conflict, but one in which we are sustained through it by the Father and his great love.

4. Conclusion

I have been putting our consideration of the life of faith into its framework in God's timetable. It is vitally important to understand the nature of the day in which we live. We trust in God's providential care, but we do not demand the end before it is due.

The discussion of our adversaries is also a reminder that the Christian life is not merely a business of rule-keeping, but is a conflict arising from relationships; it is not, finally, morality, but salvation which we are talking about.

Key verse

The Spirit himself bears witness with our spirit that we are children of God, and if children, then heirs—heirs of God and fellow heirs with Christ, provided we suffer with him in order that we may also be glorified with him. (Rom 8:16-17)

Quotation

"Then said Mr Valiant: 'I am going to my fathers, and though with great difficulty I am got hither, yet now I do not repent me of all the trouble I have been at to arrive where I am … My marks and scars I carry with me, to be a witness for me that I have fought his battles who now will be my rewarder.' When the day that we must go hence was come many accompanied him to the River side, into which, as he went he said 'Death, where is thy sting?' And as he went down deeper, he said, 'Grave, where is thy victory?' So he passed over, and the trumpets sounded for him on the other side." (John Bunyan, *The Pilgrim's Progress*)

Key terms
- The world
- The flesh
- The devil
- Adoption
- Suffering
- Perfectionism

For further thought
- In our time, is there a greater danger of idolizing creation or of forbidding any involvement with creation? What will an appropriate Christian balance look like?
- What strategies would you adopt for the defeat of the spiritual enemies described in this chapter?
- What is the nature of Christ's victory over the devil?
- Is it possible to spend too much time contemplating the power and purposes of Satan? Too little time?
- A major apologetic question is raised in this chapter: "How or why can an all-loving, all-powerful God allow suffering, especially among his people?" How should we answer?

For further reading
- Thirty-Nine Articles, articles 9 and 12-16
- Westminster Confession, chapter 12
- Packer, *Knowing God*, chapters 19 and 21
- Bray, chapter 12

22

THE LIFE OF FAITH: ITS PATTERN

Key concept: Christ is the Lord of the life of faith, as we follow him and keep his commandments.

1. Introduction

The gospel of the kingdom of God as preached by Jesus became, for his apostolic messengers, the gospel of *Christ's* kingdom—the message that Jesus Christ is Lord (see Rom 14:7-9, 17-18). In it we see the reassertion of the rule of God repudiated by Adam and Eve and continually flaunted, even in Israel, since then. As part of God's kingly rule, the covenant by which he creates and orders his people (through words of promise and command) is instituted.

God's salvation is gracious and his gift is forgiveness. But the invitation to receive his gift involves repentance and faith—that is, the capitulation of the human will and the trusting submission of oneself to him decisively and forever. He saves us by ruling over us, for we need to be saved from our proud independence.

That is why so much of Scripture is taken up with law, wisdom, exhortation, rebuke and example. It is not that this is a way to salvation. But the saved people of God seek to walk in this way, because "whether we are at home or away, we make it our aim to please him" (2 Cor 5:9). The Christian is one who has made Jesus Lord and regards himself or herself as the willing servant of this Lord, seeking only to obey, for it is the Lord's right to seek that obedience. It is our worship of him.

It is clear, then, that much of Christianity is taken up with what may loosely be called 'morality'. But despite the tendency to pervert the gospel by turning it into a moral system, it is by no means simply a code of behaviour. For Christianity takes its start from a relationship—a relationship, furthermore, which arises from love and is based on forgiveness received by faith. Since the gospel reveals that our justification is by faith, one of the chief motives of moralism is done away with. Christian behaviour stems from faith in Jesus Christ, and depends upon his sovereign rule over our lives.

This means, as well, that in looking for the context of Christian morality we are not seeking abstract universal principles capable of guiding the human race. There are principles able to be universalized in Christian teaching, but they all rest upon the prior need for a relationship with God through Jesus Christ, and they are all expressed in specific covenant literature, namely, the Bible. As befits such a relationship, the Bible is made up of commands, exhortations, proverbs, examples and invitations to delight in the Lord. It is like the voice of a good Father, full of wisdom and joy. If we wish to live well, we need to "make it our aim to please him" (2 Cor 5:9), which will involve studying to know the mind of God as revealed throughout all of Scripture, applying ourselves to be the sort of person his word dictates, and looking for the good works which God has prepared for us to walk in (Eph 2:10). Thus, "whatever you wish that others would do to you, do also to them" is often taken as a general piece of wisdom for good living, but Jesus doesn't say, "for this is the way to a truly happy life"; he says, "for this is the Law and the Prophets" (Matt 7:12). The instruction takes on its deepest meaning for the person who knows the full revelation of God in Scripture.

Christian obedience is, therefore, at once simple and complex. It is simple because it involves seeking to please the Lord; it is complex because life is complex, and the word of the Lord in Scripture corresponds to that complexity and variety.

In Romans 6, Paul speaks of us repudiating our former slavery to sin and instead having become "obedient from the heart to the standard of teaching to which you were committed, and, having been set free from sin, have become slaves of righteousness" (vv 17-18). In this chapter, I will try to delineate what this "standard of teaching" may demand of us as we make Christ our Lord.

2. Following Christ

In the Gospels, the followers of Jesus are called "disciples"—that is, ones who are his pupils, who learn from him. The name survived in the early church (e.g. Acts 20:30) and expresses part of the appropriate relationship which Christians have with their Lord: we learn from him (e.g. Matt 11:29, 23:10). Indeed, the last commission of the risen Lord to his apostles was to "make disciples ... teaching them to observe all that I have commanded you" (Matt 28:19-20).

Part of the learning that the disciple is committed to is the imitation of Christ. The disciple is especially exhorted to follow Christ in the way of the cross—a requirement which, as Luke makes clear, is intended to be fulfilled in the daily death to oneself involved in repentance: "If anyone would come after me, let him deny himself and take up his cross daily and follow me" (Luke 9:23).

There are two ways in which this type of following is limited, however. In the first place, we must not confuse the Lord and the servant. The Lord's cross saves the world; the servant's cross is incapable of saving even the servant. Second, as the passage in Luke shows, the imitation of Christ is not to be thought of in some literal manner (e.g. in the physical sign of 'stigmata', or in leaving home, or in being single) but in a far more profound way, in heart and spirit. In this respect the Gospels are impressive, for they give little on which we may make the mistake of the outward imitation of Christ; we have, for example, no clue at all as to his physical appearance. Nor do they offer encouragement to the old liberal piety encapsulated in the immensely popular book *In His Steps*, where we are urged to think in every situation "What would Jesus do?"[49] The use of imagination in such a way is bound to result in images of Jesus, mental or physical, and images have a way of misleading their creators.

The Christian question is not so much "What *would* Jesus do?" as though we could work out whether Jesus would have accepted this job offer or enrolled in that university course. The Christian question is "What *did* Jesus do?" He laid down his life for the salvation of sinners. As Dietrich Bonhoeffer said, "When Christ calls a man, he bids him come and die".[50]

The pattern of Christ's death and resurrection mark the beginning and continuance of the Christian experience (e.g. Rom 6:1-4). In particular, Scripture lays great stress on imitating Christ's love, especially as that love expresses itself in forgiveness (Eph 4:32-5:2; 1 Pet 2:18-23; Col 3:13-15; John 13:34-35; Matt 18:21-35, 5:43-44). The last reference is a reminder that the following of Christ is no new concept, for a basic Old Testament injunction was "You shall be holy, for I the LORD your God am holy" (Lev 19:2). In fact, as with God and Israel—where it was the holiness of God which demanded the holiness of his people—so all the more it is our union with Christ which expresses itself in fruitful obedience (John 15:5). Furthermore, this is simply the beginning of the process which is the culmination of the Christian life, namely, to be remade

---

49 CM Sheldon, *In His Steps*, Pacific Publishing Studio, 2010 [1896].
50 D Bonhoeffer, *The Cost of Discipleship*, SCM Press, 2015, p 44.

in the image of Christ. Again and again the New Testament promises this wonderful conclusion, and in so doing urges us to pursue the process now (John 13:12-17; Mark 10:43-45; Rom 8:29; 1 Cor 15:49; 2 Cor 3:18; Eph 4:20-24; Col 3:10-11; 1 John 3:1-3).

If, however, our behaviour is determined by the pattern of Christ and our union with him, and if it is best summed up in the word 'love', where does the injunction, the rule, the law fit? For much covenantal stipulation is called 'law' and the New Testament as well as the Old Testament knows this category. Has the law been superseded?

3. The law of Christ

In a significant phrase, Paul described himself as "not being outside the law of God but under the law of Christ" (1 Cor 9:21). The law was of massive importance to Jesus' contemporaries, and he made very clear that he endorsed it completely: "until heaven and earth pass away, not an iota, not a dot, will pass from the Law until all is accomplished" (Matt 5:18). And yet he was also dissatisfied both with their interpretation of the law and with the style of their adherence to the law (e.g. 5:21f, 23:1f). He cleared from the law the additions which arose from attempts to bring it down to size, to diminish it. His exposition of the law gave it a great power, for, according to him, the righteousness of his disciples had to exceed that of the scribes and Pharisees (5:20).

But there was more to the teaching of Jesus than merely a re-statement of the law. His work introduced a new covenant. The Sinai expression of God's law was attached to the old covenant; it served a function to do with the time and place in which it was given, but that function was affected by the cross of Christ:

> Now before faith came, we were held captive under the law, imprisoned until the coming faith would be revealed. So then, the law was our guardian until Christ came, in order

that we might be justified by faith. But now that faith has come, we are no longer under a guardian, for in Christ Jesus you are all sons of God, through faith. (Gal 3:23-26; cf. Hebrews 8-10)

It is not surprising, then, that so massive a shift in covenant relationship should result in a change in legal stipulation. Jesus himself said as much in regard to food laws, for example (Mark 7:18-19). It is for this reason that we find Paul using the paradoxical language of 1 Corinthians 9:

> To the Jews I became as a Jew, in order to win Jews. To those under the law I became as one under the law (though not being myself under the law) that I might win those under the law. To those outside the law I became as one outside the law (not being outside the law of God but under the law of Christ) that I might win those outside the law. (vv 20-21)

There are those who wish to find here a complete repudiation of law in favour of a life of being led by the Spirit (see Gal 5:18). They seem to see this as a following of the 'inner light' or whatever spontaneous urgings come to mind, thinking this to be more spiritual than the study of the 'dead word' of Scripture. Others take it to mean that the Old Testament has completely passed away as a practical guide to Christian behaviour and that the New Testament alone should be our rule.

But it should be noted that Paul takes neither of these courses. He does not repudiate law as such—he is "under the law of Christ". And in his writings he is forever exhorting, commanding, stipulating, quoting—whether words of Jesus or words of the Old Testament. That there is a body of written material which has ongoing authority for every Christian, authority for belief and conduct, cannot be doubted. As he remarks, referring to a narrative in the Old Testament book of Numbers, "Now these things happened to them as an example, but they were written down for our instruction, on whom the end of the ages has come" (1 Cor 10:11). Whatever Paul means by his words about the law, he does not mean that the Old Testament has no ongoing validity (even the legal sections) or that there does not exist a "standard of teaching" (Rom 6:17) to which Christians commit themselves.

Certainly, however, our relationship with biblical law and, in particular, the Sinai enactment is to be determined by our relationship with Christ. In essence, this means four things.

a. We are free from the law's condemnation

Although the old covenant was never intended to be a way of salvation, it contained within itself condemnation in two ways.

First, because Israel failed to keep it, the condemnatory provisions were invoked again and again. With or without the specific Sinai provisions, failure to do God's will merits death, as Adam and Eve found. The Sinai code was explicit on this point, and those who failed to keep it suffered God's judgement. It functioned—and it functions still—as a constant reminder that "the wages of sin is death" (Rom 6:23; see also 3:19-20). Paradoxically, those who attempted to rely on their obedience to it to achieve blessing likewise met with condemnation (Gal 3:10).

Secondly, because the provision for forgiveness through sacrifice was self-evidently inadequate and could bring no lasting peace to the worshipper (Heb 10:1-4), those under the old covenant were under condemnation. But the work of Christ on the cross has brought once-for-all peace and forgiveness. Through it, we have genuine freedom from the curse of the law; we are no longer "under the law" but "under grace" (Rom 6:15). We can never, therefore, look upon law in the same way again, for we are now "under the law of Christ".

b. We have the Spirit of God

The new covenant is a covenant of the Spirit, where God fulfils his promise, "I will put my law within them, and I will write it on their hearts" (Jer 31:33). Under the new covenant, God is present by his Spirit with his people in an intimate way, not (as Jeremiah 31:33 shows) contrary to his law but so that "the righteous requirement of the law might be fulfilled in us" (Rom 8:4). That is why a text such as Galatians 5:18 contrasts being "led by the Spirit" and being "under the law". Those who are under the law are under the law's curse; those who are led by the Spirit belong to Jesus Christ and are led into the things which no law condemns (5:22-24).

c. We are free from observance of the Sinai code

In Romans 7, Paul presents an illustration drawn from marriage. The revolution brought about by the new covenant is equivalent to that of a woman marrying again after the death of her first husband. The law which guided the first marriage was not wrong (although it led to fruitlessness because of sin; v 5), but it cannot be used as a yardstick for the second marriage. Christ is our new partner, and through him the old law is finished, or, as Hebrews says, "obsolete" (8:13). We now belong to him in order that we may be fruitful to God under his lordship.

Paul's word for this is 'body': we "have died to the law through the body of Christ" (7:4). This is a clue to what he thinks of the relationship between the old and the new. The old is not wrong (it is "holy and righteous and good"; v 12) but it is inadequate and weak. What it contains, however, is the foreshadowing of Christ, for Christ is now the "substance" or "body" (see Colossians 2:16-23, especially verse 17).

Paul is not, therefore, repudiating law; he is far from saying that God's will is not made known to us for us to obey it, nor even that the Sinai enactment is totally worthless as a guide to God's will (see

Eph 6:1-3). But the law needs to be in and through Christ. This means, for instance, that we have been freed from the need to observe those rules and regulations which go to make up the ceremonial and ritual law of the Old Testament. Furthermore, our relationship with God is centred on Christ with all that this means for motivation, assurance, knowledge and the presence of the Spirit.

d. We are to look to love as the key to the law

When Paul wishes to sum up the law he says, "the one who loves another has fulfilled the law ... love is the fulfilling of the law" (Rom 13:8, 10). Once again, we need to note (as the context demonstrates) that Paul is not replacing the law with love. "Love" itself must be filled with content, and the Scriptures, including the Sinai covenant, tell us what God considers to be loving behaviour.

But "love" functions to interpret "law". Broadly speaking, Scripture contains three types of material: basic short statements such as the ten commandments; 'case law', such as the material in Exodus 21-23; and the summary statement of the law that we should love God and our neighbour. All three types are needed for us to understand the will of God in our own situation. The law can never be exhaustive. We need the statements to provide a general principle, we need the case law to illustrate how the principles are applied in specific cases, and we need the law of love to remind us that all law should be interpreted in spirit, and in favour of "the other".

4. The kingdom of Christ

Is it sufficient, however, to think of following Christ, and the law of Christ as being the source or pattern for Christian obedience? Many would point to a third factor, namely, the kingdom of Christ. They would argue that the danger with what has been discussed so far is that it is too individual; the 'kingdom' language gives scope for thinking about the social aspects of Christian obedience, and the very word 'kingdom' suggests the wider scope, with its political overtones. They would argue that the problem with stopping short of this is that, excellent as the model of Christ and the law of Christ are, they do not form an intellectually coherent program of analysis and reform. The practice of doing good to all people as we have the opportunity (Gal 6:10) hardly confronts the deep-rooted problems of political exploitation, hunger, disease and corruption. It is therefore argued that we must seek to establish the norms of the ultimate kingdom in today's society.

What this means, in practice, depends upon the point of view. To take two cases, there are those who speak of 'social justice', whereas others are keen to reassert the importance of the personal morality which they see embodied in the ten commandments for the health of society. Both groups would say that they wish to see the values of the kingdom of God appear in society as a whole; both groups are fervent social critics; both groups appeal to aspects of Exodus (such as the release of slaves on the one hand, and the giving of the law on the other) as models for a just society.

Taken overall, however, the exodus is a shadow of the redemption that comes in Christ, and the kingdom of Christ is no different from the lordship which we are commissioned to preach, summoning all peoples to repentance and faith, and declaring the forgiveness of sins. Some regard this as a 'spiritual gospel' and contrast it unfavourably with a 'social gospel' which, it is said, actually achieves real change in an unhappy world. But to speak like this is to betray a painfully low conception of the power of Christ's lordship, the reality of forgiveness and the importance of the age to come.

The ultimate redress of wrong in the world will occur when Christ returns; and there is a danger in thinking that we are responsible for setting up his kingdom here and now. Our power and wisdom are both small, our sin is inveterate, and the Christian has not been given a political blueprint for a perfect society, even in the Sinai law. On the other hand, the faithful proclamation of Christ's lordship (the so-called 'spiritual gospel') is itself a political and social act, and where that gospel is accepted it rightly brings social change. The evangelist is the spear-head of social reform, as those who obey and submit to Christ's lordship cannot be content to see the suffering of people through injustice, cruelty and indifference. It is not an accident that Christians have been at the forefront of reforms to prison conditions, slavery, child labour, education, and the treatment of animals, to name just a few improvements in society.

It is for this reason that evangelism is so often forbidden and evangelists harassed and persecuted by the political agents of society. The gospel creates groups of citizens whose higher allegiance is to God rather than kings and dictators, citizens who will do good despite tyranny. It creates literacy and education, bringing power to the powerless. It has been at the forefront of providing medical help worldwide. It promotes honesty in business. It saves people from dependence on drugs such as alcohol. It challenges greed and confronts the societal damage caused by gambling. It speaks the truth about the horror of abortion on demand. It releases people from bondage to evil spirits and transforms their view of the world. It creates groups of caring persons apart from the government, the public service or the family who seek to support the weak and depressed in society. It reconciles antagonists and encourages sexual fidelity and family life, thus promoting the emotional and physical health of citizens.

In short, the distinction between a spiritual gospel and a social one is pernicious. The 'spiritual gospel' is thoroughly social in its implications—although it must be agreed, once again, that it does not entail a particular political or social program. Such programs may well be needed and there are, no doubt, various economic, social and political structures which are more compatible with the gospel than others. But the kingdom of Christ by its very nature, while being thoroughly involved in this world, is also a kingdom for the world to come. In the absence of a blueprint for society before "the day of the Lord", the Christian does well to concentrate on the Lord's present strategy of gospel preaching followed by the good works of repentance.

It needs to be said that this is not a plea for a quiescent Christian public life. Christians ought to be socially active in combating evil and in providing care and support for the weak and defenceless. It is thoroughly necessary to address the word of God about justice to government, to business and to educational institutions. But there is not one single form of involvement, nor one recipe for improvement, nor any substitute for evangelism. John Pollock writes this of William Wilberforce:

> Wilberforce believed, nonetheless, that England's destiny lay safest in the hands of men of clear Christian principle, and that submission to Christ was a man's most important political as well as religious decision.[51]

5. Conclusion

The power of the world, the flesh and the devil are constants in this evil age in which we live. It is no accident that the Lord Jesus speaks so confrontingly about taking up the cross daily (Luke 9:23), or that Paul describes our lives in military terms (Eph 6:10-20). But we have been saved through the blood of Christ, we are indwelt by the Spirit of God, and we are now living in the kingdom of God, serving the Lord Jesus Christ. His word to us, with its wonderful variety and riches, is his precious gift to enable us to know his will. It is a public document, addressed to all Christians. What the Lord requires of you, he requires of me. We are not dealing with a host of private and invisible suggestions.

But we are still sinners, prone to wander. What else does the Lord

---

51 J Pollock, *Wilberforce*, David C Cook, 2013, p 66.

give us to sustain us in the way? We turn now to the work of the Spirit of God and the place of faith and prayer in living the life of faith.

———

Key verse
But thanks be to God, that you who were once slaves of sin have become obedient from the heart to the standard of teaching to which you were committed, and, having been set free from sin, have become slaves of righteousness. (Rom 6:17-18)

Quotation
"Hence, as our heavenly Father has in Christ freely come to our aid, we also ought freely to help our neighbour through our body and its works, and each should become as it were a Christ to the other that we may be Christs to one another and Christ may be the same in all, that is, that we may be truly Christians." (Martin Luther, *The Freedom of a Christian*)

Key terms
- Christian ethics
- Obedience
- Legalism
- Antinomianism
- Discipleship

For further thought
- If we are justified by faith alone, why is so much of Scripture comprised of commands?
- Why do we seek to obey Scripture? What various biblical reasons can you name?
- Is Christian obedience more about rules or character?

- What do you understand the word 'legalism' to mean? What is objectionable in it?
- What is the difference between asking "What *would* Jesus do?" and asking "What *did* Jesus do?" Which question better captures the biblical emphasis?
- What do you mean when you urge people to follow Jesus?
- In what ways does the lordship of Christ shape the way that we think about politics?

For further reading
- Thirty-Nine Articles, article 7
- Westminster Confession, chapters 16 and 19
- Horton, chapter 13

23

THE LIFE OF FAITH: ITS RESOURCES, PART 1

Key concept: The life of faith is lived by the power of the Spirit of God and through faith in God.

1. Introduction

In the past two chapters we have seen, first, that the life of faith is lived out in the difficult context of the present age, in which we are confronted with forces as powerful as the world, the flesh and the devil, and, secondly, that we are called to the highest standard of character and behaviour through our allegiance to the Lord Jesus Christ.

God has not left us without aid, however. He is himself our strong rock and defender; in New Testament terms, he has brought us into a life-giving and sustaining union with Christ. This invasion of our lives by our great and gracious Lord is the source of all our hope: he "became to us wisdom from God, righteousness and sanctification and redemption" (1 Cor 1:30). We have already seen how his life and word sustains and nourishes us, and we turn now to the further resources that we have in Christ as we seek to live in ways that please him. Pre-eminently, of course, it is by the power of the Holy Spirit that we are being transformed into the likeness of Christ, "from one degree of glory to another", until we bear "an eternal weight of glory beyond all comparison" in the age to come (2 Cor 3:18, 4:17).

2. The Holy Spirit

We have already said much about the person and work of the Holy Spirit in chapters 6, 12 and 16. Indeed, all the chapters from 16 onwards have, in a way, been an exposition of the work of the Spirit; in a sense, this section functions merely to draw the discussion together.

In particular, the Spirit has been presented as the third person of the Godhead, sent in this present age by the ascended Christ to his people, who, by the word of God, calls men and women to God their Father through faith in Christ and is the presence of God in their lives, enabling them to serve Christ and grow like him. The great Pentecostal outpouring of the Spirit marks the inauguration of the new covenant. It means that the apostles and their contemporary believers were unique in that they passed from the old covenant to the new. We now live in the new age, under the word of God, which is to be read from now on through Christ. We can see in the structure of the book of Acts groups of people receiving the same gift of the Spirit as a sign that God had accepted them as the gospel message went into all the world. Thus we see the coming of the Spirit to the Samaritans, to the Gentiles, and to John the Baptist's disciples as the old gave way to the new (Acts 8, 10-11, 19).

The New Testament revelation of the Spirit is too rich to offer a satisfying summary here, but by the use of some of the key words associated with the ministry of the Spirit, the following constitutes an introductory survey.

Receiving the Spirit

The promises of Jesus that his disciples would be indwelt by the Spirit of God (John 14:15-17) and so by the Father and the Son (14:23) came to pass when he was glorified and poured out the Spirit on the day of Pentecost (Acts 2:33). This was not for the apostles alone, for at the end of Peter's speech he called upon all his hearers to repent and be baptized so that they too may receive the gift of the Spirit with the forgiveness of sins (2:38). The new age had dawned and the Spirit was now the possession of all who put their trust in Christ. No further step is required beyond the initial ones associated with becoming a believer.

The New Testament uses various expressions to convey the truth of this initial experience, when the Spirit who regenerates becomes the Spirit who indwells and unites us to Christ. Occasionally, it is referred to as being baptized in or by the Spirit. We turn to this phrase first because of its connection with the initial preaching of John the Baptist (Mark 1:8). In fact it appears rarely but it demonstrates the relationship of Christ with the Spirit—he baptizes with the Spirit and so, we may assume, inaugurates the new age of the Spirit foretold by the Old Testament prophet Joel (2:28f). In its other two New Testament appearances (Acts 11:15-17; 1 Cor 12:12-13), a similar application of the Baptist's prophecy is being made. Both instances have to do with the inclusive nature of salvation. In Acts 11, it is the astonishing fact that the Gentiles are to be part of the people of God; in 1 Corinthians 12, it is that all are "baptized into one body—Jews or Greeks, slaves or free ..."

Central to both passages is the idea that salvation necessarily involves this experience of the Spirit. In Acts, in particular, the simple step of faith in Jesus has led to the miraculous outpouring that Peter (quoting the Lord Jesus) calls being "baptized with the Holy Spirit", indicating that the Pentecostal gift could be described in the same way (Acts 11:16-17). The very point of 1 Corinthians 12 is that all Christians have been Spirit-baptized by definition. This in itself shows how extraordinary is the error that refers to baptism in the Spirit as an event subsequent to conversion and experienced by some but not all Christians. The very point of the expression in Acts 11 and 1 Corinthians 12 is the reverse.

Another notable and related term used in the Pauline literature is the "seal" of the Spirit:

> In him you [i.e. the Gentiles] also, when you heard the word of truth, the gospel of your salvation, and believed in him, were sealed with the promised Holy Spirit, who is the guarantee of our inheritance until we acquire possession of it, to the praise of his glory. (Eph 1:13-14; cf. 4:30; 2 Cor 1:22).

The point of this passage is the same as Acts 11: the Gentiles are included and the Spirit is given (as at Samaria in Acts 8, with Cornelius in Acts 10 and at Ephesus in Acts 19) as the seal or proof of God's approval. One of the distinguishing marks of the Christian, and of the brotherhood, is the communion of the Holy Spirit (see also Acts 5:32, where "obey" is equivalent to "receive the gospel").

In these passages it should be noted that the way to receive the seal, or the baptism of the Spirit, is by faith in Jesus. John makes the same point: "If anyone thirsts, let him come to me and drink. Whoever believes in me, as the Scripture has said, 'Out of his heart will flow rivers of living water'" (John 7:37-38). As Jesus taught, simply believing in him was the precondition for receiving the promised Spirit. There is no need for separate negotiations to receive the Spirit, as though salvation were a two-stage process. Believe in Jesus and the Spirit comes.

This 'indirectness' remains typical of the Spirit's work. Jesus told his apostles that he would send the Spirit, whom he described as "another Helper ... the Spirit of truth" (John 14:16-17) who would dwell with them. But in his coming is the coming of Father and Son (14:18-23), and the Spirit is the teacher who will teach of the things of Christ (14:25-26, 15:26-27) and who convicts about the judgement to come (16:7-15). In short, the Spirit's role is to glorify Jesus, for as Jesus says, "he will take what is mine and declare it to you" (16:14).

The 'relational' role of the Spirit is reflected also in Paul's writings. The Spirit enables us to cry "Abba! Father!" (Gal 4:6; Rom 8:14-17) and to address Jesus as Lord (1 Cor 12:1-3). The Spirit binds us to our fellow Christians in the body of Christ (12:12-13). He enables us to pray as we ought (Rom 8:26-27). The Spirit is a great uniter.

The fullness of the Spirit

John says of Jesus, "For he whom God has sent utters the words of God, for he gives the Spirit without measure" (John 3:34). He captures here the frequent connection in Scripture between the word and the Spirit. In the Old Testament, to be sure, the coming of the Spirit also stood for God's enabling of a person which sustained them for military or political action in his service (e.g. Judg 15:14). But often it had to do with the prophetic gift (Num 11:26-30). When the New Testament speaks of being filled with the Holy Spirit, it seems to have the capacity to utter mostly in view (e.g. Acts 7:55-56, 13:9-10). Certainly this is the case in the one instance when we are admonished to "be filled with the Spirit, addressing one another in psalms and hymns and spiritual songs, singing and making melody to the Lord with your heart ..." (Eph 5:18-19).

Thus, whereas the baptism with the Spirit is an initial and unique endowment, being filled with the Spirit is best thought of as something that can be repeated. It is, indeed, something we may seek when confronted with the obligation of ministry and the knowledge that we minister in God's strength and not our own. It is clearly linked, therefore, to the gifts of the Spirit, which will be discussed below.

The leading of the Spirit

Twice Paul speaks of the need to be led by the Spirit (Rom 8:14; Gal 5:18). There is a common tendency to take this phrase out of its context and apply it to 'guidance', as though, by inward promptings, the Spirit is responsible for telling us what to do in the ordinary decisions of life. In this connection theologian BB Warfield speaks wisely, describing the biblical reference as having to do with the conquest over the flesh in a continuous rather than sporadic way and of the Spirit giving firm, compulsory leadership, which he describes as "working continually in the sinner". He concludes:

> [The text] stands here not to drive us to despair, because we see we have sin within us, but to kindle within us a great fire of hope and confidence because we perceive we have the Holy Spirit within us.[52]

I would add that the firm, compulsory leadership of the Spirit is expressed by the word of the Spirit, who has inspired the Scriptures. In short, the best way to be led by the Spirit is to obey the Scriptures, for this is the voice of the Spirit. As we seek to please the Lord, we are walking by the Spirit (Gal 5:16, 25) who has given us life.

The fruit of the Spirit

The actual phrase "the fruit of the Spirit" only occurs once in Scripture (Gal 5:22), but the concept that the Spirit brings holiness or sanctification is widespread. For example, Ezekiel prophesied: "And I will put my Spirit within you, and cause you to walk in my statutes and be careful to obey my rules" (Ezek 36:27; cf. Jer 31:33).

The presence of a holy God demands holiness of life: "For this is the will of God, your sanctification ... For God has not called us for impurity, but in holiness. Therefore, whoever disregards this,

---

52 BB Warfield, 'The leading of the Spirit—Romans 8:14' [sermon], *Monergism*, 1903, accessed 17 January 2022 (monergism.com/leading-spirit-romans-814).

disregards not man but God, who gives his Holy Spirit to you" (1 Thess 4:3, 7-8; cf. 1 Cor 6:11, 19).

In these two references, we see the presence of the Spirit as promise and as challenge. In the first place, as those who are in Christ we are already saints, already holy: "And because of [God] you are in Christ Jesus, who became to us wisdom from God, righteousness and sanctification and redemption" (1 Cor 1:30). This is the truth about us, and without it we could not be the children of God and have access to him. This is what is sometimes called our 'positional sanctification'.

But in this life, holiness is also a calling, a progress—or 'progressive sanctification'. We can become holy only because of our possession of the Holy Spirit. Without him our efforts are useless. On the other hand, our possession of the Spirit provides us with the motive to seek holiness. In seeking holiness we must remember, of course, that the Spirit's presence in our lives is totally the result of what Jesus has done for us. To use an old insight, what God does *in* us follows what he does *for* us. It is our identification with Christ on the cross and the forgiveness of sins which makes us holy, and which paves the way for the coming of the Spirit; we receive him through faith in Christ (Gal 3:1-5). Our motive in seeking holiness can never be that we wish to be saved thereby.

Having noted that point, we may proceed to draw out the implication of the Spirit as promise and challenge. As promise, his presence necessarily transforms us; his fruit appears in our lives; the work is entirely his. As challenge, we must "put to death the deeds of the body" (Rom 8:13) and give ourselves without reserve to the unremitting warfare against the flesh which involves pain and self-denial and the taking up of the cross. Our sanctification is entirely our own work, done entirely by the Holy Spirit. We are reminded of Philippians 2, where Paul tells us to "work out [our] own salvation with fear and trembling", but then instantly reminds us: "for it is God who works in you, both to will and to work for his good pleasure" (Phil 2:12-13). Thus, as Paul remarks, part of the fruit of the Spirit is "self-control" (Gal 5:23). This co-operation between the Christian and the Spirit—in which the Christian does all, only to acknowledge that God does all—is integral to the growth in holiness, or likeness to Christ, that ought to mark the Christian life (2 Cor 3:18).

We ought to note that, as time passes, a sense of regression rather than progression often appears to be true of the Christian's experience, leaving them vulnerable to those who wish to promote an easy path to sanctification through a 'second blessing' or 'victory life'. Four responses can be made:

a. Second-blessing teaching, as well as having no secure base in Scripture, arises from inadequate views of the deep-seated nature of sin and the reality of justification by faith as the means of dealing with sin once and for all.
b. Perceptions of regression may well be accurate and should be dealt with by confession, forgiveness and repentance. But there is no short-cut to holiness and no Christian progress which will move us beyond the cross.
c. Perceptions of regression may also arise, however, through an increasingly sensitized conscience. Our sense of growing sinfulness may only be our growing consciousness of the sin that has always been present. It may be, paradoxically, a sign of progress.
d. The Scriptures do speak of Christian maturity, and we need to be careful of a model of the Christian life in which only the growth of a child is allowed for and not the steadiness of the adult.

The gifts of the Spirit

Although this exact phrase does not appear in Scripture, the concept is present in 1 Corinthians 12:4-11. We distinguish "gifts" from "fruit", service from sanctification, but clearly the distinction is arbitrary and misleading. If the gifts are exercised by the unsanctified, they will be thoroughly misdirected; they will be used to exalt the gifted rather than to serve the body. On the other hand, those led by the Spirit will hardly be conscious of the question of gifts as love opens their eyes to avenues of service. It is tragic for us to become obsessed with gifts at the expense of love (the main point of 1 Corinthians 13); such an obsession is consistent with self-centred worldliness rather than the Holy Spirit.

Paul's teaching on gifts in 1 Corinthians 12 is meant to encourage the believers to accept one another with all their variety of talent, and to remember constantly their unity in the body of Christ. It is also meant to locate the source of the gifts so that we can thank God for them and not allow for self-aggrandizement. The differing lists in the New Testament (cf. Rom 12:3ff) show that there is no call for all nominated gifts to be present in each church. Paul's thoroughgoing emphasis is on service—he values the gift that builds up the other person (1 Corinthians 14) and he insists, using some of the most elevated language of the Bible, on the primacy of love (1 Corinthians 13). He gives to no-one the right to use a gift simply because he or she possesses it. At the same time, he encourages us to serve each other with the perception of faith and the zeal of love (Rom 12:3-13).

Basic to the doctrine of the gifts of the Spirit is the same teaching that we have seen throughout the Bible: all things come from God, all things belong to God; creation and redemption are from him. The church is a human gathering and it may be understood in a human way. The fact that it is a body and that to each of the members "is given the manifestation of the Spirit for the common good" (1 Cor 12:7) is yet another reminder to us that the church itself flourishes and lives only from God's good hand upon it: "Not by might nor by power, but by my Spirit, says the Lord of hosts" (Zech 4:6).

3. Faith

I include 'faith' as a resource because it is a gift of God and because, as we have already seen, it is the vital point, humanly speaking, of our relationship with God. Faith is the principle of our ongoing relationship, not merely the beginning of it. The faith that justifies is the faith that sanctifies, for Christ, the object of our faith, is one.

According to the Anglican homily on this subject, faith "cannot be kept secret"; when occasion offers "it will break out, and show itself by good works".[53] The nature of faith explains why this is so. Faith is directed towards the love of God, especially as expressed in the cross, and so cannot help but give itself to God in grateful obedience. If faith does not lead to such obedience, it cannot be genuine faith (Jas 2:24-26).

Furthermore, since faith rests upon God's promises, it takes its shape and strength from those promises. This means that faith alone has the power to keep God's precepts. Thus, for example, there are many occasions when to keep the precepts of God is irritating, inconvenient, difficult, costly or even dangerous. Often it is simply unreasonable by human standards. In such cases only those who trust the promises of God will obey freely and gladly and for the right reason, because they are looking to please God, they know that God's wisdom is best, and they know God will not fail. Such was the attitude of Abraham, for example, when faith made him ready to sacrifice Isaac (Genesis 22).

Only the eye of faith can see matters in their true perspective. Faith enables a person to do the right good for the right reason. To take one example, God assures men that they should "rejoice in the

---

53 'Homily 1.4: Of the true and lively faith', *Anglican Forums*, n.d., accessed 17 January 2022 (forums.anglican.net/threads/homily-1-4-of-the-true-and-lively-faith.1964). The Anglican Homilies is a series of sermons written in the 16th century and designed to teach and uphold reformed theology in the Church of England (at a time when many ministers were unwilling or unable to preach true and robust doctrine).

wife of your youth, a lovely deer, a graceful doe" (Prov 5:18-19). If we believe that, it will guard us against the temptation to infidelity when the worldly and unbelieving perspective is very different.

It follows, therefore, that although (to all appearances) good works may be done by non-Christians, they are not, in fact, what they seem. The unbeliever, by definition, does not do good works as from faith in Christ, and this deficiency is a fundamental flaw. Faith without works is dead, but true faith is the necessary source of an obedience which pleases God. Growth in holiness must, therefore, concentrate on strengthening faith.

4. Prayer

Faith's most characteristic expression is prayer, and faith is the secret of true prayer. As we trust, so we pray. Hence the New Testament urges us to put our complete confidence in God as we pray and to abandon those doubts which are so inconsistent with our prayers (Jas 1:5-8; Mark 11:22-23). Jesus exhorted his disciples to secrecy in prayer so that the genuineness of their faith may be tested: their prayer was before God and received no reward from the plaudits of people (Matt 6:5-6). Nor were they to "heap up empty phrases" (6:7), trusting in the magical efficacy of human words in quantity or rhetorical skill, for this is inconsistent with faith.

By forbidding doubt, Jesus was not giving a psychological recipe for successful prayer, as though anything we may choose to ask for will be granted to us as long as we achieve the right frame of mind. Jesus was exhorting us to faith, and faith is humble submission to the will of God. It was faith which made Jesus pray, "Abba, Father, all things are possible for you. Remove this cup from me. Yet not what I will, but what you will" (Mark 14:36). The secret of the prayer of faith is that it be in accordance with the will of God, for this is the condition of the granting of all prayer—nor would we have it any other way, for God's wisdom is best. When we pray in humble submission, we may confidently leave the matter with God knowing that his answer will be sure, wise and loving. We do not have to dictate the form or timing of his actions.

Our aim in prayer, then, is to pray in accordance with God's will. Thus our prayers will be moulded by what we know of God. What is it that we know? Four great truths should guide us.

a. There is one God

The Bible directs our prayers to God alone. Lesser beings such as 'saints' and angels are not prayed to. In biblical piety, exclusive attention is focused on God. True faith rests on him alone.

b. There is one sovereign God

There is little point in prayer to a god who lacks the power to respond. But, in fact, it is the presupposition of biblical prayer that God is almighty and well able to achieve both the casting of mountains into the sea or the forgiveness of sins. We have seen that such things as regeneration, the control of the weather and the twists of history are likewise in his hands. We may, therefore, be confident of his power to answer our requests.

c. There is one sovereign, revealed God

Those who do not know God are filled with doubt and confusion about what to pray to him. They will pray many different prayers, with many flattering remarks and even sacrifices of various kinds in the hope that they may be heard. Others will pray to many gods or spirits. Christian prayer, in contrast, is based on what God has revealed. God's covenant reveals his purposes and opens a vast field for prayer where we may be certain of praying within the will of God. The Lord's Prayer, for example (Matt 6:9-13; Luke 11:2-4), relies on the known character and plan of God and puts our needs into the context of those revealed intentions.

There is no mysticism in the Bible—if by 'mysticism' we imply a route to God which bypasses verbal revelation. It is by responding to and being guided by the words of Scripture that our prayers are best formed. This is the deepest meaning behind the practice of praying in the name of Jesus. Although praise abounds in scriptural religion, it is the proclamation of the wonderful name and deeds of the Lord, not the mindless and illogical repetition of words favoured by some. Nor is there any embarrassment whatever about petitionary prayer—such prayer is just as honouring to God as praise, or even more so. Where some see a logical problem at work—'If God is sovereign anyway, why pray? Surely just praise him'—the Christian sees here the rule for his or her prayer life. The God who is in control of all things invites us, commands us, to call on him in prayer, and promises to hear and respond. As it is often observed, it is the Pharisee who merely thanks; it is the tax collector who asks (Luke 18:9-14).

d. There is one sovereign, revealed and gracious God

By trusting in Christ we receive God's Spirit, who enables us to call God "Abba, Father". This means that we may approach him with reverent boldness. He does not, of course, always answer our prayers as we would wish. His large promises of earthly blessing are to be understood in terms of what he knows is best for us. He is infinitely wise and good, and we may trust him to give us what we need. Jesus insisted that God is not a mean and reluctant donor but a generous and kind Father.

But the generosity of God must be reflected in our own prayers and in the attitude of our own hearts. The New Testament insists that they who would approach God must themselves demonstrate forgiveness. An unbreakable link is forged between prayer and forgiveness (e.g. Mark 11:25).

5. Conclusion

Luke 11:13 tells us that the loving Father gives generously of his Holy Spirit to those who ask him. Here is an ever-appropriate prayer of faith as we endeavour to live the Christian life! But our discussion has not exhausted the resources with which God blesses us. We turn next to the church.

Key verse

For God has not called us for impurity, but in holiness. Therefore whoever disregards this, disregards not man but God, who gives his Holy Spirit to you. (1 Thess 4:7-8)

Quotation

"Nothing is more characteristic of the prayers recorded in the Bible than the spirit of reverence by which they are pervaded." (Charles Hodge, *Prayer*)

Key terms
- Positional sanctification
- Progressive sanctification
- Pentecost
- Prayer
- Baptism in the Spirit
- Fruit of the Spirit
- Gifts of the Spirit

For further thought
- Describe the fullness of the Spirit and the baptism of the Spirit.
- What are the marks of being led by the Spirit?
- Why are faith and forgiveness so significant for prayer?

- How does the sovereignty of God coexist with the Bible's teaching on prayer?
- Paul speaks not of the fruits of the Spirit, but of the fruit (singular). Does the distinction matter?
- What are the similarities between the "fruit" of the Spirit and the "gifts" of the Spirit? What are the differences?
- Should a Christian pursue 'sinless perfection'?

For further reading
- Westminster Confession, chapter 20
- Martin Luther, *The Freedom of a Christian* (1520)[54]

---

54 This work is sometimes known as *A Treatise on Christian Liberty* and is widely available online. It can be accessed for free, along with other resources from the period, in K Birkett, *Classics of the Reformation*, Matthias Media, 2017 (matthiasmedia.com.au/products/classics-of-the-reformation).

24

THE LIFE OF FAITH: ITS RESOURCES, PART 2

Key concept: The life of faith is lived in the fellowship of the church of God.

1. Past, present and future

In one sense, all the material between chapter 12 and this chapter has been a bypath. Chapter 12 was entitled 'The covenantal nation' and it brought us to the point at which God lovingly determined to set up his rule once more after the catastrophic disobedience of Adam and Eve, resulting in the choice of a people. Of these, Abraham became the Father of a great nation, the recipient of God's gracious covenant, and the one through whom all nations were to be blessed. I then described the creation of the covenant nation, with its institutions and laws, and something of its history. Its constitution was from God, and therefore proper for his purposes, but its fulfilment was to be through the one perfect Israelite, Jesus, God's great "Yes" to all his promises (2 Cor 1:20).

We have seen the transformation of this people through Christ and, in particular, its widening out in accordance with the promise to Abraham to include the Gentiles. The alienated are reconciled, those without God are now given access to him, and the ones who were strangers are now family (Eph 2:13-16). In subsequent chapters we have traced the events which led to this, the accomplishment and application of redemption. In this chapter the focus will be on the people of God as we experience our present participation in it and draw strength from it. But just as what God has done to create his covenantal nation in the past is essential to understanding the present, so, too, it is helpful to consider the future and see the way in which God plans to conclude his great work.

2. The people of God and their city

It would be possible to think of eternal life as consisting of the individual enjoyment of God. The redeemed person may gaze and gaze with sublime rapture at the vision of God's glory, and be conscious of nothing else at all. Or else the redeemed may be absorbed into God as drops of water are absorbed into the ocean and lose their individual identity and consciousness altogether.

Neither of these views seems to fit the picture of heaven in the New Testament. In the first place, it is not 'heaven' which is spoken of as though it is a static state of existence after death. The language of the Bible continues its 'historical' categories and the 'end' or 'goal' of God is described as a consummation where the old becomes transformed into the new when Christ returns to change our lowly bodies to be like his glorious body (Phil 3:20-21).

But the consummation is also the consummation of relationships. Of course, the relationship with God is central here—to depart and be with Christ, for example (Phil 1:23), or to "know fully, even as I have been fully known" (1 Cor 13:12). But just as there is nothing here to encourage the notion of 'absorption', there is also nothing to encourage the idea of merely individual enjoyment. Indeed, the Bible uses the category of the city and, in particular, Zion—or Jerusalem—to describe the end. The Scriptures begin with human beings in a park, but they end with the redeemed as citizens of a great city:

> And I saw the holy city, new Jerusalem, coming down out of heaven from God, prepared as a bride adorned for her husband. And I heard a loud voice from the throne saying, "Behold, the dwelling of God is with man. He will dwell with them, and they will be his people, and God himself will be with them as their God." (Rev 21:2-3)

We could pause to wonder at this scene, but for the moment I want to indicate some important features. First, it is a pure city: a division has occurred, and the sinners are excluded (Rev 21:27, 22:15). Second, entrance to the city is through the cleansing of sin in the cross (22:14). Third, this city is the place of fulfilment of God's plans for humanity (21:4, 6-7, 24; 22:1-5), which include peace, joy, love, the enjoyment of the glory of the nations, and the dominion or reign that God gave humanity at the beginning (22:5). Fourth, at the very centre of everything is God himself, ruling from his throne, worshipped by all and tending his people as a shepherd tends his flock (cf. 7:15-17). Fifth, the citizens of the city are called the people of God, just as Israel was the people of God, though in terms of Revelation this people is doubtless made up of "a great multitude that no-one could number, from every nation, from all tribes and peoples and languages" (7:9).

The conclusion of all things is no private, individual vision of God, but a corporate one, in which we share with others who make up the same people—*his* people, the people of God. That is our hope.

But is there any sense in which we already enjoy our hope? Two factors would immediately suggest so. First, there is the fact that the future is described in terms of the past—ideas such as Jerusalem, people, temple, Eden and so on. Second, there is our knowledge of the way in which, since the coming of Jesus, the age to come has penetrated the present age and we experience something of both together.

A text from Hebrews illustrates the point. After reminding his readers that, unlike Israel of old, they were not standing before Mount Sinai, the writer goes on:

> But you have come to Mount Zion and to the city of the living God, the heavenly Jerusalem, and to innumerable angels in festal gathering, and to the assembly of the firstborn who are enrolled in heaven, and to God, the judge of all, and to the spirits of the righteous made perfect, and to Jesus, the mediator of a new covenant, and to the sprinkled blood that speaks a better word than the blood of Abel. (Heb 12:22-24)

The thought world of Hebrews is rather different from that of Revelation (though a contrast can be overdone). But once more it is the city which provides a vision of the end, once more God is in the midst, once more admission is by the blood of Jesus, once more a people is present, and once more there is the consummation (or 'perfection') of humanity.

But two special points deserve mention. First, the word for 'church' appears in this passage, but is translated as "assembly"—which is its prime meaning, but what is undoubtedly significant in this context is that it must suggest the Christian assembly. Our present and our future is to be gathered around the throne of God. Second, there is the location in time: "you *have come* ..." The believers' present experience is on view—they now partake of the future. The writer warns them to "offer to God acceptable worship" (Heb 12:28), by which he especially means approaching God through Jesus and then living for him in this world. Paradoxically, he observes: "For here we have no lasting city, but we seek the city that is to come"

(13:14). In short, they have entered the city which is to come, the city which Paul calls "our mother", "the Jerusalem above" (Gal 4:26).

Much that is basic to an understanding of what we call 'church' can be found in these two passages. There is only one true church, made up of peoples from all nations redeemed by the blood of Jesus Christ who gave his life for her on the cross (Eph 5:25), summoned together and founded on the teaching of Christ and his apostles, indwelt and made holy by the presence or Spirit of God, focused in worship on the throne of God, reigning with God forever. There is no solitary Christianity, for every believer belongs by birth to this fellowship and cannot leave it without leaving Christ.

And yet our current experience of God's people is intermittent, not permanent. What can we say of this?

3. The people of God in exile

Israel lived together in a certain land with a temple, a city, a priesthood and a kingship, all of which were tangible and provided a potential focus for unity. The revolution that is Jesus Christ has transformed the people of God so that it is international—indeed, worldwide. The old landmarks now exist, but in their fulfilled, glorious and spiritual form. We are united by land, city, priesthood, kingship and Spirit. But it is now impossible for us to congregate physically as Israel once congregated (or 'churched') at Mount Sinai.

In a most profound sense, as Hebrews 12 shows, we have indeed assembled or congregated. There is one assembly and we are always part of it even when we are on our own. But how are we to think of God's people now as we await the fulfilment of that particular hope? Three New Testament words offer help.

Exiles

We have already noted these words from Hebrews: "we seek the city that is to come" (13:14). Peter describes us as "exiles of the

Dispersion" (1 Pet 1:1) and describes the future in terms of the inheritance "kept in heaven for you" (1:4). To him we are "God's people" (2:10) but "sojourners and exiles" (2:11). Akin to this is Paul's description of the Philippian church having a "citizenship … in heaven" (Phil 3:20).

Brothers

Peter speaks of the dispersed and suffering believers as a "brotherhood throughout the world" (1 Pet 5:9), thus reminding us of our family membership with all who, like us, are exiles but who belong to the Lord Jesus Christ.[55] It is natural and proper that we should address one another in a fraternal way and, more importantly, treat each other thus (e.g. Rom 12:9-13, 15:7; Gal 6:10). It is tragic that such things as denominationalism should stop us recognizing the "brotherhood".

Assembly

I have already indicated that we are 'assembled' even now in the one true and glorious church which contains all the saints both 'dead' and alive. But it is essential to see that the same word is used of the local assemblies which meet from time to time. That is not to say that one can simplistically work back from the picture of church in Revelation to what we should do now. The word 'church' means not so much 'community' as 'assembly' or 'congregation', though no doubt as time passed the assemblies also formed communities. From time to time Christian people gather in order to meet with Jesus ("where two or three are gathered in my name, there am I among them"; Matt 18:20) and there is the church. The New Testament has a particular way of relating this gathering to the one true church

---

[55] "Brotherhood" here refers to a fellowship of believers that comprises both men and women.

(i.e. the heavenly assembly of Hebrews 12). It is not thought of as part of the church, or a section or branch of the church. It is the church, or better still, a manifestation or expression of the one true church which exists now and will appear at the end of history (cf. 1 Corinthians 1:2—church local—and Ephesians 1:22—church universal). The New Testament does not define the church as we tend to do by building or location or time or liturgy or ministry or connection with other local assemblies. The real issue is whether Christ is in the midst of his people—whether they have gathered to meet him in his word and by his Spirit.

4. Pictures of God's people

Once it is clear that any gathering of God's people to meet with Jesus in his word and by his Spirit can be called 'church', we can benefit most truly from the metaphors that the New Testament uses of this assembly. These metaphors can apply most directly and fully to each assembly—so that the local church should not be regarded as *part of* the body of Christ; as an expression of the one true church, it *is* the body of Christ (cf. 1 Cor 12:27).

There are many metaphors of the church in the New Testament, and the study of them is well worthwhile. But I have selected four chief ones which will enrich our understanding.

Bride

Both Paul and Revelation use this metaphor (Eph 5:21-33; Rev 21:2), which goes back to the relationship between the Lord and Israel (Hosea 1-3; Ezekiel 16; 2 Cor 11:2), and beyond that to the marriage of man and woman in Genesis 2. In Ezekiel, the stress is on the helplessness of the bride, the gracious choice of the husband, the extent of his generous bounty, her subsequent beauty, and her infidelity. The last point is, of course, the obverse of the loyalty that such a bride owes to such a husband. In Paul and in Revelation, the purity and beauty of the bride is remarked on; in both cases, it is the result of the husband's loving care. In Paul, the need for obedience to the husband's word and fidelity is also at issue, but always in response to the husband who nourishes, cherishes and gives up his life for her. Paul also dwells on the union between husband and wife, which is a symbol of the union between Christ and the church.

Flock

Once again this metaphor has Old Testament roots, with Israel being regarded as the Lord's flock (e.g. Zech 10:3; Isa 40:11). The Lord is the owner and protector of the sheep; they, for their part, owe him allegiance, which they display by keeping his word. These themes are taken up in John 10, where Jesus is "the good shepherd" and his sheep are identified as the ones who hear and respond to his voice. As the bridegroom dies for the bride, so the shepherd dies for the sheep (vv 11, 15). Emphasis also falls on the other sheep "not of this fold" (i.e. Gentiles) who will heed the voice of the shepherd so that there may be "one flock, one shepherd" (v 16). These are mainly themes which we have observed in connection with the bride metaphor, but there is the additional point with the flock that others are regarded as pastors or shepherds in a subsidiary way and warned to give excellent care to the sheep (Acts 20:28; 1 Pet 5:1-5).

Temple

The Old Testament temple was regarded as the dwelling place or palace of the Lord and was, of course, situated in Jerusalem. Jesus warned his Jewish hearers that he was building a new temple, which he identified as his own body (John 2:19-22). Stephen's speech in Acts 7 was in part a warning that the days of the temple were numbered (see verses 48-50). But both Paul and Peter identified the temple, not just with Jesus, nor with the individual believers, but with the church. Peter described his readers as "living stones" that are "being built up as a spiritual house, to be a holy priesthood, to offer spiritual sacrifices acceptable to God through Jesus Christ" (1 Pet 2:5).

The clash of metaphors is necessary to contain the truth that God's people are both temple and priesthood, the fulfilment of the Old Testament. Paul likens the Jews and Gentiles together in the one church to the temple, the main point being that the temple is filled with God's presence and glory: they "are being built together into a dwelling place for God by the Spirit". Most importantly, though, this temple is "built on the foundation of the apostles and prophets, Christ Jesus himself being the cornerstone"; it is in Christ that "the whole structure, being joined together, grows into a holy temple in the Lord" (Eph 2:20-22).

Body

This is the most famous of the metaphors and care must be taken, for that reason, not to turn it into the whole doctrine on its own. In Ephesians, Christ is "the head of the church, his body" (5:23; cf. 5:28-30), and the emphasis falls on the care of the head for the body and the obedience of the body to the head (5:21-33). In 1 Corinthians, the focus shifts and the church is the body, with the interest being in the variety within unity provided by the analogy, as well as in the provision for the life of the body represented by the gifts. It is notable that the Corinthian church is regarded as the body of Christ in itself (12:27), not part of the body; notable, too, that the gifts of the body are *for* the body. The metaphor is never turned outward, as though the body exists to serve the world or the church is viewed as an extension of Christ's incarnate body. But the profound unity between Christ and his people and between the members themselves is certainly one of the chief implications of the doctrine.

These metaphors and the others of the New Testament add variety and depth to our vision of the church, and over time they should profoundly affect how we think about the local church and our involvement in it. But in each one Christ is absolutely central, and especially Christ's death as the saving act and Christ's word as the governing principle. Whatever the doctrine of the church, whatever our experience of church, if these two elements are either missing or muted, something is very deficient.

5. God's people in action

What do the people of God do when they meet? The simple and usual answer is that they 'worship'. This answer is not wrong since, with the Lord in their midst, it is fitting that they should reverence God, like Isaiah in the temple or the saints of Revelation.

Nonetheless, there are difficulties with the usual answer: First, the New Testament does not emphasize worship words in connection with the earthly assembly. Second, the use of such words may obscure the fact that our worship of God entails every part of life. Third, the word puts so much emphasis on our relation to God that it may divert attention from our fellow Christians. It is striking that, in two crucial New Testament passages, we are instructed to address *one another* in "psalms and hymns and spiritual songs" (Eph 5:19; Col 3:16). Fourth, the word suggests that we meet in order to do something to or for God, and there is therefore a danger that we distort the gospel of God's gracious approach to us.

Colossians 3:14-17 gives us a brief insight into the assembly. There is great emphasis on the word of God as the basis of the meeting, and on teaching and learning as being integral to it. It is the word which should guide, enrich and edify, and nothing must hinder the word. Paul instructs Christians to "let the word of Christ dwell in you richly", and the gathering is to place a heavy emphasis on "teaching and admonishing", on the sharing of an intelligible message "so that the church may be built up" (v 16; 1 Cor 14:5). By his word—and this means especially the word of the gospel—God approaches us and dwells in our midst. We should conduct ourselves in such a way as to promote the word in our midst.

A more extended picture arises from the study of 1 Corinthians, and especially chapters 11 to 14. We could summarize the teaching of this material by saying that as we meet we are to submit to the word of God, show love for one another, build each other up by the gifts which are ours, and do everything "decently and in order" (14:40). As the last phrase signifies, this reflects the nature of God himself and our obligation so to behave that we will bless one another. The gathering is marked by love.

In these days, technology means that we can be edified in our own home—and, indeed, recent global events have meant that many of God's people have had no choice but to settle for being edified in this way. But, make no mistake (as so many have discovered!), this is indeed settling for second best. For church exists for us to serve one another in love, which happens most effectively when we gather together in person.

In short, whatever the outward form of our church (and such matters as time, place, liturgy, denomination and government must surely be secondary, although important), it must be an experience in which God's people gather to seek the Lord in faith and bless one another in love. Because our unity is based on the atoning death of Jesus, it must be a forgiving and accepting fellowship (Gal 3:27-28; Col 3:12-14). The outward forms must serve the gospel which is the foundation of the congregation.

Another place at which we see the nature of the church expressed is in Paul's description of the Lord's Supper (1 Cor 11:17-34). In the eating and drinking, we "proclaim the Lord's death until he comes" (11:26). That is to say, the Supper is an enactment of the gospel, a 'visible word'. This is the foundation of the meeting and determines what occurs. The eating and drinking of the covenantal bread and wine are a reminder, or proclamation, of his death, and once again our response is repentance and faith, as it is to every preaching of the gospel. By this means we participate in Christ.

But we cannot participate in Christ without being bound to one another (1 Cor 10:16-17). This was what was so offensive in the unloving practices of the Corinthians (11:20-22). Their lack of love towards one another was a sheer denial of the love that had purchased them at the cross. To fail here was to fail at "discerning the body" (11:29) and instead to profane "the body and blood of the Lord" (11:27). Already, earlier in his letter, Paul had warned the congregation about the effects of allowing gross sin in their midst without the discipline which called for repentance (1 Corinthians 5-6). Now he deals with further evidence of their lack of love for God's word and for one another.

In short, what we call the sacrament of the Lord's Supper, or Holy Communion, is a sign of the Lord's death, to be received by faith. Partaking of it is a reminder of our incorporation in the new covenant in his blood with the supreme blessing of the forgiveness of sins (Matt 26:28). Like all preaching of the death of Jesus, if it is received rightly it strengthens our faith and is a source of strength and assurance. It is tragic to see it elevated to being the most significant element in the Christian life, especially when the reason for doing so is a confusion between the reality to which it points (Christ's body on the cross) and the sign, namely the bread and wine.

Likewise, the practice of baptism arises from the words of Christ himself (Matt 28:16-20) and 'preaches' the gospel, in this case initiation into Christ and so into his people. In particular, the use of water signifies the washing away of sin and the new life involved in being saved. It enacts the grace of God and the response of the sinner. The New Testament gives no direct guidance on the exact mode of baptism or the vexed question as to whether it is to be reserved for those who can answer for themselves or may be applied to infants as was circumcision in the Old Testament. I favour infant baptism, because it enacts the grace of God to fallen sinners and his power to regenerate even those who have yet to hear the gospel outwardly. But there is, of course, the grave danger that the practice of infant baptism gives false assurance and leads to nominalism.

Just as the word 'worship' is associated with church in a somewhat misleading way, so too is the word 'mission'. It is popularly said that the church exists for mission. Depending on the viewpoint of the speaker, 'mission' may itself be defined as evangelism or, more broadly, may include many other forms of Christian obedience.

The danger here is that 'mission' will become an especially churchly activity, rather than being the constant response of every Christian to God's love. There is every reason why individuals and societies should engage in mission without any formal link with local churches. Indeed, it may be argued that church is the fruit of mission rather than an agent of mission. Such a view puts the contrast rather too starkly, and in fact there is truth in both perspectives: the church both has a mission and is the fruit of mission. As we see from 1 Corinthians 14:23-25, it was expected that outsiders would be present in church and that they would be challenged to worship God.

Finally, something should be said about church unity. In one sense, there can be no concern—there is only one church and it cannot be divided, for God has created it, and God is holding it. And yet in another sense, it is for us to maintain the unity which is given—especially in the local manifestation of the church (cf. Eph 4:1ff). But we ought to seek fellowship with the brotherhood throughout the world. The churches which confess Christ belong to one another (e.g. 1 Cor 11:16) and it was natural that they should develop links and even a network as time went by. In due course they became what we call 'denominations' or 'churches'. This was, on the whole, a positive development. But there is no need to regard this as demanding organic unity, and too much time and effort has gone into creating such unity, which often amounts only to denominational mergers with remaining splinter groups (or, sometimes, more than 'splinters'!).

6. Conclusion

Some recent distortions of the doctrine of the church have involved turning it into a club, so much emphasis has been placed on human encounter. What we need to grasp is that the church is God's people, God's flock, saved with the blood of his own Son and meeting with his word and Spirit in their midst. It is only as we realize that he is present and react accordingly that we will truly be able to meet the Lord Jesus in his word and bless one another in love.

Key verse

Let the word of Christ dwell in you richly, teaching and admonishing one another in all wisdom, singing psalms and hymns and spiritual songs, with thankfulness in your hearts to God. And whatever you do, in word or deed, do everything in the name of the Lord Jesus, giving thanks to God the Father through him. (Col 3:16-17)

Quotation

"Let me offer you in sacrifice the service of my thoughts and my tongue, but first give me what I may offer you." (Augustine)

Key terms

- Universal/local church
- Visible/invisible church
- Sacraments
- Lord's Supper
- Worship
- Assembly
- Body

For further thought
- What are the essential features of a genuine church? How can we distinguish "church" from any gathering of Christians?
- What is the relationship between the universal church and the local church?
- How will our gatherings be shaped by the knowledge that church is not about our movement towards God, but about his movement towards us in Christ?
- What is the value to the Christian of the Lord's Supper? What would it take for a Christian to be excluded from the Lord's Supper in the local church?
- What is necessary for an 'online church' to be a true church meeting?
- What is worship?

For further reading
- Thirty-Nine Articles, articles 19, 20, 25, 26 and 28-31
- Westminster Confession, chapters 21, 25-31
- Bray, chapter 29
- Horton, chapters 15-16
- Milne, chapters 23-24

25

THE LIFE OF FAITH: ITS RESOURCES, PART 3

Key concept: The life of faith is lived with the help of the ministry of the word of God.

1. Introduction

One of the chief resources of the life of faith is other Christians, especially as we gather in order to meet Christ and one another. Those whose focus is on the grandeur of buildings, or liturgy, or the importance of priesthood are sometimes critical of what they regard as the downplaying of church in evangelical Christian experience. But this is to prefer the outer to the inner; evangelicalism which is true to itself has always valued 'fellowship', or the communion of believers, for mutual strengthening and edification. It has not necessarily undervalued liturgy and buildings, but it has always seen that these are secondary, and it has always encouraged so-called 'lay' Christians to minister to each other freely, especially in family life. They have seen, too, that 'formal' church life can hinder the growth of the relationships in which love is expressed and received.

But although denominational or congregational order may properly be quite varied—being formal or informal, or both at different times—there are certain principles of order which reflect theology and which need to be observed in all situations. In this area the informal is as likely to err as the ritualistic, the free as much as the structured. It is to these principles that we now turn.

2. God and human agency

As we have seen, the Bible safeguards the priority of God in salvation at every point. The process of salvation occurs because of his plan, and it is his power at work when great things happen. His people are urged to make constant prayer to him, for only in him is there hope and salvation.

The purposes of God are advanced, however, by the use of human agents. Noah, for example, both preached and built—in a sense his salvation lay literally in his own hands. Abraham is the chosen instrument of God to bring blessing upon all the families of the earth. Moses, Joshua, Deborah, Hannah, Samuel and David were all used by God to do his will.

Nor can the reality of their contribution be doubted. It is as Moses' arms are raised that Israel triumphs over Amalek but, nonetheless, the soldiers must wield their weapons and fully extend their efforts. It is for this reason that it is entirely legitimate to praise and thank God's agents even though, in the end, all praise and thanks belong to God alone. It was through faith that they "conquered kingdoms, enforced justice, obtained promises, stopped the mouths of lions" (Heb 11:33).

The relationship between God and his servants is illustrated by Paul in his words about Christian ministry in 1 Corinthians 3. Here Paul described himself and Apollos as "servants through whom you believed, as the Lord assigned to each. I planted, Apollos watered, but God gave the growth" (vv 5-6). Paul sees himself as entitled to

God's reward or blame as God's fellow worker, but he insists both that the result of his labour belongs to God and that the very work itself is God's.

In allowing that men and women are God's agents in his work, however, the Bible allows no room whatever for glory to accrue to them. This is the point of the passage just quoted, and elsewhere Paul is at pains to demonstrate that the apostolic ministry was one of obscurity, pain and dishonour: "But we have this treasure in jars of clay to show that the surpassing power belongs to God and not to us …" (2 Cor 4:7-12; cf. 10-13).

Indeed, there are cases of God using the ignorant and totally unworthy as his ministers (e.g. John 11:51; Isa 45:1f). Certainly, too, the human agents of God were fallible and sinful, and the Bible does not hesitate to reveal their deficiencies.

It is worth noting that from the beginning all of humankind is engaged in 'ministry'—that is, in the service of God and others. For this must be included in the instructions to Adam and Eve to rule the world as God's image-bearers. It follows, naturally, that God regards all of Israel as a priestly royalty; he calls them "my treasured possession among all peoples, for all the earth is mine" (Exod 19:5).

Within Israel, however, there were different types of ministry by which God ruled. We may think of judges, prophets, priests and kings, for example; the first two were given at particular times; provision was made for the latter two to sustain a regular pattern. There were also elders and judicial figures in the towns and villages, and it ought not to be forgotten that parents occupied a special place in the rule of God's people through families (e.g. Exod 20:12; Deut 6:1-9). In all these cases the rule was meant to be in accordance with the covenant stipulation.

The key ministry of the old covenant was that of Moses. He was a prophet who combined within himself, although not fully, the task of being priest and king. He demonstrated the centrality of the revealed word for Israel's existence. Through him came not only the saving leadership by which Israel emerged from bondage, but also the principles by which Israel's life was to be governed. This included both general and specific principles; it included moral, civic and cultic principles. It became the task of the prophets to recall Israel to the Mosaic covenant; it was the task of the kings to rule in accordance with that covenant; it was the task of the priests to explain and provide for the provisions of the covenant; it was the task of these ministries, in short, to sustain the holiness to which the nation was called.

Yet even Moses was not exalted. In the end, he did not lead the people into the promised land, since his service of God was not without its faults (Deut 32:48-52). God does not share his glory, even with Moses, for even Moses was a sinner like the rest of us.

3. The ministry of Jesus

The contrast between Jesus and Moses is one of the astonishing features of Jesus' ministry. Even Moses falters and fails: Jesus never does. This fact alone alerts us to the uniqueness of Jesus' ministry; and yet he is also the pattern for all Christian service from every Christian.

In the days of Jesus there existed a sophisticated and highly educated ministry conducted by the scribes. They were ordained to teach and to administer the law, and they were highly respected, being given such titles as 'Rabbi' ('doctor'), 'Father' and 'Master'.

Jesus himself exercised a ministry which received no human accreditation (John 7:15). He was highly critical of the ostentatiousness, unscrupulous behaviour, hypocrisy and preference for human authority shown by the scribes. He does not attack Moses but the interpreters of Moses (Matt 23:2-3). In describing the character of his own mission, he calls himself one who came to serve: "For even the Son of Man came not to be served but to serve, and to give his life as a ransom for many" (Mark 10:45).

In speaking of himself as one who came to serve, Jesus is self-consciously identifying with the servant of Isaiah, and especially Isaiah 53. In so doing he is emphasizing that his supreme and unique service is that of his death upon the cross.

This death is connected with his work of preaching. He came to preach (Luke 4:43), and the purpose of his preaching was to summon the lost into his kingdom (5:31-32). The twofold work of preaching and dying is brought together in the image of the good shepherd (John 10), who gathers his sheep into the fold and, unlike the false shepherds, is prepared to die for them. The use of the shepherd image also reminds us that the servant can rule: there is no inconsistency in the idea of a king being the servant of his people. It is not the fact of leadership which Jesus disputes with his servant language, but the manner in which it is exercised.

There is the obvious uniqueness of Jesus' death for his people. But when that is said, the ministry of Jesus provides the most profound pattern for all Christian ministry, whether it is the general calling of all believers to live for their Lord and each other, or the specific tasks of Christian ministry that God also gives (cf. Phil 2:1-11; 2 Cor 4:5).

Thus, in calling disciples to follow him, Jesus is not summoning them to an entirely different ministry. In the face of the disciples' jostling for position he exhorts them: "it shall not be so among you. But whoever would be great among you must be your servant, and whoever would be first among you must be slave of all" (Mark 10:43-44). In the same spirit, he lays down that "If anyone would come after me, let him deny himself and take up his cross daily and follow me" (Luke 9:23). When he washes the disciples' feet, he stresses that he alone can save but also that they should give themselves in the service of one another (John 13:1-20).

It is worth noting that the vision of costly service applies particularly to the evangelistic ministry to which all are directed. When confronted by Greeks, who represent the world of Gentiles beyond

Judaism, Jesus speaks immediately of his own suffering and death and then goes on to apply it to the suffering and death of the Christian (John 12:20-26). Any Christian ministry (and, in this case, evangelistic ministry) is irresistibly accompanied by suffering and the death of self. We can hardly be true followers of Jesus if we have no vision of the harvest which awaits beyond the church and do not seek our own role in helping to reap it. After all, we hear Paul say: "I try to please everyone in everything I do, not seeking my own advantage, but that of many, that they may be saved". He immediately adds: "Be imitators of me, as I am of Christ" (1 Cor 10:33-11:1).

Ministry, then, is not the sole prerogative of some within the church. There is mutual ministry and there is the service of the gospel in the world. On the other hand, as in Israel, so in the church there are different ministries, and to them we now turn.

4. Apostolic ministry

"The household of God", Paul tells us, is "built on the foundation of the apostles and prophets, Christ Jesus himself being the cornerstone" (Eph 2:19-20; cf. Rev 21:14). This apostolic ministry was the creation of Christ himself during his earthly life and, with the Old Testament prophets, it formed the basis of the church.

The New Testament witnesses both a fulfilment and a transformation of Old Testament ministries as with Old Testament laws and practices. It is most remarkable that the priestly category is never applied to Christian leadership (except metaphorically in Romans 15:16). It reaches its appointed end in Christ himself and, as in Exodus 19:5, in all of the people (1 Pet 2:10). Nor is there any suggestion that Christians are to be ruled by an earthly king-like figure, as was the case for Israel, with a place and a capital city. The apostles preach "another king, Jesus" (Acts 17:7).

On the other hand, the unique event of the Word become flesh is accompanied by the creation of a 'new' order of ministry, one which bears a special relationship to that event and to the person who was central to it. Luke represents Jesus choosing twelve disciples and making them apostles, a word indicative of an 'ambassador', one who is the authorized representative of a person. The place of Judas was taken by Matthias, who was chosen as one who "accompanied us during all the time that the Lord Jesus went in and out among us"; it was his task to join the others as "a witness to [Jesus'] resurrection" (Acts 1:21-22).

Luke largely focuses the apostolic ministry on their being witnesses. When the need arose for administrative work, the apostles declined to be involved on the grounds that it was not right that they "should give up preaching the word of God to serve tables" (Acts 6:2), but they ensured that the need was met through the appointment of seven men usually referred to as 'deacons' (6:3-6). We do not have a description of apostles acting as elders in a local congregation; indeed, it is James, the Lord's brother, who presides at the meeting of apostles and elders in Acts 15. On the other hand, in a key passage we have the description of a church which was thoroughly committed to apostolic doctrine: "And they devoted themselves to the apostles' teaching and the fellowship, to the breaking of bread and the prayers" (2:42). This is the point, too, in the apostolic presence at Samaria (8:14-16), at Caesarea (10:23-24) and in the Jerusalem Council (15:22).

In John's Gospel, Jesus' choice of the twelve is especially emphasized. They were "his own" and he "loved them to the end" (13:1). Once again there is an emphasis on the witness that the apostles will bear Christ, a witness to the historical fact of his life (14:26, 15:27). Like Luke, John particularly mentions the coming of the Spirit in this connection; in his case, however, he explains that the Spirit will remind the apostles of the words of Jesus and guide them into all the truth (14:26, 16:13). These are special promises to the apostles, not directly to all believers. It means that their words are the touchstone of truth (13:20, 17:14-21).

In short, the apostolic ministry occupies a vital place in the history of God's salvation. It is unique and irreplaceable, although, like the ministry of Jesus itself, there are aspects of it which provide a model for other Christian ministries. But the church is continually refreshed by returning to the apostolic witness, and this cannot be replaced by any other body of writings. Nor can the apostles be replaced by any other group of persons. The apostolicity of the church is to be found in its adherence to the apostles' teaching (cf. Eph 2:20), not in a succession of ministers such as bishops.

5. The ministry of the word

Christ gathers his flock and rules it by his word. In this task, all Christians have a part to play (1 Thess 5:11; Eph 4:29; Col 3:16) and, in particular, each household must be instructed by responsible Christians (1 Tim 3:4; Titus 2:3-4; Eph 6:4). Likewise, the local church is described in family or household terms, with implications for how we treat each other and for the qualifications for leadership —for example, that teaching elders should be men (1 Tim 2:8-15, 3:1-16).

Ephesians 4:11-16 speaks of Christ's gifts in terms of persons: apostles, prophets, evangelists, pastors and teachers. When these gifts are active there is the upbuilding of the church into the likeness of Christ, especially through all members working in response to the teaching. The common feature of each of the gifts mentioned is that they are to do with the communication of the word of God (assuming that in verse 11 pastor-teacher, or shepherd-teacher, is the same person). In this sense there is only one ministry, although it may find expression in different ways.

The creation of local congregations was accompanied by a need for local leadership. In some places, at least, this was met by the appointment of elders (or 'presbyters' or 'overseers'; Acts 14:23).

'Elders' and 'overseers' appear to be different names for the same people. The word 'overseer' can also be translated 'bishop'. In later church history, the two titles were distinguished from each other, a development which, although not contradicting the New Testament, is not mandated within it. The New Testament structure seems to have been parallel to the situation in synagogues, although it is not certain that every church was the same in constitution and government. There is, however, evidence of the relatively widespread existence of an appointed leadership (e.g. Heb 13:17; 1 Pet 5:1-3; Acts 20:17, 28; 1 Thess 5:12; Phil 1:1; 1 Tim 3:1ff; 2 Tim 2:2). As well, Paul was accompanied by "co-workers" and "fellow workers", and there seem to have been other peripatetic ministers.

The structure of church life is not set down, but the importance of pastoral care is indicated by the careful instructions given about the qualifications of those chosen to exercise it (1 Tim 2:8-3:7), the need to guarantee succession (2 Tim 2:2), and the fact that it may be paid for (1 Cor 9:6-12; Gal 6:6; 1 Tim 5:17-18). Note, too, that apart from moral and spiritual qualifications, the aptitudes required for leadership are those required to rule or manage a household (1 Tim 3:5), and especially that the leader be "able to teach" (3:2; 2 Tim 2:24). Something of the nature of the work may be gleaned from the titles accorded to it: steward (Titus 1:7), pastor and teacher (Eph 4:11), and overseer or bishop (Acts 20:28).

The pastor, or shepherd, rules the flock by expounding and applying the word of God; this is the essence of the pastoral ministry (Acts 20:17-35). The task involves serving the word of God in private as well as in public, "in season and out of season" (2 Tim 4:2). The task cannot be confined to ministry to the existing flock; the "lost sheep" are the concern of every Christian; how much more are they the concern of those who are specifically designated "ambassadors for Christ" and "shepherds"?

There is a great deal in 1 and 2 Corinthians about the principles of ministry, and a survey reveals the following points:

a. The ministry is regarded as doing the work of God in the power of God. It does not, therefore, depend upon rhetorical skills or human cunning (1 Cor 1:18ff). Nor should ministers be the object of cultic devotion and loyalty (1:12, 3:5-9).
b. The ministers are servants of God, doing "the work of the Lord" (1 Cor 3:5, 16:10); secondarily, they are servants of their fellow believers (2 Cor 4:5).
c. The task of the minister is to feed the congregation with the word (1 Cor 3:1-3). To this end they are "stewards" of the word (4:1-2), neither inventing it nor changing it. Nor can they "lord it over" the faith of others (2 Cor 1:24).
d. The word of the minister must be accompanied by a life which itself teaches (1 Cor 4:16-17); this may well also involve suffering (4:8-13). Suffering, not power, is likely to be the Christian path (2 Corinthians 10-13); in suffering, the grace of God is magnified (4:7-12, 6:3-10).
e. It is permissible but not mandatory for the ministers to be paid (1 Cor 9:1-18).
f. The minister is under God's special scrutiny (1 Cor 4:4, 9:27; cf. Jas 3:1).
g. The essence of the ministry is the proclamation of reconciliation; the ministers are ambassadors for Christ (2 Cor 5:19-20). This proclamation is necessarily accompanied by profound, caring, personal relationships in which the application of the gospel is worked out in discipline, in suffering, and in joy. But the minister's serving role is not inconsistent with authority and rule any more than a parent's role is (1 Cor 16:16).

While there is a lack of rigidity about ministerial office and church government in the New Testament, it should not be assumed that there is support for the modern idea that authority only resides in the preached word and that the minister only has authority when he is preaching (and then only when he is preaching the truth).

Such an idea is inconsistent with the nature of pastoral care that we see already developed in the early church (e.g. Heb 13:17; 1 Thess 5:12-13). Indeed, we can see in the New Testament the beginnings of what later developed into networks of churches under leaders especially responsible for doctrine and support. There are many legitimate ways for what we now call denominations to be governed, but crucial to the way chosen is the integrity of character and doctrinal commitment of the leadership.

It is also important to notice the connection between word and sacraments. As we have already seen (in chapter 24), Christ appointed the sacraments of baptism and the Lord's Supper to be 'visible words'. They are the gospel preached by participation. The emphasis in baptism falls on the grace of God in which our sins are washed away and new life is granted to us, while the emphasis in the Lord's Supper falls on our union with Christ, and so with one another, in his death for our sins. The sacraments depend for their efficacy on the word of God, which explains them, and to which they point.

It is of key importance, then, that the sacrament be conducted by one who teaches the word, so that word and sacrament do not become dissociated from one another, leading ultimately to superstitious abuse of the sign itself.

6. Conclusion

The New Testament insists that the congregation be ruled by love. The mutual relationships of Christians are to be characterized by forgiveness and by bearing one another's burdens, thus fulfilling "the law of Christ" (Gal 6:2).

Christian ministry is, therefore, co-extensive with the people of God. We are to excel in our humble service of one another. We are brothers and sisters, and even those who are prominent by virtue of special responsibility must not lord it over the rest (1 Pet 5:3; 3 John 9);

nor are they to allow themselves the place and prestige which would be associated with their position in a merely human context (Matt 23:8-12). Nonetheless, the flock should honour and respect those who lead for the work they do (1 Pet 5:1-5; 1 Tim 5:17-18).

The headship of Christ over his church is exercised in part by the gifts of his Spirit. No exhaustive list of such gifts may be found in the New Testament; Christ's sovereignty is not restrained. The Christian is a steward, using Christ's gifts as the situation demands (1 Pet 4:10-11). The aim is to build up and to strengthen, not to provide personal satisfaction for the gifted person. The possession of a gift does not entitle a person to use the gift.

Above all, we bless one another by meeting under the direction of Christ's word, receiving the word and expressing it as we are able: in creed, in song, in speech, in reading (1 Cor 14:26). Then, in obedience to that admonition and encouragement, we bring into use those gifts with which we have been graced by Christ, so far as they are needed. We are to have a right estimate of ourselves (Rom 12:3-8), not despising others, and not demanding uniformity (1 Corinthians 12). The church does not create ministry; it recognizes it. God is the judge of it.

Our mutual ministry also involves discipline. This is not the responsibility of the leadership alone but of every Christian. It begins with admonition and exhortation, is conducted with gentleness and humility, and is aimed at the restoration of the person (Gal 6:1-5). If the offender is entirely unrepentant of a serious public offence, it will lead to a withdrawal of fellowship until there is repentance (Matt 18:15-20; 1 Corinthians 5-6; cf. 2 Cor 2:5-11).

Mutual ministry of any sort arises from love for the church and must be regulated by this love (1 Corinthians 13). Too rigid an exercise of the 'official' ministry has hindered it in the past; but the vigorous exercise of gifts without the discernment of love brings it into disrepute.

Key verse

"You know that those who are considered rulers of the Gentiles lord it over them, and their great ones exercise authority over them. But it shall not be so among you. But whoever would be great among you must be your servant, and whoever would be first among you must be slave of all. For even the Son of Man came not to be served but to serve, and to give his life as a ransom for many." (Mark 10:42-45)

Quotation

"All the ministries and offices which Christ instituted into His church are centred in the Word." (Herman Bavinck)

Key terms

- Ministry
- Congregation
- Denomination
- Priesthood
- Leadership
- Apostles
- Marks and notes of the church

For further thought

- In what ways is the church "built on the foundation of the apostles and prophets" (Eph 2:20)?
- What do you understand by church unity—its form, and its necessity?
- What are the likely strengths and weaknesses of denominations? What are the likely strengths and weaknesses of an independent church?
- To what extent should a church be governed democratically?
- Do we need a priesthood? Do we have one?

- What qualities are to be looked for in a pastor, and why? (The 'Pastoral Epistles' of 1-2 Timothy and Titus are especially important here.)
- What should 'servant leadership' look like in the church? In the home? In the marketplace?

For further reading
- Thirty-Nine Articles, articles 21, 23, 24, 26, 32-34 and 36-39
- Westminster Confession, chapters 32-34
- Bray, chapter 30
- Horton, chapter 17
- Milne, chapters 25-26

26

THE LIFE OF FAITH: ITS HOPE

Key concept: The life of faith is lived by hope in the coming of Christ the Lord.

1. The one who is our hope

There is an indissoluble connection between hope and health: when we have lost all hope, we are on the verge of losing our human functioning; but when we have hope, we feel that the future contains promise—even though the past cannot be altered and the present cannot be grasped. By looking forward, we retain balance and cheerfulness even in desperate and painful times.

What is true of an individual is also true of a family or a nation. When hopelessness assails us, we become lethargic or angry. Revolutions are inspired when the hopeless are given hope, however spurious. Because hope is to do with the future, it is the vehicle by which the future invades the present and shapes it. We hope for some desired goal and we bend our steps towards it, the future dominating the present. In this capacity hope gives meaning and purpose to our lives. Indeed, medical research is beginning to show a connection between a hopeful faith and physical and mental well-being. This is all the more important in a world in which there has been something of an epidemic of anxiety and depression, especially among younger people.

So far I have been speaking mainly of the psychological aspect of hope—what may also be called 'longing'. It is, of course, very closely linked with faith; in a way it may be called faith with a forward gaze. It shares with faith this dual characteristic: first, that it is part of mental health and helps create stable, happy persons; and second, that it may, nonetheless, be based on illusion. The psychological benefit may still be apparent, at least in the short term, despite the illusory character of the faith or hope. An optimist may be wildly astray and yet will achieve a degree of happiness while dreams persist. A fool's paradise is still a paradise of sorts.

But, as I have also hinted, hope can also be a goal rather than a mere state of mind. Thus, for example, you may have a political and social goal of achieving a classless and non-discriminatory society, the diminution of the family, equality of the sexes in all things, higher education for all, emancipation from demeaning work, the abolition of the state, and economic rewards based on need rather than achievement. To achieve such goals will require human effort in law-making, in education, in moral instruction, perhaps even in revolution. Such a vision will require generations to accomplish, but a vision is still needed to inspire and provoke. Usually, such an all-encompassing vision is based on an optimistic view of the capacity and inherent goodness of human beings.

In the Scriptures, God reveals the Christian hope. It is many-sided, but central to it is the return, or second coming, of Jesus Christ. Our faith in God rests on his promises, and promises are, by their very nature, forward-looking. When we investigate the promises we see that they may best be summed up in Christ. Whatever eschatology Christians develop (and there are several variations open to us), the great test for the reliability and accuracy of such an eschatology is this: does it focus hope on the one who is our hope, Jesus Christ? No amount of fascination with the details of the future, whether the intricacies of the unfolding of history or the furniture of heaven, can replace that as the essence of our beliefs about what lies ahead. Paradoxically, the Christian hope is provenly effective at improving the lot of the individual and the experience of justice in society, not by providing a political program, but by recognition of human sinfulness and obedience to the word of God as we wait for the coming of Christ. Love of God and love of neighbour are powerfully transformative, but they are not utopian.

In the final two chapters, the *parousia* (or coming again of Jesus) will be the watershed. In this chapter we will focus on the nature of his return and the events leading up to it; in the next we will concentrate on the state of affairs ushered in by his manifestation to the world. Of course, from the beginning of this book we have been thinking of God's future, since the gospel and the Bible are always forward-looking. Christian doctrine is set within a narrative.

2. The nature of his coming

Some passages of Scripture speak of Jesus' coming (Acts 1:11), where others speak of his coming *again* (John 14:3), of his appearing (Col 3:4; 1 Tim 6:14), of his descent (1 Thess 4:16), or of his being revealed (2 Thess 1:7). Each description has its own nuance. But it is clear from them all that his return will differ significantly from his first appearing, which was restricted in time and space, being more or less local. His coming will not be invisible and selective, as was (and is) the coming of the Holy Spirit.

According to Luke 17:20-37 and similar passages, the nature of his coming will be sudden, divisive and decisive.

a. Sudden

Again and again in passages to do with his coming, there are warnings that any prior signs will not be so clear as to awaken the sleeper or to give unambiguous indication that he is coming. I will discuss the signs of his coming below, but the fundamental point is that no-one can predict with certainty when this event will be (Luke 17:20-23; cf. Mark 13:32-37).

b. Divisive

The sudden end of history will reveal the human race to be divided between those who know God and those who do not. There will undoubtedly be surprises awaiting many, for families and churches will discover that human judgement and God's judgement do not coincide (Luke 17:34-35; cf. Matt 7:21-23). And yet, for those who are truly looking to Christ, there will be joy in his appearing.

c. Decisive

The return of Jesus Christ will mark the end of this stage of history. It will not be just another event in a long chain. In a way, his first coming was like that; and even if through dramatic climate change or a nuclear war the human race were to be reduced to a tiny number, these too would be events within the process of history. But the return of Christ will put history on an entirely new plane: "every eye will see him" (Rev 1:7); "for as the lightning flashes and lights up the sky from one side to the other, so will the Son of Man be in his day" (Luke 17:24).

What this adds up to is the 'given-ness' and the certainty of it all. Unlike the worldly hopes, which will not come to pass without human toil and sacrifice, the Christian hope comes from God, as his gift. The Christian doctrine of the fall and our slavery to sin always challenges the utopian language of the humanistic ideologies which are premised on human goodness. We do not bring the kingdom of God or create it, though we may pray for it. Whatever we do in this life under the impetus of God's rule (and it ought not to be inconsiderable), and however much it may be remembered in the age to come, it will still not create that age. From first to last, the kingdom belongs to God.

We have seen that the heart of Jesus' message was the coming of the kingdom or rule of God. We have seen also that by the time the New Testament message reached its fullness, the kingdom had both come and yet remained to come. Thus the passage in Luke 17 begins with the mysterious (to his first hearers) statement "the kingdom of God is in the midst of you" (v 21). Jesus was declaring himself to be the king. The preaching that Jesus Christ is Lord is the proper message for this age; it may be over-schematized, but we may speak of the present age as being "the kingdom of Christ" (1 Cor 15:20-28). When Christ is revealed, it will be the revelation for all to see his lordship, it will be the overthrow of his enemies, including death, and it will be the signal for the consummation of all things in the kingdom of God.

3. The time of his coming

It is extraordinary how frequently in history believers have tried to calculate the date of the second coming; extraordinary because Jesus himself declared his own ignorance: "But concerning that day or that hour, no-one knows, not even the angels in heaven, nor the Son, but only the Father" (Mark 13:32). What has drawn them on, no doubt, has been the nature of the apocalyptic language of Old Testament and New Testament, and especially passages such as Mark 13 which speak in terms of signs by which some sense can be made of history, and some information gleaned about its progress. But three things should have increased caution: first, what we are told about where we now are in history; second, the nature of prophetic language; and third, the careful study of the passages involved.

First of all, we must remember what we have seen when Jesus declared that the kingdom of God was in their midst (Luke 17:20-21). The coming of Jesus, and especially the great triumph of his death, resurrection and ascension, inaugurated the age to come. This means that ever since Jesus ascended, we have been living in what the Bible calls "the last days", experiencing something of the powers of the age to come (such as the ministry of the Spirit), but nonetheless still awaiting the end (e.g. Heb 1:2, 6:4-6). We have been resurrected with Christ, but we await the resurrection promised for his appearing (Col 3:1-4). Thus the signs of the last days are already here, and have been ever since Christ left. We must be aware that his coming will be at any time, and the existing signs minister to our awareness of this.

Secondly, the Bible itself helps us to understand prophetic language. According to Jesus, the Old Testament contained a great deal about him: "everything written about me in the Law of Moses and the Prophets and the Psalms" (Luke 24:44). Indeed, from apostolic days onwards Christians have concurred gladly with that judgement and have seen Christ "in all the Scriptures" (24:27). But consider whether this is possible from the other point of view; with the Old Testament in hand—and only the Old Testament—could you write a Gospel, or be confident of giving an account of Jesus? The prophetic language is not so clear that one would be able, with any confidence, to write history in advance. It is only when Christ comes that we see how he fulfils the prophecies.

This phenomenon is well worth remembering when we are over-confident about our ability to predict the future based on New Testament prophecy. The most faithful reader of the Old Testament would have been surprised at the events of the life of the real Jesus—surprised, but accepting and believing. In the same way, when he comes again he will not in any way falsify what is written, but the reality will be beyond our present imagining.

That brings us to the third point. When we study the passages involved, whether in the synoptic Gospels or the epistles or Revelation, it is also worth asking: what is the function of the passage? When we do this, we will see that it is not to give us a detailed map of the future (though what it says about the future is, of course, true), but rather to make sure that our present attitudes are right. This is the reason, for example, that we are warned that the coming of the Lord will be "like a thief in the night" (1 Thess 5:2). In the face of this, we must be constantly ready, not counting down toward his return, but counting on his return.

This also clarifies what a passage like Mark 13 is about. The passage refers to the destruction of the temple as its starting point, and the disciples ask, "when will these things be, and what will be the sign when all these things are about to be accomplished?" (v 4). Jesus' answer gives many signs—wars and rumours of wars, false prophets, earthquakes, famines and the "abomination of desolation" (v 14). If he is giving them a warning about his return at the end of the age, it is noteworthy that these signs occurred virtually at once and have gone on ever since. If he is referring, in the first place at least, both to his own impending death and to the destruction of Jerusalem, as seems possible, the signs still function in the same way: to prepare his hearers for the events rather than to satisfy intellectual curiosity about the details of the future and the timing of it.

Once this point is perceived—and once we become aware that it is by accepting exhortations such as enduring to the end (v 13), being on guard (v 9), and being wakeful but not anxious (vv 11, 35) that we best receive the teaching of these passages—we may also see whether there is material in them for some idea of how history is going to turn out. After all, the destruction of Jerusalem did occur, and tradition has it that the Christian community left the city in time, obeying Mark 13:14. Thus the New Testament gives us both particular events in history, but also events which occur in every generation. Some examples follow.

a. The fall of Jerusalem and the destruction of the temple

This occurred within the lifetime of the generation to whom Jesus addressed his words in Mark 13:1-2, 14-23 and Luke 19:41-44.

b. The evangelization of the world

Jesus predicts that "the gospel must first be proclaimed to all nations" (Mark 13:10). This need not be taken as equivalent to the evangelization of the world in our modern sense, but rather as a reference to the gospel going forth from the Jews among the Gentiles. Compare Paul's claim in Colossians 1:23: "the gospel that you heard, which has been proclaimed in all creation under heaven …"

c. The salvation of Israel

In Romans 9-11 Paul gives a sort of overview of history, largely concerned with the way in which Jews and Gentiles have responded to the gospel. He sees a "remnant" of Israel "chosen by grace" (11:5) for the present; but he also sees the "full inclusion" of Israel (11:12). He concludes: "a partial hardening has come upon Israel, until the fullness of the Gentiles has come in. And in this way all Israel will be saved …" (11:25-26).

Some take this to mean a full-scale turning by the Jews to Christ before the end of history, or even something like the coming into existence of the present state of Israel. But the wording may equally mean that during history, side by side, elect Gentiles and Jews are being summoned into God's kingdom until, in the end, "all Israel will be saved"—that is to say, all *true* Israel: those who have turned to God through Christ, seeing in him the fulfilment of the promises of the Old Testament.

d. The coming of "the man of lawlessness"

In 2 Thessalonians 2, Paul corrects the misunderstanding of the Thessalonian Christians that the day of the Lord may already have come by reminding them that it will be preceded by "the rebellion" when "the man of lawlessness is revealed, the son of destruction, who opposes and exalts himself against every so-called god or object of worship, so that he takes his seat in the temple of God, proclaiming himself to be God" (vv 3-4).

The man of lawlessness has sometimes been identified with "the antichrist" of 1 John 2:22, but this seems unlikely; they are more like colleagues in godlessness—the one political, the other religious (cf. Revelation 12-13). In the case of the antichrist, however, John notes: "Children, it is the last hour, and as you have heard that antichrist is coming, so now many antichrists have come. Therefore we know that it is the last hour" (1 John 2:18).

John's words may well give us an interpretative clue. In the New Testament perspective, the last days have already begun and, even if they stretch over several thousand years, they remain the last days for all that. Within these last days we have various outbursts of antichrist "lawlessness". They always remind us that we are living in the last days and that we must therefore be ready for the coming of Jesus, but they are not in themselves readily identifiable as the final outburst before the end.

e. The thousand-year reign of Christ

The biblical reference to such a millennium is in Revelation 20:1-10. Broadly speaking, there have been three explanations of it:

i. Some would locate the thousand years within history, beginning at a particular date and culminating with the return of Christ. They would say that the thousand-year reign of Christ will be marked by an ever-increasing advance for the gospel. Their position is called 'postmillennialism', since Christ's return is thought of as being after (post) the thousand years. Many in this group would say that the thousand years (which may be a literal or a figurative number) has already commenced.

ii. Some would locate the thousand years as an extension of history to take place after the return of Christ. Since Christ's return precedes the thousand years, their position is called 'premillennialism'. The thousand-year period would be characterized by the gradual triumph of the gospel in the world.

iii. Some would locate the thousand years as the whole of history between the first and second coming of Christ, regarding the reference in Revelation as being of a figurative length rather than literal, and the preaching of the gospel during this period as the binding of Satan (v 2). This view is called amillennialism ('a' meaning 'not'), although it teaches that Christ's return will occur after the figurative thousand years is over.

I favour the third option, which in my view best suits the nature of the book of Revelation and the way in which numbers are used within apocalyptic literature, as well as the teaching of the rest of the New Testament. Once again, however, I would argue that we are not to be looking for the evidences of the thousand-year reign, but rather should always be prepared for the appearing of Christ the Saviour.

4. The purpose of his coming

The New Testament teaches that Christ will come again to judge the world (Acts 10:42). The next chapter will study that topic in more detail. But we can say at once that Christ's return is to gather and save his people. Paul depicts him as descending and his people coming to meet him: "And the dead in Christ will rise first. Then we who are alive, who are left, will be caught up together with them in the clouds to meet the Lord in the air, and so we will always be with the Lord" (1 Thess 4:16-17). Elsewhere he speaks of his people "being gathered together to [Christ]" (2 Thess 2:1) and of

Christ being "glorified in his saints, and ... marvelled at among all who have believed" (1:10).

Certainly the testimony of the New Testament is that Christ is to be the focal point of this great occurrence. His lordship is preached now; then it will be demonstrated in no unclear way: "at the name of Jesus every knee should bow, in heaven and on earth and under the earth, and every tongue confess that Jesus Christ is Lord, to the glory of God the Father" (Phil 2:10).

The New Testament reveals that the whole creation came into being through the Son (Col 1:16; John 1:3); that the whole creation is sustained by the Son (Col 1:17; Heb 1:3); that the whole creation was brought into being for the Son (Col 1:16); and that the whole creation was reconciled through the Son (1:19-20). That reconciliation involves the pacification and unwilling surrender of those who oppose him to the end, whether thrones, dominions and principalities, or men and women. In the end, every knee will bow to Christ, whether those who worship him or those who reject him (Phil 2:9-11). But, in the end, when God brings righteousness to pass and all the enemies of Christ, including death itself, are destroyed, all this will be summed up in him:

> In him we have redemption through his blood, the forgiveness of our trespasses, according to the riches of his grace, which he lavished upon us, in all wisdom and insight making known to us the mystery of his will, according to his purpose, which he set forth in Christ as a plan for the fullness of time, to unite all things in him, things in heaven and things on earth. (Eph 1:7-10)

In the next chapter we will consider what this means for men and women. But, as we shall see, this consummation is not unconnected with God's purposes for us as they were foreshadowed in the opening chapters of Genesis.

5. Conclusion

First John tells us that "it is the last hour" (1 John 2:18) and in so doing gives the New Testament perspective on the present time. The length of the last hour hardly matters (2 Pet 3:1-10); it is the type of time, or quality of time, that counts. Wherever we are on the time scale, we are living in the last hour. It is appropriate, then, that we should adopt the attitudes and behaviour of those for whom only one last great act of God is left, and one that may occur at any time.

In our treatment of the life of faith, we have already observed that the last hour is characterized by elements of "the age to come", such as the Spirit of God, as well as by elements of the "present evil age", such as the world, the flesh and the devil. We are heirs, but we have not yet received our full inheritance. And yet during this period we are sustained and strengthened by hope—not the optimism which comes mainly from the possession of a sunny disposition, but the hope that arises from trusting in the solid promises of God himself. That hope is described in various ways in the New Testament—for example, Peter uses the language of the old covenant and speaks of "an inheritance that is imperishable, undefiled, and unfading, kept in heaven for you" (1 Pet 1:4)—but at the centre of every hope is Jesus Christ himself and his coming again (1:7-9). We do not need maps of the future when he is our hope.

Death still stalks humanity. He is "the last enemy" (1 Cor 15:26). We would be foolish to say that he has lost his power to hurt and to terrify. But the Christian hope is the resurrected Lord, the firstfruits of those who have fallen asleep. The New Testament often speaks of those who have died in Christ as being "asleep", not meaning that they have entered a world of dreams, but rather that, from the point of view of we who remain, they are alive but absent for a time. They are at peace. For them, washed in the blood of the Lord who deals with all sin, there is no experience of 'Purgatory' (an idea which is not in Scripture and which contradicts the fullness of the grace of God). From their own point of view, there can be no doubt that they have the fruition of Christian faith in passing straight into the presence of their Lord when they pass from this world: "We are of good courage, and we would rather be away from the body and at home with the Lord" (2 Cor 5:8); "My desire is to depart and be with Christ, for that is far better" (Phil 1:23).

Key verse

For the Lord himself will descend from heaven with a cry of command, with the voice of an archangel, and with the sound of the trumpet of God. And the dead in Christ will rise first. Then we who are alive, who are left, will be caught up together with them in the clouds to meet the Lord in the air, and so we will always be with the Lord. Therefore encourage one another with these words. (1 Thess 4:16-18)

Quotation

"Life can only be understood backwards, but it must be lived forwards." (Søren Kierkegaard)

Key terms

- Hope
- Second coming
- Parousia
- Millennium
- Apocalypse
- Eschatology

For further thought

- What aspects of Christ's return are certain? What aspects are uncertain?

- Will history give us any clue to the timing of Christ's return?
- In your judgement, does our day and age have too much focus on Christ's return, or too little? What does a healthy balance look like?
- What is the 'hope' on offer from various cultural, social and political movements in our world? How does the Christian hope differ?
- Does the Christian hope hinder or foster efforts to improve the world?
- What should we make of 'near-death experiences'?

For further reading
- For chapters 26-27 of this book, see *Concise Theology*, part 4
- Thirty-Nine Articles, article 22
- Horton, chapter 18
- Milne, chapters 27-28

27

CHRIST THE LORD AND THE END OF HISTORY

Key concept: In the end, all will be raised, all will be judged, and God will be glorified.

1. Introduction

The Bible begins with the orderly process of God the Creator bringing all things into existence, creating humanity—male and female—in his own image, commissioning them to rule the world under his sovereignty, and coming to his rest on the seventh day. It continues with the rebellion of Adam and Eve against the sovereignty of God, a rebellion that throws into doubt the whole future of the race and succeeds in corrupting us and poisoning the relationships in which God placed us. With the environment, with the animal kingdom, with the opposite sex, exist tensions and difficulties, and we regard God himself as the enemy.

The gospel preaching of Jesus, that the kingdom of God is at hand, is a reassertion of both the rights and the purposes of God. Jesus invites men and women to submit themselves for the day on which God will come in his judgement. By so doing, they are identifying with the future and the fulfilment of God's plans.

John the Baptist preached the same message. In the case of Jesus, however, he did not merely preach the message; he was at the very centre of the message. In the interim period before the full coming of the kingdom of God, the message is the lordship of Christ and faith in him. This is, of course, because he is the Son of God. But, more than that, he is man as well as God, the one man who is the mediator between God and humanity. As such, he is the pattern for humanity, the last Adam into whose image all who belong to him will ultimately conform. He is what we should be.

In this final chapter, having already seen that the New Testament identifies Jesus as the one who will come again, we now see what his return will mean for humanity, and how humanity's fulfilment in God's purposes comes to its conclusion.

2. The resurrection

The resurrection of Jesus Christ from the dead is God's great positive affirmation over the one who was rejected. In it he is "declared to be the Son of God in power according to the Spirit of holiness … Jesus Christ our Lord" (Rom 1:4). By raising him from the dead God gives proof to all people that he will judge the world in righteousness "by a man whom he has appointed" (Acts 17:31).

But there is more to the resurrection than that. The fact that the resurrection occurred on the first day of the week suggests a new age, a new beginning. In any case, we are told that Jesus' resurrection powerfully affects our own Christian lives now, and that we have been "raised with Christ … for you have died, and your life is hidden with Christ in God" (Col 3:1-3).

As with all eschatology there is the present tension between what is and what is yet to be, but clearly the resurrection has transported us, in some sense, into the age to come. Furthermore, Paul sees Christ as "the firstfruits of those who have fallen asleep. For as by a man came death, by a man has come also the resurrection of the dead" (1 Cor 15:20-21).

In short, Christ is the pattern for our future, the man who is the image and guarantee of all his followers. He is the pioneer, and if his resurrection did not take place there would be no hope whatever for us: "If Christ has not been raised, your faith is futile and you are still in your sins" (1 Cor 15:17).

The resurrection of which Christ is the firstfruits is portrayed in the New Testament as affecting all humanity—those who belong to Christ and those who do not: "an hour is coming when all who are in the tombs will hear his voice and come out, those who have done good to the resurrection of life, and those who have done evil to the resurrection of judgement" (John 5:28-29). This is not inconsistent with what Paul says, but he does not focus his attention on the resurrection of unbelievers.

We have little information about the nature of the resurrection body. The two passages of most significance are 1 Corinthians 15:35-38 and 2 Corinthians 4:7-5:10. In the first of these (as also with Philippians 3:20-21), it is clear that our resurrection bodies will be in the pattern of Christ the Lord's. Whether the body in which he appeared to his disciples represented the final stage of his changed and glorious body, we do not need to speculate. Sufficient to say, with Paul, that the glory of the resurrected body will be such that it transcends the present earthly body as the full-grown plant transcends the seed. He contrasts the perishable with the imperishable, the dishonourable with the glorious, the weak with the powerful, the physical with the spiritual (1 Corinthians 15:42-44, with the last of these contrasts meaning that the new body will be controlled by the Spirit).

The words that seem most to characterize his description are 'immortality' and 'glory'. Our immortality is not the absolute immortality which belongs to God alone, but is entirely dependent upon him. It means that we can never be touched by death again—that we have, in John's terms, eternal life. Death's power to hurt comes from sin, which means, therefore, that we shall be without sin. Indeed, we will have the glorious freedom of not being able to sin.

'Glory' is the word that most dominates 2 Corinthians 4-5. Here the apostle is focusing on a different problem, namely that of death before the return of Jesus. He contrasts his present outward experience of affliction, perplexity and persecution—first with his true inner nature, which is "being renewed day by day", and second with the glory that is to come: "For this light momentary affliction is preparing for us an eternal weight of glory beyond all comparison …" (2 Cor 4:16-17). Paul therefore finds himself groaning in this life and hence longing to "put on" the resurrection body that God has prepared for him (5:2-3).

There is little else to be said about the body that we are to be given. That we are to be embodied, that we are to be like Christ, that we are to be immortal and glorious, is enough. There are many other questions—such as whether we will recognize each other (which seems likely, given the communal nature of salvation)—about which no definitive answer may be given. The key thing is that "we will always be with the Lord", and so with his people (1 Thess 4:17).

Opinion is divided about when we are to receive our new bodies. Some argue that we receive them at the moment of our death, judging that this is Paul's meaning in 2 Corinthians 5:1-10. Others would argue that there is an interim period when we are certainly "with the Lord" but when we remain as yet to be resurrected, just as there was a delay between the death of Jesus and his resurrection on the third day. There is difference of opinion, too, on the connection between the body that is put into the earth and the resurrection body. The Lord Jesus' tomb was empty—he was raised in the same body. But some argue that Christ's was a unique case and that the heavenly dwelling of 2 Corinthians 5:1 is altogether new, although the person who inhabits it remains the same throughout the experience. On balance, I prefer the view that we will be awaiting our resurrection, rather than being given a body immediately. This seems to accord better with the delay between the death and the resurrection of Jesus, and his words to the dying thief, "today you will be with me in paradise" (Luke 23:43). I also think that 1 Corinthians 15 means that however great the transformation, there remains a connection between our present body and that which is to come.

3. The judgement

The fact of judgement is one of the doctrines most repudiated and disliked both within and without the church. For many years the secular world has been uneasy with judgement and punishment of all sorts. It is true that in the educational process a positive and encouraging attitude achieves far more than a negative and censorious one. And yet, even in contemporary education, reality ultimately intrudes and we have to agree that, although it is good to be nearly right, it is far better to be actually right. In the case of crime, the community is often double-minded, wanting criminals to be punished, yet readily accepting explanations which ameliorate the offence and reduce the judgement.

It is not surprising, therefore, that talk of God's judgement should seem so threatening and so bizarre. That God loves is agreed; that he should be wrathful is thoroughly disputed. The secular attitude has affected many within the church; in particular, many believers have rejected the concept of hell. They would prefer to believe in universal salvation or in annihilation rather than a state of eternal punishment.

It is extremely important that in areas of Christian doctrine which the world finds unpalatable, we turn to the Scriptures. The world's view may be correct, and we may simply be reflecting old-fashioned worldly views rather than the actual teaching of the

Bible. On the other hand, the world and the word of God may be at variance with each other, and we are being challenged to hold the Bible's point of view by faith despite a hostile culture. We will find, however, that if we do adhere to Scripture its teaching will make sense at a deeper level.

In fact the idea of judgement by God must be regarded as one of the Bible's leading themes: "in the day that you eat of it you shall surely die" (Gen 2:17) contains the first note of warning; the Lord's judgement is then extended against the serpent (3:14-15), the woman (3:16) and the man (3:17-19) in turn. Cain is punished for murder (4:11f), and then the whole world is judged and overthrown (apart from Noah and his family) in the flood. On page after page of the scriptural text, the Lord shows himself willing to punish sin. It is part of the name by which he is revealed:

> "The Lord, the Lord, a God merciful and gracious, slow to anger, and abounding in steadfast love and faithfulness, keeping steadfast love for thousands, forgiving iniquity and transgression and sin, but who will by no means clear the guilty, visiting the iniquity of the fathers on the children and the children's children, to the third and the fourth generation." (Exod 34:6-7)

The book of Judges, the former prophets and the latter prophets all teach and give examples of God's judgements on his own people and on others in the arena of history. The idea of a day of the Lord in which a final judgement will be delivered also seems present (e.g. Amos 5:18-20), and apocalyptic writings such as Daniel undergird it (Dan 12:1-4). The New Testament does not ameliorate the idea in the slightest:

> The wages of sin is death ... (Rom 6:23)

> "Whoever does not believe is condemned already ..." (John 3:18)

> And the sea gave up the dead who were in it, Death and Hades gave up the dead who were in them, and they were judged, each one of them, according to what they had done. (Rev 20:13)

The name of God as given in Exodus 34 is a reminder of an important aspect of the judgement. The word 'judgement' itself sounds (and indeed can be) negative and condemnatory. But God is a righteous judge (Ps 96:13) whose concern is not to overthrow and condemn but to act with truth and faithfulness, putting things right and bringing justice, mercy and peace. He drives Adam and Eve from the garden, but he clothes them as well (Gen 3:21).

One of the most significant biblical passages on judgement is Romans 1:18-3:31. Paul reveals that God's wrath is experienced in history as a response to the ingratitude and sinfulness of humanity. Indeed much of that sin both merits God's wrath and is part of the punishment. But at the same time he notes that this present experience of God's wrath is not a final one, for God's decree is that "those who practice such things deserve to die" (1:32).

Rather, God's kindness is holding back the day of final reckoning: "you are storing up wrath for yourself on the day of wrath when God's righteous judgement will be revealed" (Rom 2:5). Peter attributes this to the patience of God in "not wishing that any should perish, but that all should reach repentance" (2 Pet 3:9). On that day God's impartiality will also be revealed: "He will render to each one according to his works" (Rom 2:6). Although Paul concedes that this may mean praise for some, his conclusion is gloomy, for in fact "all have sinned and fall short of the glory of God" (3:23).

We see, therefore, that the teaching of Scripture (and this can be illustrated from the rest of the New Testament) is that God is judge, that his judgement is apparent in this life, and that his judgement will come to full fruition in a day of judgement when he will, in righteousness, deal with the human race decisively, comprehensively and eternally: "on that day when, according to my gospel, God judges the secrets of men by Christ Jesus" (Rom 2:16). Three features of this judgement require further comment.

a. By whom is the judgement made?

As we have seen, the judgement is consistently related to the Lord God. But there are also passages in Scripture which indicate that the Father has committed the judgement to his Son: "he is the one appointed by God to be judge of the living and the dead" (Acts 10:42). As Paul teaches, "he has fixed a day on which he will judge the world in righteousness by a man whom he has appointed" (17:31). John also relates this to the role of Jesus as the Son of Man (John 5:27), doubtless with reference to Daniel 7. It is worth noting, as well, that believers are linked with God in the work of judgement (1 Cor 6:3).

b. On whom does judgement come?

The last text mentioned reveals that angels are to be judged. Normally, however, the Scriptures concentrate on the children of Adam and Eve, and press the point that there is no escape from judgement; it is universal. As far as believers are concerned, the greatness of our salvation is such that the New Testament declares that we have already passed through judgement; or rather that the judgement of Christ on the cross was our judgement:

> For God did not send his Son into the world to condemn the world, but in order that the world might be saved through him. Whoever believes in him is not condemned, but whoever does not believe is condemned already, because he has not believed in the name of the only Son of God. (John 3:17-18)

Nonetheless, there are other passages which reveal that believers, too, are to face the judgement, notably 2 Corinthians 5:10: "For we must all appear before the judgement seat of Christ, so that each one may receive what is due for what he has done in the body, whether good or evil". It is usual (and doubtless correct) to see this not as a judgement for salvation but as a tribunal on the quality of our obedience to God. We have the warning about our work in 1 Corinthians 3:5-15: "each one's work will become manifest, for the Day will disclose it, because it will be revealed by fire, and the fire will test what sort of work each one has done ... If anyone's work is burned up, he will suffer loss, though he himself will be saved, but only as through fire" (vv 13, 15).

It is useless to pretend that God rewards all equally; that is manifestly not the case. Our fundamental happiness in the next age will arise from the satisfaction with which we perceive the rightness of God's judgements. There will be no jealousy or anger, only joy in the grace of God (Eph 2:7). Perhaps it is the case that there will also be differences in the responsibilities we bear, as may be suggested by the parable of the ten minas (Luke 19:11-27). In any case, we ought to give far more thought than we do to the question of whether we are pleasing the Lord, and to the relationship between his pleasure in us and our own futures (2 Cor 5:9-10).

c. What are the criteria of judgement?

The basic requirement of God is complete obedience to his word, and any failure of obedience merits his disapproval. James observes that to sin at one point is to breach the whole law, for that sin is an offence against the law-giver (Jas 2:10-11). In this the words and even the thoughts of a person, the sins of commission and the sins of omission, are all significant (Matt 12:36-37, 15:19; Heb 4:12; Luke 10:31-32).

But, as we have already seen, there is another over-riding principle. For the name of God is mercy and forgiveness, and his Son came into the world for salvation. As we stand before God's judgement seat we see that Christ has been appointed judge, and we recollect the word of God:

> Who shall bring any charge against God's elect? It is God who justifies. Who is to condemn? Christ Jesus is the one who died—more than that, who was raised—who is at the right hand of God, who indeed is interceding for us. (Rom 8:33-34)

We have indeed already passed from death to life and, however testing our experience of the judgement may be, we are experiencing the discipline of children, not the condemnation of the criminal (Heb 12:3-11). Revelation speaks of those whose names are written in "the book of life", and it is they who are to share the glory of the new Jerusalem, while anyone whose name "was not found written in the book of life … was thrown into the lake of fire" (Rev 20:11-15).

It is as Revelation takes us to the scene of the "great white throne and him who was seated on it" with "the dead, great and small, standing before the throne, and books were opened" (Rev 20:11-12) that we are able to think with all due seriousness of who we are and what the world is. For despite the infinite variety of human life across space and time, all are heading for one destination. We are to be united at this point, and all are to be held accountable for their lives—with different degrees of accountability, it is true, but accountable nonetheless. The searching gaze of a perfect judge will be upon us, and there will be no escape from "the eyes of him to whom we must give account" (Heb 4:13).

Everything in this life is put into its proper place by that moment. It explains why, on the one hand, we must do what pleases God in this life, and yet, on the other, our pleasing of God is also for the next life. It explains the urgency of evangelism. It explains the necessity for the cross and for our preaching of the cross. It gives meaning to every aspect, however small, however momentous, in our lives. It identifies every human being as important and the life they live, however humdrum and trivial it appears, as eternally significant. In short, the fact of judgement, far from exhibiting God's contempt for the race, demonstrates his immense love for us. You apply your judgement to that which is precious, and it may well be that the gravest sense of loss felt by those whose names are not in the book of life will be their understanding that they have failed to worship the God who loves like this.

4. Beyond the day of judgement

The Bible presents us clearly with the fact that the human race will be permanently divided into those "in Adam" and those "in Christ" on the day of judgement. Comparatively little is said of the fate of those in Adam. The Gospel of John records that "whoever believes in the Son has eternal life; whoever does not obey the Son shall not see life, but the wrath of God remains on him" (3:36). These words of the Lord Jesus are as striking as any in Scripture: "It is better for you to enter the kingdom of God with one eye than with two eyes to be thrown into hell, 'where their worm does not die and the fire is not quenched'" (Mark 9:47-48).

Metaphoric as the expression doubtless is, we cannot ameliorate its severity, for we must still ask what it depicts. Attempts to suggest that hell is less than a permanent state seem to founder on such expressions.

At the heart of the biblical pictures of judgement there is the concept of broken relationships. This was both the first sin and the punishment for the first sin. We are made for communion with God and with each other, and the failure of that communion is the worm which does not die:

> "I never knew you; depart from me, you workers of lawlessness." (Matt 7:23)

> They will suffer the punishment of eternal destruction, away from the presence of the Lord and from the glory of his might … (2 Thess 1:9)

We are speaking here of an inconsolable loss, of a grief that will not dissipate because it is linked to guilt and shame. If this is the case, the sharp pangs of conscience that most of us experience occasionally are a sort of foretaste of what may be the bitterness of destruction.

We do not know whether such a fate awaits few or many. God is sovereign, and his saving choice, according to Revelation, encompasses "a great multitude that no-one could number, from every nation, from all tribes and peoples and languages" (7:9). God is infinitely merciful and all powerful. His power is at work in people's lives in a way which is invisible to us, not least when they have been prayed for.

5. Eternal life

Once again, the Bible does not take us far in describing the joys of the age to come. What we do see, however—and this must surely be more than sufficient for us—is that Christ Jesus is at the centre of our future. We will be with him. We will be like him, living for him in perfect safety and peace for all eternity.

God's people will be resurrected and in the image of "the man of heaven". We will inherit the kingdom of God (1 Cor 15:49-50), which means that we will share in the victory of Christ in which he conquers "every rule and every authority and power", including the last enemy: death itself (15:24-26). In this present age we have seen Christ as the one man who has fulfilled God's plans for the race, the one man who rules the world, in line with Genesis 1 and Psalm 8 (see 1 Corinthians 15:27, and especially Hebrews 2:5-18). With his return will come the moment for the complete restoration of all who are in him when "the last Adam" becomes the head of a new race, in fact through the resurrection of all who are in him. Thus "in Christ" the situation of Genesis 1 and 2 will be restored and surpassed, and, at the head of this people, having subjected all things to himself, Christ our representative will make obeisance to the Father, "that God may be all in all" (1 Cor 15:28).

Hebrews 4 speaks of this as the "rest", but there is no need to think of it as static any more than God's seventh day rest (Gen 2:2-3) was static, or the Israelite's possession of their rest was static. Rather, just as Israel had rest from her enemies in the promised land (2 Sam 7:1), so we too have safety from the world, the flesh and the devil. 'Fulfilment' may be a better word, but it is a fulfilment that is active in love and righteousness. Peter speaks of the dissolution of the old creation and the coming of "new heavens and a new earth in which righteousness dwells" (2 Pet 3:13). It seems, then, that just as our future is to be embodied, so too our future is to be within a new creation.

But at the heart of whatever the Bible teaches about the age to come, there is the experience of love.

Ephesians speaks about God saving us, "that in the coming ages he might show the immeasurable riches of his grace in kindness towards us in Christ Jesus" (Eph 2:7). In 1 Corinthians, Paul gives us a glimpse of a world dominated by love:

> Love bears all things, believes all things, hopes all things, endures all things. Love never ends … when the perfect comes, the partial will pass away. When I was a child, I spoke like a child, I thought like a child, I reasoned like a child. When I became a man, I gave up childish ways. For now we see in a mirror dimly, but then face to face. Now I know in part; then I shall know fully, even as I have been fully known. So now faith, hope, and love abide, these three; but the greatest of these is love." (1 Cor 13:7-8, 10-13)

Whatever the future is to be, it is to be the triumph of love, a triumph of the true maturity of the human race in God's kingdom. In this age we are but children; it is in the age to come that we shall reach the maturity of adults, and be the recipients of "an eternal weight of glory beyond all comparison" (2 Cor 4:17). We will be at home, at last, in and with the Lord.

———

Key verse
Then I saw a new heaven and a new earth, for the first heaven and the first earth had passed away, and the sea was no more. And I saw the holy city, new Jerusalem, coming down out of heaven from God, prepared as a bride adorned for her husband. And I heard a loud voice from the throne saying, "Behold, the dwelling place of God is with man. He will dwell with them, and they will be his people, and God himself will be with them as their God. He will wipe away every tear from their eyes, and death shall be no more, neither shall there be mourning, nor crying, nor pain any more, for the former things have passed away." (Rev 21:1-4)

Quotation
"When thou prayest, rather let thy heart be without words than thy words without heart." (John Bunyan)

Key terms
- Heaven
- Hell
- Judgement
- Salvation
- Eternal life

For further thought
- What do we know about what our future life is going to be like?
- What is the basis and nature of any judgement experienced by Christians?
- What can we learn about our resurrection from Jesus' resurrection?
- Do the sciences of biology and physics have any relevance to our beliefs about life beyond the grave?
- What is the significance of Christ remaining fully human for all time?
- Does God's wrath clash with his love?
- How does the life to come shape the life of faith that we live now?

For further reading
- Thirty-Nine Articles, article 4
- Westminster Confession, chapters 32-33
- Bray, chapter 31
- Horton, chapter 19
- Milne, chapters 29-30

Feedback on this resource

We really appreciate getting feedback about our resources—not just suggestions for how to improve them, but also positive feedback and ways they can be used. We especially love to hear that the resources may have helped someone in their Christian growth.

You can send feedback to us via the 'Feedback' menu in our online store, or write to us at info@matthiasmedia.com.au.

APPENDICES

1

THE APOSTLES' CREED

I believe in God, the Father Almighty,
creator of heaven and earth.
I believe in Jesus Christ,
God's only Son, our Lord,
who was conceived by the Holy Spirit,
born of the Virgin Mary,
suffered under Pontius Pilate,
was crucified, died, and was buried;
he descended to the dead.
On the third day he rose from the dead;
he ascended into heaven,
and is seated at the right hand of the Father;
from there he will come to judge
the living and the dead.
I believe in the Holy Spirit,
the holy catholic Church,
the communion of saints,
the forgiveness of sins,
the resurrection of the body,
and the life everlasting. Amen.

2

THE NICENE CREED

We believe in one God,
the Father, the Almighty,
maker of heaven and earth
of all that is, seen and unseen.
We believe in one Lord, Jesus Christ,
the only Son of God,
eternally begotten of the Father,
God from God, Light from Light,
true God from true God,
begotten not made,
of one being with the Father;
through him all things were made.
For us and for our salvation
he came down from heaven,
was incarnate of the Holy Spirit and the Virgin Mary
and became truly human.
For our sake he was crucified under Pontius Pilate;
he suffered death and was buried.
On the third day he rose again

in accordance with the Scriptures;
he ascended into heaven
and is seated at the right hand of the Father.
He will come again in glory to judge
the living and the dead
and his kingdom will have no end.
We believe in the Holy Spirit,
the Lord, the giver of life,
who proceeds from the Father and the Son,
who with the Father and the Son
is worshipped and glorified,
who has spoken through the prophets.
We believe in one holy catholic and apostolic Church.
We acknowledge one baptism for the forgiveness of sins.
We look for the resurrection of the dead,
and the life of the world to come. Amen.

3

THE THIRTY-NINE ARTICLES OF RELIGION

The Protestant Reformation of the 16th and 17th centuries gave birth to various confessions of faith, which were intended to explain the faith and to bind the clergy and others together in their beliefs. One of the earliest of these confessions was the Thirty-Nine Articles of Religion of the Church of England, ratified in 1571. It belongs in the Reformed tradition of Protestantism and to this day, along with *The Book of Common Prayer* (1662) and the Ordinal, is fundamental to an understanding of Anglicanism. It was addressed very much to the issues of the day, especially the break with the Roman Catholic Church, and as a statement of biblical faith has perennial importance. The Homilies to which reference is made were authorized sermons intended to be read in the churches as the great teachings of the Reformation were preached in the land. Other confessions in English emerged in the 17th century, including the powerful Westminster Confession of Faith of 1646 (used mainly by Presbyterians) and its variants, the Savoy Declaration of 1658 (Congregationalist) and the 'Things Most Surely Believed Among Us' of 1689 (Baptist).

I. OF FAITH IN THE HOLY TRINITY

There is but one living and true God, ever-lasting, without body, parts, or passions; of infinite power, wisdom, and goodness; the Maker, and Preserver of all things both visible and invisible. And in unity of this Godhead there be three Persons, of one substance, power, and eternity; the Father, the Son, and the Holy Ghost.

II. OF THE WORD OR SON OF GOD, WHICH WAS MADE VERY MAN

The Son, which is the Word of the Father, begotten from everlasting of the Father, the very and eternal God, and of one substance with the Father, took Man's nature in the womb of the blessed Virgin, of her substance: so that two whole and perfect Natures, that is to say, the Godhead and Manhood, were joined together in one Person, never to be divided, whereof is one Christ, very God, and very Man; who truly suffered, was crucified, dead, and buried, to reconcile his Father to us, and to be a sacrifice, not only for original guilt, but also for all actual sins of men.

III. OF THE GOING DOWN OF CHRIST INTO HELL

As Christ died for us, and was buried, so also is it to be believed, that he went down into Hell.

IV. OF THE RESURRECTION OF CHRIST

Christ did truly rise again from death, and took again his body, with flesh, bones, and all things appertaining to the perfection of Man's nature; wherewith he ascended into Heaven, and there sitteth, until he return to judge all Men at the last day.

V. OF THE HOLY GHOST

The Holy Ghost, proceeding from the Father and the Son, is of one substance, majesty, and glory, with the Father and the Son, very and eternal God.

VI. OF THE SUFFICIENCY OF THE HOLY SCRIPTURES FOR SALVATION

Holy Scripture containeth all things necessary to salvation: so that whatsoever is not read therein, nor may be proved thereby, is not to be required of any man, that it should be believed as an article of the Faith, or be thought requisite or necessary to salvation. In the name of the holy Scripture we do understand those Canonical Books of the Old and New Testament, of whose authority was never any doubt in the Church.

Of the Names and Number of the Canonical Books
Genesis
Exodus
Leviticus
Numbers
Deuteronomy
Joshua
Judges
Ruth
The First Book of Samuel
The Second Book of Samuel
The First Book of Kings
The Second Book of Kings
The First Book of Chronicles
The Second Book of Chronicles
The First Book of Esdras
The Second Book of Esdras

The Book of Esther
The Book of Job
The Psalms
The Proverbs
Ecclesiastes or Preacher
Cantica, or Songs of Solomon
Four Prophets the greater
Twelve Prophets the less

And the other Books (as Hierome saith) the Church doth read for example of life and instruction of manners; but yet doth it not apply them to establish any doctrine; such are these following:
The Third Book of Esdras
The Fourth Book of Esdras
The Book of Tobias
The Book of Judith
The rest of the Book of Esther
The Book of Wisdom
Jesus the Son of Sirach
Baruch the Prophet
The Song of the Three Children
The Story of Susanna
Of Bel and the Dragon
The Prayer of Manasses
The First Book of Maccabees
The Second Book of Maccabees

All the Books of the New Testament, as they are commonly received, we do receive, and account them Canonical.

VII. OF THE OLD TESTAMENT

The Old Testament is not contrary to the New: for both in the Old and New Testament everlasting life is offered to Mankind by Christ, who is the only Mediator between God and Man, being both God and Man. Wherefore they are not to be heard, which feign that the old Fathers did look only for transitory promises. Although the Law given from God by Moses, as touching Ceremonies and Rites, do not bind Christian men, nor the Civil precepts thereof ought of necessity to be received in any commonwealth; yet notwithstanding, no Christian man whatsoever is free from the obedience of the Commandments which are called Moral.

VIII. OF THE THREE CREEDS

The Three Creeds, Nicene Creed, Athanasius's Creed, and that which is commonly called the Apostles' Creed, ought thoroughly to be received and believed: for they may be proved by most certain warrants of holy Scripture.

IX. OF ORIGINAL OR BIRTH-SIN

Original Sin standeth not in the following of Adam, (as the Pelagians do vainly talk;) but it is the fault and corruption of the Nature of every man, that naturally is ingendered of the offspring of Adam; whereby man is very far gone from original righteousness, and is of his own nature inclined to evil, so that the flesh lusteth always contrary to the spirit; and therefore in every person born into this world, it deserveth God's wrath and damnation. And this infection of nature doth remain, yea in them that are regenerated; whereby the lust of the flesh, called in the Greek, "Phronema Sarkos", which some do expound the wisdom, some sensuality, some the affection, some the desire, of the flesh, is not subject to the Law of God. And although there is no condemnation for them that believe and are baptized, yet the Apostle doth confess, that concupiscence and lust hath of itself the nature of sin.

X. OF FREE-WILL

The condition of Man after the fall of Adam is such, that he cannot turn and prepare himself, by his own natural strength and good works, to faith, and calling upon God: Wherefore we have no power to do good works pleasant and acceptable to God, without the grace of God by Christ preventing us, that we may have a good will, and working with us, when we have that good will.

XI. OF THE JUSTIFICATION OF MAN

We are accounted righteous before God, only for the merit of our Lord and Saviour Jesus Christ by Faith, and not for our own works or deservings: Wherefore, that we are justified by Faith only is a most wholesome Doctrine, and very full of comfort, as more largely is expressed in the Homily of Justification.

XII. OF GOOD WORKS

Albeit that Good Works, which are the fruits of Faith, and follow after Justification, cannot put away our sins, and endure the severity of God's Judgement; yet are they pleasing and acceptable to God in Christ, and do spring out necessarily of a true and lively Faith; insomuch that by them a lively Faith may be as evidently known as a tree discerned by the fruit.

XIII. OF WORKS BEFORE JUSTIFICATION

Works done before the grace of Christ, and the Inspiration of his Spirit, are not pleasant to God, forasmuch as they spring not of faith in Jesus Christ, neither do they make men meet to receive grace, or (as the School-authors say) deserve grace of congruity: yea rather, for that they are not done as God hath willed and commanded them to be done, we doubt not but they have the nature of sin.

XIV. OF WORKS OF SUPEREROGATION

Voluntary Works besides, over, and above, God's Commandments, which they call Works of Supererogation, cannot be taught without arrogancy and impiety: for by them men do declare, that they do not only render unto God as much as they are bound to do, but that they do more for his sake, than of bounden duty is required: whereas Christ saith plainly, When ye have done all that are commanded to you, say, We are unprofitable servants.

XV. OF CHRIST ALONE WITHOUT SIN

Christ in the truth of our nature was made like unto us in all things, sin only except, from which he was clearly void, both in his flesh, and in his spirit. He came to be the Lamb without spot, who, by sacrifice of himself once made, should take away the sins of the world, and sin, as Saint John saith, was not in him. But all we the rest, although baptized, and born again in Christ, yet offend in many things; and if we say we have no sin, we deceive ourselves, and the truth is not in us.

XVI. OF SIN AFTER BAPTISM

Not every deadly sin willingly committed after Baptism is sin against the Holy Ghost, and unpardonable. Wherefore the grant of repentance is not to be denied to such as fall into sin after Baptism. After we have received the Holy Ghost, we may depart from grace given, and fall into sin, and by the grace of God we may arise again, and amend our lives. And therefore they are to be condemned, which say, they can no more sin as long as they live here, or deny the place of forgiveness to such as truly repent.

XVII. OF PREDESTINATION AND ELECTION

Predestination to Life is the everlasting purpose of God, whereby (before the foundations of the world were laid) he hath constantly decreed by his counsel secret to us, to deliver from curse and damnation those whom he hath chosen in Christ out of mankind, and to bring them by Christ to everlasting salvation, as vessels made to honour. Wherefore, they which be endued with so excellent a benefit of God be called according to God's purpose by his Spirit working in due season: they through Grace obey the calling: they be justified freely: they be made sons of God by adoption: they be made like the image of his only-begotten Son Jesus Christ: they walk religiously in good works, and at length, by God's mercy, they attain to everlasting felicity.

As the godly consideration of Predestination, and our Election in Christ, is full of sweet, pleasant, and unspeakable comfort to godly persons, and such as feel in themselves the working of the Spirit of Christ, mortifying the works of the flesh, and their earthly members, and drawing up their mind to high and heavenly things, as well because it doth greatly establish and confirm their faith of eternal Salvation to be enjoyed through Christ, as because it doth fervently kindle their love towards God: So, for curious and carnal persons, lacking the Spirit of Christ, to have continually before their eyes the sentence of God's Predestination, is a most dangerous downfal, whereby the Devil doth thrust them either into desperation, or into wretchlessness of most unclean living, no less perilous than desperation.

Furthermore, we must receive God's promises in such wise, as they be generally set forth to us in holy Scripture: and, in our doings, that Will of God is to be followed, which we have expressly declared unto us in the Word of God.

XVIII. OF OBTAINING ETERNAL SALVATION ONLY BY THE NAME OF CHRIST

They also are to be had accursed that presume to say, That every man shall be saved by the Law or Sect which he professeth, so that he be diligent to frame his life according to that Law, and the light of Nature. For holy Scripture doth set out unto us only the Name of Jesus Christ, whereby men must be saved.

XIX. OF THE CHURCH

The visible Church of Christ is a congregation of faithful men, in the which the pure Word of God is preached, and the Sacraments be duly ministered according to Christ's ordinance in all those things that of necessity are requisite to the same.

As the Church of Jerusalem, Alexandria, and Antioch, have erred; so also the Church of Rome hath erred, not only in their living and manner of Ceremonies, but also in matters of Faith.

XX. OF THE AUTHORITY OF THE CHURCH

The Church hath power to decree Rites or Ceremonies, and authority in Controversies of Faith: And yet it is not lawful for the Church to ordain any thing that is contrary to God's Word written, neither may it so expound one place of Scripture, that it be repugnant to another. Wherefore, although the Church be a witness and a keeper of holy Writ, yet, as it ought not to decree any thing against the same, so besides the same ought it not to enforce any thing to be believed for necessity of Salvation.

XXI. OF THE AUTHORITY OF GENERAL COUNCILS

General Councils may not be gathered together without the commandment and will of Princes. And when they be gathered together, (forasmuch as they be an assembly of men, whereof all be not governed with the Spirit and Word of God,) they may err, and sometimes have erred, even in things pertaining unto God. Wherefore things ordained by them as necessary to salvation have neither strength nor authority, unless it may be declared that they be taken out of holy Scripture.

XXII. OF PURGATORY

The Romish Doctrine concerning Purgatory, Pardons, Worshipping, and Adoration, as well of Images as of Reliques, and also invocation of Saints, is a fond thing vainly invented, and grounded upon no warranty of Scripture, but rather repugnant to the Word of God.

XXIII. OF MINISTERING IN THE CONGREGATION

It is not lawful for any man to take upon him the office of publick preaching, or ministering the Sacraments in the Congregation, before he be lawfully called, and sent to execute the same.

And those we ought to judge lawfully called and sent, which be chosen and called to this work by men who have publick authority given unto them in the Congregation, to call and send Ministers into the Lord's vineyard.

XXIV. OF SPEAKING IN THE CONGREGATION IN SUCH A TONGUE AS THE PEOPLE UNDERSTANDETH

It is a thing plainly repugnant to the Word of God, and the custom of the Primitive Church, to have publick Prayer in the Church, or to minister the Sacraments in a tongue not understanded of the people.

XXV. OF THE SACRAMENTS

Sacraments ordained of Christ be not only badges or tokens of Christian men's profession, but rather they be certain sure witnesses, and effectual signs of grace, and God's good will towards us, by the which he doth work invisibly in us, and doth not only quicken, but also strengthen and confirm our Faith in him.

There are two Sacraments ordained of Christ our Lord in the Gospel, that is to say, Baptism, and the Supper of the Lord.

Those five commonly called Sacraments, that is to say, Confirmation, Penance, Orders, Matrimony, and extreme Unction, are not to be counted for Sacraments of the Gospel, being such as have grown partly of the corrupt following of the Apostles, partly are states of life allowed in the Scriptures; but yet have not like nature of Sacraments with Baptism, and the Lord's Supper, for that they have not any visible sign or ceremony ordained of God.

The Sacraments were not ordained of Christ to be gazed upon, or to be carried about, but that we should duly use them. And in such only as worthily receive the same they have a wholesome effect or operation: but they that receive them unworthily purchase to themselves damnation, as Saint Paul saith.

XXVI. OF THE UNWORTHINESS OF THE MINISTERS, WHICH HINDERS NOT THE EFFECT OF THE SACRAMENT

Although in the visible Church the evil be ever mingled with the good, and sometimes the evil have chief authority in the Ministration of the Word and Sacraments, yet forasmuch as they do not the same in their own name, but in Christ's, and do minister by his commission and authority, we may use their Ministry, both in hearing the Word of God, and in receiving of the Sacraments. Neither is the effect of Christ's ordinance taken away by their wickedness, nor the grace of God's gifts diminished from such as by faith and rightly do receive the Sacraments ministered unto them; which be effectual, because of Christ's institution and promise, although they be ministered by evil men.

Nevertheless, it appertaineth to the discipline of the Church, that inquiry be made of evil Ministers, and that they be accused by those that have knowledge of their offences; and finally being found guilty, by just judgement be deposed.

XXVII. OF BAPTISM

Baptism is not only a sign of profession, and mark of difference, whereby Christian men are discerned from others that be not christened, but it is also a sign of Regeneration or new Birth, whereby, as by an instrument, they that receive Baptism rightly are grafted into the Church; the promises of forgiveness of sin, and of our adoption to be the sons of God by the Holy Ghost, are visibly signed and sealed; Faith is confirmed, and Grace increased by virtue of prayer unto God. The Baptism of young Children is in any wise to be retained in the Church, as most agreeable with the institution of Christ.

XXVIII. OF THE LORD'S SUPPER

The Supper of the Lord is not only a sign of the love that Christians ought to have among themselves one to another; but rather is a Sacrament of our Redemption by Christ's death: insomuch that to such as rightly, worthily, and with faith, receive the same, the Bread which we break is a partaking of the Body of Christ; and likewise the Cup of Blessing is a partaking of the Blood of Christ.

Transubstantiation (or the change of the substance of Bread and Wine) in the Supper of the Lord, cannot be proved by holy Writ; but is repugnant to the plain words of Scripture, overthroweth the nature of a Sacrament, and hath given occasion to many superstitions.

The Body of Christ is given, taken, and eaten, in the Supper, only after an heavenly and spiritual manner. And the mean whereby the Body of Christ is received and eaten in the Supper is Faith.

The Sacrament of the Lord's Supper was not by Christ's ordinance reserved, carried about, lifted up, or worshipped.

XXIX. OF THE WICKED WHICH EAT NOT THE BODY OF CHRIST IN THE USE OF THE LORD'S SUPPER

The Wicked, and such as be void of a lively faith, although they do carnally and visibly press with their teeth (as Saint Augustine saith) the Sacrament of the Body and Blood of Christ, yet in no wise are they partakers of Christ: but rather, to their condemnation, do eat and drink the sign or Sacrament of so great a thing.

XXX. OF BOTH KINDS

The Cup of the Lord is not to be denied to the Lay-people: for both the parts of the Lord's Sacrament, by Christ's ordinance and commandment, ought to be ministered to all Christian men alike.

XXXI. OF THE ONE OBLATION OF CHRIST FINISHED UPON THE CROSS

The Offering of Christ once made is that perfect redemption, propitiation, and satisfaction, for all the sins of the whole world, both original and actual; and there is none other satisfaction for sin, but that alone. Wherefore the sacrifices of Masses, in the which it was commonly said, that the Priest did offer Christ for the quick and the dead, to have remission of pain or guilt, were blasphemous fables, and dangerous deceits.

XXXII. OF THE MARRIAGE OF PRIESTS

Bishops, Priests, and Deacons, are not commanded by God's Law, either to vow the estate of single life, or to abstain from marriage: therefore it is lawful for them, as for all other Christian men, to marry at their own discretion, as they shall judge the same to serve better to godliness.

XXXIII. OF EXCOMMUNICATE PERSONS, HOW THEY ARE TO BE AVOIDED

That person which by open denunciation of the Church is rightly cut off from the unity of the Church, and excommunicated, ought to be taken of the whole multitude of the faithful, as an Heathen and Publican, until he be openly reconciled by penance, and received into the Church by a Judge that hath authority thereunto.

XXXIV. OF THE TRADITIONS OF THE CHURCH

It is not necessary that Traditions and Ceremonies be in all places one, and utterly like; for at all times they have been divers, and may be changed according to the diversities of countries, times, and men's manners, so that nothing be ordained against God's Word. Whosoever through his private judgement, willingly and purposely, doth openly break the traditions and ceremonies of the Church, which be not repugnant to the Word of God, and be ordained and approved by common authority, ought to be rebuked openly, (that others may fear to do the like,) as he that offendeth against the common order of the Church, and hurteth the authority of the Magistrate, and woundeth the consciences of the weak brethren.

Every particular or national Church hath authority to ordain, change, and abolish, ceremonies or rites of the Church ordained only by man's authority, so that all things be done to edifying.

XXXV. OF THE HOMILIES

The second Book of Homilies, the several titles whereof we have joined under this Article, doth contain a godly and wholesome Doctrine, and necessary for these times, as doth the former Book of Homilies, which were set forth in the time of Edward the Sixth; and therefore we judge them to be read in Churches by the Ministers, diligently and distinctly, that they may be understanded of the people.

Of the Names of the Homilies
1. Of the right Use of the Church.
2. Against peril of Idolatry.
3. Of repairing and keeping clean of Churches.
4. Of good Works: first of Fasting.
5. Against Gluttony and Drunkenness.
6. Against Excess of Apparel.
7. Of Prayer.
8. Of the Place and Time of Prayer.

9. That Common Prayers and Sacraments ought to be ministered in a known tongue.
10. Of the reverend estimation of God's Word.
11. Of Alms-doing.
12. Of the Nativity of Christ.
13. Of the Passion of Christ.
14. Of the Resurrection of Christ.
15. Of the worthy receiving of the Sacrament of the Body and Blood of Christ.
16. Of the Gifts of the Holy Ghost.
17. For the Rogation-days.
18. Of the State of Matrimony.
19. Of Repentance.
20. Against Idleness.
21. Against Rebellion.

XXXVI. OF CONSECRATION OF BISHOPS AND MINISTERS

The Book of Consecration of Archbishops and Bishops, and Ordering of Priests and Deacons, lately set forth in the time of Edward the Sixth, and confirmed at the same time by authority of Parliament, doth contain all things necessary to such Consecration and Ordering: neither hath it any thing, that of itself is superstitious and ungodly. And therefore whosoever are consecrated or ordered according to the Rites of that Book, since the second year of the forenamed King Edward unto this time, or hereafter shall be consecrated or ordered according to the same Rites; we decree all such to be rightly, orderly, and lawfully consecrated and ordered.

XXXVII. OF THE CIVIL MAGISTRATES

The King's Majesty hath the chief power in this Realm of England, and other his Dominions, unto whom the chief Government of all Estates of this Realm, whether they be Ecclesiastical or Civil, in all causes doth appertain, and is not, nor ought to be, subject to any foreign Jurisdiction.

Where we attribute to the King's Majesty the chief government, by which Titles we understand the minds of some slanderous folks to be offended; we give not to our Princes the ministering either of God's Word, or of the Sacraments, the which thing the Injunctions also lately set forth by Elizabeth our Queen do most plainly testify; but that only prerogative, which we see to have been given always to all godly Princes in holy Scriptures by God himself; that is, that they should rule all estates and degrees committed to their charge by God, whether they be Ecclesiastical or Temporal, and restrain with the civil sword the stubborn and evil-doers.

The Bishop of Rome hath no jurisdiction in this Realm of England.

The Laws of the Realm may punish Christian men with death, for heinous and grievous offences.

It is lawful for Christian men, at the commandment of the Magistrate, to wear weapons, and serve in the wars.

XXXVIII. OF CHRISTIAN MEN'S GOODS, WHICH ARE NOT COMMON

The Riches and Goods of Christians are not common, as touching the right, title, and possession of the same, as certain Anabaptists do falsely boast. Notwithstanding, every man ought, of such things as he possesseth, liberally to give alms to the poor, according to his ability.

XXXIX. OF A CHRISTIAN MAN'S OATH

As we confess that vain and rash Swearing is forbidden Christian men by our Lord Jesus Christ, and James his Apostle, so we judge, that Christian Religion doth not prohibit, but that a man may swear when the Magistrate requireth, in a cause of faith and charity, so it be done according to the Prophet's teaching, in justice, judgement, and truth.

4

SCRIPTURE INDEX

REFERENCE	PAGE	REFERENCE	PAGE
Genesis		6:5	55, 137, 138
1	105, 223, 372	9:5-6	133
1-2	84, 373	9:6	249
1-3	68, 70, 131-132	11	275
1:27	133	12:1-3	39, 155, 163
1:31	107, 274	14:19	84
2	323	15:1-6	39
2:2-3	373	15:6	39, 156
2:15	275	16:7f	96
2:17	366	17:1-14	39
2:18	146	18:14	94
2:23	146	20:3-7	249
2:24	147	22	310
3	278	25:23	264
3:1	243	45:7-8	264
3:5	98	45:8	110
3:14-15	366	50:18-20	264
3:14-19	248	50:20	110
3:15	136		
3:16	366	**Exodus**	
3:17-19	274, 366	Book of	296
3:21	122, 367	2:23-25	156
4:11f	366	3-4	104

3:1-6	51	34:6-7	116-117, 366
3:2	52	34:7	118
3:6	43		
3:8	156	**Leviticus**	
3:14	104	5:14-6:7	183
4:11	65	7:1-7	183
4:11-12	42	18:19-23	147-148
4:22	168	19:2	120, 290
14:21	112	19:3	147n
19-20	115	19:33-34	147
19:1-8	39		
19:5	335, 338	**Numbers**	
19:5-6	39	5:5-8	183
19:6	84	11:17	80
19:18	115	11:26-30	305
19:21	115	18:1	185
20:1-17	39	18:22	185
20:3	84	18:32	185
20:7	104, 105		
20:8-12	147n	**Deuteronomy**	
20:12	335	4:12	40
20:14	147n	6:1-9	335
20:18f	115	6:4	84
21-23	295	6:4-5	41
23:3	148	6:4-9	147n
23:4	147	6:10-15	84
23:6	148	7:6-8	122
23:7	59, 99, 254, 257	7:6-11	264
24	185	8:3	43
24:1-11	39	9:4-5	264
24:7	39, 48	13:6-10	147n
24:8	39, 183	18:15-22	157
24:10	115	21:18-21	147n
24:15-17	116	22:8	147
29:43	116	27:17	147
32:10	118	29:22	274
33:11	52	30:2	239
33:21-23	116	30:6	240
33:23	52	32:48-52	336
34	367		
34:5	116		
34:6	122		

Judges
Book of	366
6:34	80
15:14	87, 305

1 Samuel
Book of	41, 52
10:6	87
16:13	80

2 Samuel
Book of	41, 52
7:1	373
7:14	81
7:16	167
12:1-15	135
24:1	278

1 Kings
Book of	41, 52
8:33	239
8:39	95
22:20	110
22:34	110
22:37	110

2 Kings
Book of	41, 52

1 Chronicles
Book of	40n
21:1	278

2 Chronicles
Book of	40n

Ezra
Book of	40n

Nehemiah
Book of	40n

Esther
Book of	40n

Job
Book of	40n, 144
1:21	125
38-41	106
38:4	106
38:7	97-98, 106
42:2	94, 106, 113
42:7-9	98

Psalms
Book of	39, 40n, 144
2	52
8	151, 169, 204, 372
8:5-6	150
8:9	107
11:4-7	118
14:1	27
16	200
19:1	55
19:1-6	28
19:7	55
49:7-9	182
51:5	136
52-65	120
52:8	120
54:5-6	120
55:22	120
57:3	120
57:10	120
59:10	120
59:16	120
61:7	120
62:8	120
63:3	120
65:1-4	120
71	119
85:10	120
90	97
90:2	97

90:10	145
93	15
94:4-11	95
95	52
96:13	367
104:15	108
104:27-30	108
104:31	107
104:35	109
110	157,
110:1	203
110:6	172
119:89-91	94, 110, 223
127	147, 147n
139	96
139:1-6	95
148:2-5	97

Proverbs
Book of	40n, 144, 146
1:7	5
1:8-9	147n
4:1-6	147n
5:18-19	310-311
8	99
11:21	147
15:3	95
16:1	264
16:4	264
16:9	95
17:6	147, 147n
19:18	147n
19:21	264
21:1	96

Ecclesiastes
Book of	40n
1:2	144
12:6-7	145
12:8	144

Song of Solomon
Book of	40n, 146

Isaiah
6:1-5	90
6:3	118
6:3-5	109
10:5-11	110
11:1-5	87
11:1-9	108
11:1-10	157, 167
11:1-11	15
11:11-17	240
40:3	166
40:11	324
40:12	107
40:15	107
40:15-17	94
40:22	107
40:28	97, 107
40:28-29	107
41:22	95
42:8	117
43:9	95
44:6-8	95
45:1f	335
45:21-22	79
53	160, 162, 176, 182, 185, 337
53:2	176
53:5	176
53:10	183
55:8	186
55:10-11	223, 231-232
55:11	228
61:1-2	123
64:6	180

Jeremiah
7:12-15	84
17:9	55, 137
27:5	108
31	46, 183

31:31f	160, 240
31:31-34	15
31:33	40, 294, 306

Lamentations
Book of	40n

Ezekiel
11:17-20	240
16	323
16:1-14	264
20:9	104
36:16-38	160
36:22f	105
36:22-36	15
36:25-27	228n
36:26-27	240
36:27	306

Daniel
Book of	40n, 84
1	84
2:19	84
2:20-23	84
2:36-45	15
2:44	85
2:47	85
4:3	85
5:14	84
6:26-27	85
7	85, 168, 368
7:13	85
7:14	168
7:27	85
12:1-4	366
12:2	201

Hosea
1-3	323
6:7	155
11:1	81, 168

Joel
2:28f	303

Amos
4:7	274
4:13	84, 95
5:8-9	96
5:18-20	366
9:7	264
9:11-15	167
9:15	160

Jonah
3:10	98

Micah
5:2-6	157

Habakkuk
1:13	99, 111, 118, 119
2:4	111

Zechariah
4:6	309
9:9	167
10:3	324

Matthew
1:21	104, 166, 168
1:23	166
3:2	11
3:11-12	11
4:1-11	169, 170, 279
4:3	278
4:4	43
5	86
5:1-12	45
5:17-20	43
5:18	291
5:20	291
5:21f	291
5:25-26	143

5:27-30	46	19:28	168, 226
5:27-32	147n	21:1-11	167
5:43-44	290	21:9	168
5:43-48	99	21:12-13	171
6:5-6	311	21:18	168-169
6:7	311	22:42-45	167
6:9-13	312	23:1f	291
6:12	142	23:2-3	336
6:12-15	278	23:8-12	344
7:2	143	23:10	289
7:12	288-289	23:29-39	172
7:21-23	350	25:31	168, 172
7:23	371	25:41-46	249
8-9	71	26:26-29	160
10:10	69	26:28	328
10:28	143	28:16-20	45, 47, 96, 172, 202, 204, 328
10:29-30	110		
10:33	143	28:18	172
11:2-15	171	28:19	88, 91
11:3	32	28:19-20	289
11:11	80	28:20	96, 172
11:19	255		
11:25-27	266	**Mark**	
11:25-30	173	Book of	12
11:27-28	271	1	87
11:28	255, 265	1:1	11
11:29	289	1:2-3	166
12:1-14	42, 45	1:3	165
12:36-37	95, 369	1:4	238
13	71	1:7-8	80
13:44	17	1:8	303
15:19	369	1:9-11	171
16	167	1:9-13	80
16:13-16	33	1:10	16, 172
16:17	34	1:10-11	81
18:15-20	344	1:11	173
18:20	322	1:12	172
18:21-35	290	1:14-15	11, 37-38, 79, 180, 237
18:23-35	142	1:15	80, 224, 238, 240
19:4-5	43	1:24-25	167
19:4-6	147	1:38	12, 180
19:6-22	45	2:9	86

2:20	181	12:24	42
3:6	181	12:26	42
3:27	279	13	183-184, 351, 353
3:31-35	14	13:1-2	354
4	16	13:4	353
4:26-32	13	13:9	353
4:35-41	86	13:10	354
4:38	168	13:11	353
6:8	69	13:13	353
7:9-13	147n	13:14	353
7:14-23	108	13:14-23	354
7:18-19	292	13:20	269
7:18-23	138	13:22	269
7:19	45	13:32	169, 351
7:20-23	139	13:32-37	350
8:27	182	13:35	353
8:27-29	165	14-16	183-184
8:29	31	14:24	183
8:31-33	181	14:36	16, 169, 311
8:35	182	15:10	184
8:36-37	182	15:14-15	184
9:2-8	171	15:15	169
9:7	173	15:34	184
9:24	243	15:37	169
9:42-50	143	15:38	184
9:47	119	15:39	184
9:47-48	371	16:6	184
10:18	99		
10:21	169	**Luke**	
10:35-45	181-182	Book of	166
10:37	203	1:15	228
10:42-45	345	2:40	169
10:43-44	337	2:52	169
10:43-45	291	4:1-13	170
10:45	16, 176, 182, 183, 187, 336	4:43	337
10:46	69, 71	5:31-32	337
10:48	167	6:24-26	143
11:22-23	311	7:47-50	244
11:23	242	8:8	224
11:25	313	8:15	224
12:1-11	143	9:23	289, 298, 337
12:1-12	171, 181	10:29-37	147

10:31-32	369	1:18	17, 52
11:2-4	312	2:19-21	160
11:13	314	2:19-22	324
12:6	95	3	228
12:6-7	110	3:1-8	18, 123
13:1-5	144	3:5-6	226
13:22-30	267	3:14	205
15:1-10	132	3:16	132, 265
15:11-32	121	3:17-18	368
16:19-31	43, 143	3:18	366
17:5-6	243	3:34	229, 305
17:20-21	33, 352	3:36	143, 248, 371
17:20-23	350	4:24	98, 99
17:20-37	349	5:18	173
17:21	14, 351	5:27	368
17:24	350	5:28-29	363
17:34-35	350	5:39-40	76
18:9-14	251, 313	6:37	266
18:35	69, 71	6:63	229
18:38	167	7:15	336
19:11-27	369	7:37-38	304
19:41-44	354	7:37-39	18
21:23	274	8:34	100, 136
22:20	42	8:44	278
23-24	198	8:46	170
23:34	255	8:58	86, 173
23:43	255, 365	9:1-3	144
24:25-27	264	10	337
24:27	352	10:11	268, 324
24:39	169	10:15	324
24:44	58, 352	10:16	324
24:44-47	43, 172	10:17	86
		10:17-18	187
John		10:18	172
1:1	30, 41n, 86, 87, 173	10:27-28	269
1:1-3	47, 105	10:30	87
1:3	223, 357	10:35	58
1:11	162, 166	11:35	168
1:13	266	11:49-53	53
1:14	30, 94, 117, 165, 173, 174	11:51	335
1:16-17	161n	12:20-26	338
1:17	117	12:20-32	172

12:27-28	169	19:21	168
12:31	136, 225, 279	19:28	169
12:31-32	176, 185, 190	19:34	169
13:1	339	20:17	203
13:1-20	337	20:22-23	209
13:12-17	291	20:28	33, 86, 173
13:20	339-340	20:29	202
13:27	279		
13:34-35	290	**Acts**	
14	202	1	202
14:3	349	1:8	14
14:6	230	1:9	202
14:7-10	87	1:11	202, 349
14:15-17	303	1:21-22	339
14:16	88	2:17	201
14:16-17	209, 304	2:17-18	160
14:16-20	18	2:23	110, 186, 264
14:17	88, 89	2:23-24	200
14:18-23	304	2:27	200
14:23	89, 210, 303	2:33	16, 172, 203, 204, 209, 303
14:25-26	304	2:36	205
14:26	88, 339	2:38	238, 241, 303
14:28	87	2:42	339
15:1-11	211	3:22	160
15:5	290	4:12	55, 104
15:26	172, 209	4:25	44, 52
15:26-27	304	5:1-11	274
15:27	339	5:3	280
16:7	203	5:3-4	87, 88
16:7-15	305	5:29	148
16:12-15	47, 210	5:31	18
16:13	339	5:32	304
16:14	305	6:2	339
16:16	203	6:3-6	339
17:3	9, 10, 17, 20	6:4	230
17:6-19	47	7:48-50	324
17:9	204, 265	7:55-56	305
17:14	275	8	302, 304
17:14-21	339-340	8:5	17
17:20	47, 204	8:14-16	339
17:20-21	265	10	304
18:36	13	10-11	302

10:23-24	339
10:42	205, 356, 368
10:42-43	18
10:47-48	161
11	303-304
11:15-17	303
11:16-17	303
11:18	240, 241
12:23	274
13:8-10	280
13:9-10	305
13:32-33	201
13:48	266
14	55
14:16-17	27
14:17	108
14:23	340
15	339
15:16-18	160
15:22	339
16:7	210
16:9	260
16:14	94, 260
17	55
17:7	17, 338
17:11	44, 74
17:22-31	27
17:24-25	101, 109
17:24-29	108
17:27	109
17:28	55
17:30	231, 265
17:30-31	240, 241, 245-246
17:31	197, 362, 368
19	302, 304
20:17	341
20:17-35	341
20:20-21	238
20:21	17
20:25	17
20:28	173, 324, 341
20:30	289

Romans

1:1-2	44
1:2	53
1:3	167
1:3-4	224
1:4	200-201, 362
1:16	187, 224
1:16-18	248
1:18	99, 109, 189
1:18-31	143
1:18-32	249
1:18-3:20	134
1:18-3:31	367
1:19-20	34
1:19-21	28
1:20	107, 120
1:21	55, 83, 109
1:24	248
1:25	134
1:26	248
1:27	189
1:28	248
1:28-31	118
1:32	189, 367
2:3	189
2:4-11	119
2:5	143, 189, 367
2:6	367
2:6-7	134
2:12-16	28, 189, 249
2:15-16	142
2:16	95, 99, 368
2:29	240
3:2	41, 44, 63, 65
3:2-6	249
3:9	250
3:9-23	142
3:10-11	250
3:19	99, 189
3:19-20	250, 293
3:23	118, 367
3:24-25	160

3:25	190, 252	8:3-4	169, 240
3:26	190, 252	8:4	45, 282, 294
4:2-5	253	8:7-8	276
4:4-5	257	8:9	89, 172, 210, 214
4:5	59, 242, 254	8:12-13	278
4:17	107	8:13	282, 283, 307
4:25	201	8:14	306
5	169	8:14-15	86, 216
5:2	121	8:14-16	282
5:5-6	123	8:14-17	305
5:5-11	191	8:15	18, 173
5:7-8	132	8:15-16	282
5:8	121	8:16	88
5:10	134	8:16-17	284
5:12	135	8:17	213, 270, 283
5:13	249	8:19	282
5:15-18	135-136	8:20	274
5:17	212	8:20-22	281
5:18	212	8:21	105, 283
5:19	212	8:23	281, 282, 283
6:1f	124	8:24-25	282
6:1-4	277, 290	8:26	281, 282
6:1-11	201, 213, 240	8:26-27	88, 305
6:2-4	240-241	8:28	109, 270
6:4	277	8:28-30	283
6:15	293	8:28-39	110
6:17	293	8:29	151, 266, 270, 284, 291
6:17-18	289, 299	8:30	267, 284
6:23	293, 366	8:31-34	267
7	294	8:31-39	191
7-8	277-278, 281	8:33-34	370
7:4	294	8:34	204, 206
7:5	294	8:35	269
7:7-8	138	8:35-38	281
7:7-12	137, 249, 281	8:37-39	284
7:12	294	8:38	281
7:15-20	266	8:38-39	269
7:18	55, 137, 208	9-11	354
7:22	45	9:4-5	41
7:24	281	9:5	86, 173
8:1	282	9:14-26	267
8:3	170	9:17	44

9:18	265
9:19-24	134
10:9-13	173
10:14-15	225
10:17	225
11	18
11:5	354
11:11-24	161
11:12	354
11:25-26	265, 354
11:26	161
11:29	264
11:33	99
12:1-2	54
12:3-8	344
12:3-13	309
12:9-13	322
13:1-2	148
13:6-7	148
13:8	149, 295
13:10	295
14:5-6	160
14:7-9	287
14:17-18	287
15:4	44
15:7	322
15:7-13	120
15:16	338
16:20	136, 278

1 Corinthians

Book of	325
1:2	323
1:12	342
1:17	224
1:18	41n
1:18f	176, 342
1:18-25	55
1:18-31	16
1:18-2:6	186
1:23	225, 230
1:26-31	187, 268-269
1:30	301, 307
1:30-31	255
1:31	270
2:2	180
2:4-5	229
2:7	121
2:8	120, 175
2:8-9	16
2:11	88, 95
2:12-13	228
3:1-3	342
3:5	342
3:5-6	230, 334
3:5-9	110, 187, 342
3:5-15	369
3:9	230
3:11	230
3:21-23	213, 276
3:22	109, 150
4:1-2	342
4:4	342
4:8-13	342
4:16-17	342
5-6	328, 344
5:6-7	118
5:7-8	160
6:3	368
6:11	307
6:19	160, 307
7:14	147
7:31	274
7:39	212
7:40	53
8:1-8	108
8:4	83
8:5	79, 86
8:6	86, 105
9:1-18	342
9:6-12	341
9:9	158
9:20-21	292
9:21	46, 160, 291

9:27	342	15:13-19	33
10:1-11	160	15:14	196
10:11	44, 274, 292-293	15:17	196, 201, 363
10:16-17	328	15:20-21	363
10:19-31	108	15:20-23	169
10:20	83	15:20-28	14, 17, 351
10:20-22	280	15:22	135, 211, 212
10:26	280	15:23	201
10:33-11:1	338	15:23-28	151
11-14	327	15:24-26	372
11:1-3	146	15:25-28	204
11:3	87, 89, 210	15:26	358
11:16	329	15:27	372
11:17-22	227	15:28	87, 373
11:17-34	327	15:35-38	363
11:20-22	328	15:42-44	363
11:27	328	15:44	200
11:29	328	15:45	17
11:30	274	15:45-49	212
12	303-304, 309, 344	15:47-49	150, 152
12:1-3	305	15:48	169
12:3	18	15:48-49	200
12:4-11	308-309	15:49	212, 291
12:7	309	15:49-50	372
12:12-13	215, 303, 305	15:53	97
12:26	215	15:56	201, 250
12:27	323, 325	16:10	342
13	309, 344	16:16	342
13:7-8	373		
13:10-13	373	**2 Corinthians**	
13:12	18, 93, 133, 318	1:18-20	16
14	309	1:20	61, 76, 160, 224, 317
14:5	326	1:20-21	47
14:20	54, 243	1:21-22	18
14:23-25	329	1:22	304
14:26	344	1:24	342
14:37	55	2:5-11	344
14:37-38	47	3:1-6	228
14:40	327	3:5-6	44-45
15	169, 199, 204, 365	3:7-11	120
15:3-4	44	3:18	121, 291, 302, 308
15:6	198	4-5	364

4:1-6	10
4:2	230
4:4	83, 136, 279
4:5	17, 231, 337, 342
4:6	17, 120
4:7-12	335, 342
4:7-5:10	363
4:16-17	364
4:17	121, 302, 374
5:1-10	364
5:2-3	364
5:7	202
5:8	359
5:9	288
5:9-10	369
5:10	368-369
5:17	212, 276
5:17-18	227
5:18	89, 227
5:18-19	187
5:18-21	189
5:19-20	342
5:21	170
6:3-10	342
6:14-16	212
8:9	122, 132, 176
10-13	187, 335, 342
10:5	54
11:2	323
11:3	280
11:4	278-279
13:14	88

Galatians

1:4	274
2:20	132, 191, 213, 273
3:1-2	214
3:1-5	307
3:1-18	156
3:1-4:10	159
3:8	18
3:10	137, 293
3:13	162, 189
3:20	85
3:23-26	291-292
3:27-28	327
4:1-7	173
4:1-10	137
4:4	42, 169
4:4-5	162, 177
4:4-6	86
4:5-6	282
4:6	17, 89, 172, 210, 305
4:8-10	280
4:9	241, 260
4:26	321
5:4	213
5:16	306
5:17	277
5:18	88, 292, 294, 306
5:19-21	138
5:22	306
5:22-23	18
5:22-24	294
5:23	308
5:25	228, 306
6:1-5	344
6:2	343
6:6	341
6:10	296, 322

Ephesians

1:4	212, 213, 266, 270
1:4-6	122
1:7-8	123
1:7-10	357
1:9-10	205, 270
1:10	212, 265
1:11	94, 110, 265
1:12	270
1:12-14	265
1:13	212, 214
1:13-14	18, 47, 161, 304
1:15-22	14

1:21	274
1:22	323
2:1	142, 221
2:1-3	208
2:1-10	123
2:2	136, 279
2:4-10	212
2:5-6	212
2:7	97, 124, 212, 369, 373
2:8	241
2:8-9	18, 125
2:9	251
2:10	18, 109, 212, 288
2:12	41, 211
2:13-16	318
2:14f	213
2:14-15	212
2:15	46
2:18	212, 214
2:19-20	338
2:20	47, 56, 340, 345
2:20-22	325
3:19	93
4:1ff	329
4:4-6	215
4:8	44
4:8-10	203
4:11	204, 341
4:11-16	340
4:20-24	291
4:22	46
4:22-24	18
4:29	340
4:30	88, 304
4:32-5:2	290
5:5	203
5:14	44
5:18-19	305
5:19	326
5:21-33	323, 325
5:23	325
5:25	268, 321
5:28-30	325
6:1-3	294-295
6:4	340
6:10ff	94
6:10-20	280, 298
6:12	83
6:17	229

Philippians

1:1	341
1:23	318, 359
2:1-11	173, 205, 337
2:9-11	86, 357
2:10	357
2:12-13	236, 307-308
3:4	251
3:7	251
3:8	17
3:20	322
3:20-21	212, 318, 363
4:1	269

Colossians

1:9-10	243
1:13	83, 136
1:13-14	160, 190, 279
1:15	17
1:15-20	214
1:16	97, 105, 109, 357
1:17	357
1:19-20	357
1:23	354
2:3	61, 214
2:6-7	214, 269
2:9	214
2:10	214
2:11-15	160
2:13-15	190
2:14	137
2:16-23	294
2:17	159
2:21	276

Reference	Page
2:23	276
3	214, 226
3:1	201
3:1-3	362
3:1-4	352
3:3	214
3:4	349
3:5f	241
3:10	46, 201, 241
3:10-11	291
3:12f	241
3:12-14	327
3:13-15	290
3:14-17	326
3:16	56, 326, 340
3:16-17	330
3:18-4:1	147n

1 Thessalonians

Reference	Page
Book of	260
1:2-3	262
1:4-5	263
1:5	261, 262
1:6	261, 262
1:6-8	261
1:9	261
1:10	248
2:2	261, 262
2:4	261
2:7-8	261
2:9	261
2:11	261
2:13	261, 262
2:16	261, 262
2:18	280
3:2	261
3:5	261, 280
3:10	261
4:2	261
4:3	307
4:7-8	307, 314
4:8	261
4:9	262
4:10-11	261-262
4:16	349
4:16-17	356
4:16-18	359
4:17	364
5:2	353
5:9	263
5:11	340
5:12	341
5:12-13	343
5:19	88

2 Thessalonians

Reference	Page
Book of	260
1:7	349
1:8-9	249
1:9	372
1:10	120, 356-357
2:1	356
2:2-6	262-263
2:3-4	354-355
2:9-10	280
2:10	262
2:10-15	263
2:11	263
2:15	261
3:6-13	243
3:14	53
3:14-15	261

1 Timothy

Reference	Page
Book of	346
1:15	48, 76, 247, 251
1:17	96, 98
2:1-2	148
2:5	17, 85
2:5-6	247
2:8-15	340
2:8-3:7	341
3:1ff	341
3:1-16	340

3:2	341
3:4	340
3:5	341
3:16	203
4:1-5	107
4:4-5	108, 223, 276
4:10	268
5:8	147
5:17-18	341, 344
6:6-10	275
6:14	349
6:16	96
6:17-19	275

2 Timothy

Book of	346
2:2	341
2:9	142
2:24	341
3:14-17	47, 60
3:16	44, 52
3:16-17	63
4:2	341

Titus

Book of	346
1:2	58, 99
1:7	341
2:3-4	340
2:11-12	124
2:13	86, 173
3:3-7	245
3:5	226

Hebrews

1	86
1:1-2	61
1:1-3	171
1:2	352
1:3	108, 120, 223, 357
1:5-14	98
1:8	173
2	204
2:5-9	109
2:5-18	151, 372
2:6-9	150
2:7-14	169
2:10	204
2:17	169, 190
3:1-6	171
3:7	52
4	160, 373
4:12	369
4:12-13	228-229
4:13	370
4:14	160
4:15	170
5:8	169
6:4-6	352
6:5	274
7:25	204, 206
8-10	292
8:13	294
9-10	159
9:14	89, 188
10:1-4	293
10:4	159
10:11-14	186
10:30-31	99, 118
11	161
11:1	243
11:3	97
11:8	242
11:33	242, 334
11:39-40	161
12	321, 323
12:3-11	370
12:5-6	118, 144
12:22-24	320
12:28	320
13:14	320-321
13:17	341, 343

James
1:5-8	311
1:17	99
1:21	228
2:1-7	227
2:10-11	369
2:24-26	310
3:1	342
4:4	275

1 Peter
Book of	184
1:1	321-322
1:2	184, 185
1:3-5	201
1:4	160, 322, 358
1:7-9	358
1:8	202
1:11	172, 184
1:18-19	185
1:18-21	184, 185
1:23	228
1:25	228
2:4	184, 185
2:5	324-325
2:7	184
2:8	185
2:9-10	185
2:10	338
2:10-11	322
2:18-23	290
2:21	184-185
2:21-25	184
2:22-23	170
2:23	169
2:24	185, 191
3:18	184, 185
3:18-20	185
4:1	184, 185
4:10-11	344
4:13	184, 185
5:1	184
5:1-3	341
5:1-5	324, 344
5:3	343
5:8	278, 280
5:9	322

2 Peter
1:16	197
1:19	74
1:21	44, 52, 65-66
3:1-2	47
3:1-10	358
3:5	97
3:5-9	223
3:8	95
3:9	118, 367
3:13	15, 160, 373
3:15-16	75, 76-77
3:16	53

1 John
1:8-9	277
1:9	118
2:2	190
2:13	278
2:15-17	275
2:18	355, 358
2:22	355
3:1-3	291
3:5	170
3:9	277
3:13	275
4:1-6	280
4:8	99
4:8-10	190
4:10	99, 123, 188-189
4:19	260

3 John
9	343

Jude
3   61

Revelation
1:7   350
1:8   95-96
7:9   319, 372
7:15-17   319
9:11   278
12-13   355
19:1-6   119
19:16   17
20:1-10   355
20:2   278, 356
20:11-12   370
20:11-15   370
20:11-21:1   15
20:13   367
21:1-4   374
21:2   323
21:2-3   319
21:4   319
21:6-7   319
21:14   338
21:24   319
21:27   319
22:1-5   319
22:14   319
22:15   319

ACKNOWLEDGEMENTS

I would like to acknowledge with gratitude the inspiration of Tony Payne and Gary Nichols, and the extraordinary efforts of Geoff Robson, without whom this book would never have been published. My own teacher in theology, Dr Broughton Knox, had a huge influence on me and many others. And I pay tribute once again to my dear wife, Christine, whose service of the Lord and fellowship in my own efforts surpass anything I could find words for.

matthiasmedia

Matthias Media is an evangelical publishing ministry that seeks to persuade all Christians of the truth of God's purposes in Jesus Christ as revealed in the Bible, and equip them with high-quality resources, so that by the work of the Holy Spirit they will:

- abandon their lives to the honour and service of Christ in daily holiness and decision-making
- pray constantly in Christ's name for the fruitfulness and growth of his gospel
- speak the Bible's life-changing word whenever and however they can—in the home, in the world and in the fellowship of his people.

Our resources range includes Bible studies, books, training courses, tracts and children's material. To find out more, and to access samples and free downloads, visit our website:

www.matthiasmedia.com

How to buy our resources

1. Direct from us over the internet:
   - in the US: www.matthiasmedia.com
   - in Australia: www.matthiasmedia.com.au
2. Direct from us by phone: please visit our website for current phone contact information.
3. Through a range of outlets in various parts of the world. Visit **www.matthiasmedia.com/contact** for details about recommended retailers in your part of the world.
4. Trade enquiries can be addressed to:
   - in the US and Canada: sales@matthiasmedia.com
   - in Australia and the rest of the world: sales@matthiasmedia.com.au

Register at our website for our **free** regular email update to receive information about the latest new resources, **exclusive special offers**, and free articles to help you grow in your Christian life and ministry.

Also by Peter Jensen

The Future of Jesus

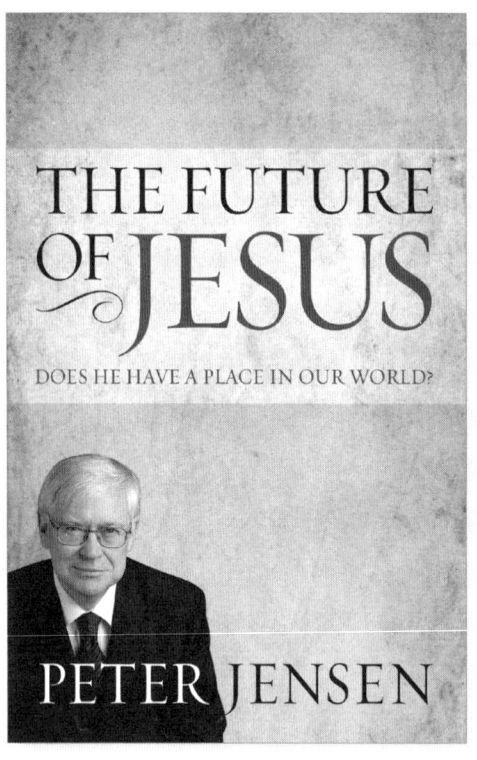

By almost any measure, Jesus has been the most influential human to have ever lived. But is the time of his influence coming to an end? Does Jesus really belong in our modern world?

In *The Future of Jesus*, Peter Jensen challenges believers and unbelievers alike to think again about Jesus. Who was he? Can we believe in his miracles? If Jesus announced the coming of the kingdom of God, why are we still waiting? Was he a failed prophet or a religious genius? And does it matter?

Dr Jensen's unfailingly intelligent investigation of these questions achieves its purpose: "What I really want to do—and what I think each of us needs to do while we still have the chance—is to talk about Jesus, and to let Jesus talk back to us."

FOR MORE INFORMATION OR TO ORDER CONTACT:

Matthias Media
Email: sales@matthiasmedia.com.au
www.matthiasmedia.com.au

Matthias Media (USA)
Email: sales@matthiasmedia.com
www.matthiasmedia.com